Elizabeth
JENNINGS

Elizabeth
JENNINGS

"THE INWARD WAR"

Dana
GREENE

OXFORD
UNIVERSITY PRESS

OXFORD
UNIVERSITY PRESS

Great Clarendon Street, Oxford, OX2 6DP,
United Kingdom

Oxford University Press is a department of the University of Oxford.
It furthers the University's objective of excellence in research, scholarship,
and education by publishing worldwide. Oxford is a registered trade mark of
Oxford University Press in the UK and in certain other countries

First Edition published in 2018

Impression: 1

Published in the United States of America by Oxford University Press
198 Madison Avenue, New York, NY 10016, United States of America

British Library Cataloguing in Publication Data

Data available

Library of Congress Control Number: 2018935711

ISBN 978–0–19–882084–0

Printed and bound by
CPI Group (UK) Ltd, Croydon, CR0 4YY

In memory of Dorothea Benson Greene
and Rosalyn Sylvester Roesel

Acknowledgments

Writing a biography is a solitary venture, but it is dependent on others to sustain one during the years of research and writings. I am grateful beyond measure to the many individuals and institutions which helped bring this first biography of Elizabeth Jennings to life. These include the late Nicholas Sheetz, collector of Jennings' papers, who first suggested that I write this biography; Mark Albrow, executor of the Jennings literary estate, who extended permission to use Jennings' voluminous writings; archivists Fran Baker (Rylands), Lisette Matano (Georgetown), and Joel Minor (Washington University) who lent their assistance; Emma Mason and Jane Dowson for their scholarly contributions. Washington University, Special Collections, and the Eugene Bianchi Fund of Emeritus College, Emory University, provided financial support.

A biography comes alive through the detail provided by those who knew Jennings and others who have studied her writings and offered insights. I am grateful to: Mark Albrow, Alan Brownjohn, Duncan Campbell, O.P., Sabine Coelsch-Foisner, Donald Hall, Peter Hannigan, Christina Hardyment, Anne Harvey, Wendy Hill, Christopher Johnson, Pat Kingerlee, Grevel Lindop, Ann Loades, Maria Antonietta Marghella, Robert Ombres, O.P., Gina Pollinger, James and Belinda Price, Roger Pringle, Gillian Reynolds, John and Christine Saward, Michael Schmidt, Anthony and Ann Thwaite, Priscilla Tolkien, Anna Walczuk, Jean Ward, and Greg Wolfe. Although I take full responsibility for the content of this biography, their insights have been invaluable.

I am fortunate to have the stimulation of fellow biographers in the Washington Biography Group, devotees of poetry in the Martha Washington Poetry Group, and friends who gave encouragement. They know who they are, but to thank them publicly I name them here: Emily Archer, Victoria Barnett, Peter and Sonja Bloom, Merrill and Tim Carrington, Missy Daniel, Deborah Douglas, Susan Henry-Crowe, Neva Herrington, Fay Key and Steve Bullington, Dolores

Leckey, Joan Neal, Kathleen O'Connor, Angela Alaimo O'Donnell, Donna Osthaus, Linda Peck, Adrienne and Andy Rosen, Kathleen Staudt, Bonnie Thurston, Valerie Trueblood, and Addison Ullrich. Permission to use Elizabeth Jennings' published and unpublished poetry and prose has been granted by David Higham Associates. Quotations of published poems are taken from *Elizabeth Jennings: The Collected Poems* edited by Emma Mason (Manchester: Carcanet, 2012).

For their forbearance in enduring my preoccupation with Elizabeth Jennings I am grateful to my daughters, Justin Greene, Kristin Blackman, Lauren Greene-Roesel, and Ryan Greene-Roesel; my sisters, Karen Greene and Mary Greene Kyle; and my spouse of fifty years, Richard Roesel, to whom I owe most. What is written here would not have been possible without his love, friendship, critique, computer wizardry, and endless good humor.

Contents

List of Figures

Prologue—Finding Elizabeth Jennings

> I believe that the literary biographer can stretch out a hand to his
> subject and invite him, invite her, to write one more work posthu-
> mously and in collaboration. Their chief business does not really
> lie in sensationalism but in attempting to chart illuminating connec-
> tions between past and present, life and work.... We know the value of
> dreams and fantasies, the shadow of the life that isn't lived but lingers
> within people, and that the lies we tell are part of the truth we live.[1]
>
> Michael Holroyd

On October 29, 1992, Elizabeth Jennings presented herself at
Buckingham Palace to be honored for her national contribution to
poetry. Dressed in an oversized duffel coat, a red wool cap, flowered
skirt and sweater, tights, and lace-up shoes, this ramshackle woman was
invested as Commander of the British Empire by Queen Elizabeth.

Who was she? The myriad descriptions applied to her boggle the
mind. She was at once "a major poet of our times;" "a triumphant
anomaly;" "Botticelli's angel—so pure, so lovely;" "the best of the
Movement poets;" "the star of our show, our discovery;" "the last poet
of what used to be called the soul;" "a major sublunary asset;" "a triumph of integrity;" "one of the best-loved British poets in the last fifty
years;" but also an "emotional anchorite;" "prissily decorous;" a writer
of "lavender-scented" poems who churned out "acres of meaningless
pieties;" a "school mistress among drunken marines;" "the bag lady of
the sonnets." To herself Jennings was "blighted," "an alien," "outcast,"
"clown," and "leper," but mostly, assuredly, a poet.

Elizabeth Jennings was one of the most widely anthologized women
poets in the second half of the twentieth century, and at her death in
2001 all major British newspapers carried lengthy obituaries, acknowledging both her forty-eight volumes of poetry, prose, and anthology,
and her many awards. She wrote of nature, friendship, childhood, religion, love and death, endearing her to a wide audience and making
her "the most unconditionally loved writer of her generation."[2] But
beneath the surface of the published corpus was a trove of more than

30,000 unpublished poems and autobiographical writings chronicling an "inward war" of a person besieged by lifelong depression, unbearable loneliness, and unrelenting fears exacerbated by religious guilt and the isolation of being a woman in the literary world.

Elizabeth Jennings lived most of her life in Oxford, in the circumscribed world of Banbury and Woodstock Roads, a world which gave her comfort and solace. It was there in her "city of spires" that evidence of her life is to be found in her parents' home on Banbury Road, the old Oxford High School, Saints Gregory and Augustine Catholic Church, St. Anne's College, the old Oxford City Library, the Walton Street Cinema, the Randolph Hotel, the many cramped rooms in north Oxford in which she stuffed her possessions, her lonely grave in the Wolvercote cemetery, and the commemorative Elizabeth Jennings Way off the Woodstock Road. Footsteps through these places resurrect recollections of her.

But it is through the voluminous unpublished writing that one can begin to piece together this uncommon life. These shards lie before the biographer like fragments of an intricate puzzle. The search for Elizabeth Jennings between the gentle angel and the elderly eccentric spinster is complicated by the fact that Jennings herself was sometimes contradictory and often non-disclosing, even secretive. She claimed to have the "gift of concealment." She wanted her life story told, but she wanted to be the one who would tell it. To this end she wrote several autobiographies, none of which was published.

Jennings was adamant that her poetry was not autobiographical, although she claimed it was "personal." On the other hand, she admitted that writing poetry was never separate from the life one leads and that each of her poems found a temporary home in her; a small part of her life was caught within her poems, "skip[ping] in between the lines." The fact is that there was little gap between Elizabeth Jennings' life and her poetry. Her published poems, and even more so her unpublished "still-born" poems, provide evidence for her life, especially when corroborated by other sources. What is patently clear is that Jennings wanted her work, not her life, to be celebrated. In her poem, "An Impertinent Interviewer," she castigates an interviewer who asks banal questions about her life and ignores her poetry. "I let her questions proceed, / Answered now and then, occasionally told / An off-white lie. I could see her trivial need, / Her intrusion which was bold. / She did not seem to care about verse indeed."[3]

Irrespective of Jennings' aversion to biography, the genre can contribute to contextualizing and understanding her achievement by anchoring her huge poetic corpus within the cultural and literary history of the second half of twentieth-century England. Of necessity she will be linked to the so-called Movement, which gave her a start as a poet, and with whose members she shared commitments to clarity, rationality, formal verse, and accessible meaning.

In the end, the Movement proved to be a faux classification, and Jennings an unclassifiable poet. She was set apart from her Movement contemporaries by gender, religion, and psychological affliction, all of which shaped her life and the verse she produced. Because she was singular and belonged to no tradition, she needed to create one. She attached herself to the likes of Herbert, Traherne, Hopkins, and others with similar affinities. Like them, she believed the poem was related to religious experience and gave access to God. By compression and intensity, the poem became a "shortcut to truth." Her poems had a spiritual dimension, and the best of them "were something more than literature."[4]

In addition to contextualizing her life and placing her among her contemporaries, a biography offers the opportunity to illustrate how the creative process takes place: where it comes from, what stimulates it, what impedes it, how it develops and changes, and how it is received. Jennings' creative process is revealed in the chronicling of her life.

Jennings titled the first iteration of her autobiography "The Inward War," a line taken from Marianne Moore—"There never was a war that was not inward." It traces the events of her early life and her inner turmoil but oddly it is not self-revelatory; much is left unsaid. In this biography an attempt will be made to integrate Jennings' inner and outer life. Without this integration a biography devolves to either adulation or denigration. The aim here is rather to understand this complicated woman in her complex historical context.

Elizabeth Jennings could be gracious, thoughtful, loyal, caring, and good company. Many thought of her as meek. But given her years under psychiatric care, her strange appearance and sometimes erratic behavior, her early admission of singularity and oddness, and her lifelong and profound sense of loneliness, it would be easy to sensationalize her life as that of a quintessential tormented and suicidal artist, curiously dressed, and laden down with multiple carrier bags which accompanied her everywhere. She admitted to "having melancholy or high spirits,"[5] and it is true that she was paranoid, extremely anxious, used alcohol to medicate herself, was a hoarder and gambler, and a Manichean as regards sex. The process of documenting her brokenness can be a trap, however, reducing her life to its eccentricities. One of the functions of this biography is to acknowledge these diverse character-istics and behaviors, indicate their consequences for her life and work, and in so doing clear away the detritus and rubble so that her poetic contribution might emerge more clearly. Her oddness is background, not foreground for more important issues. The real question is how did this woman, against extraordinary odds of psychological instability, poverty, ill health, and neediness, achieve what she did? Jennings' answer was that poetry "saved" her, but for her, poetry derived from her religion. The two were linked, she wrote: "Poetry is an art / That's close to all / Religion."[6]

Jennings' early experience of Roman Catholicism was a source of doubt, shame and guilt, but when she visited Rome in her early thirties she encountered religion as a living community. In Rome faith was made easy, and the unhappy religious experience of childhood and adolescence was altered. Her doubts were removed, her shame for-given, and she was accepted. In Rome she was no longer a minority; there she felt whole and free. It was there too that her vocation as poet was confirmed, and religion and poetry were forever linked in her mind. For her, poets were makers and hence they do "in little what God does with all his force...God / Is present in all poetry that's made / With form and purpose."[7] She wrote: Poetry was "my way / Of reaching God."[8]

Sexuality and religion were tangled together in her life as well. From an early age, largely through the influence of church and family, Jennings came to think of sex as disgusting and shameful. She was frightened by it, but it also preoccupied her. This may explain in part her attraction to priests and to the notion of hero-worship and friend-ship as the purest form of love. She always publicly maintained that she was chaste, saying her religion demanded this, although this may have been a protective shield against the sex that she feared. This also may have been a technical description of her physical behavior, but cer-tainly not of her imaginative life. Although she claimed to have admirers not lovers, she boasted that she knew about the most exquisite shared sexual delight and how hard it was to control.[9]

Another aspect of her inward war was the isolation imposed by gender and its impact on her life and work as a poet. The situation for women poets in the mid-twentieth century is artfully described by the Irish poet Eavan Boland, who was twenty years Jennings' junior and who grew up in England. Boland wrote that in the world in which she came of age, woman and poet were opposite categories, the former evoking "collective nurture," the latter "self-reflective individualism." She reminisced that she had to "shout" across this distance.[10] Lamentably, Jennings was not a shouter, and she suffered accordingly.

Social expectations for women precluded Jennings from believing she could marry and be a poet. In the end she married poetry. Up through the 1970s poetry was almost exclusively the purview of men. Women were readers of poetry but generally not creators of it. With some obvious exceptions, the writers of poetry, the reviewers, and those who made awards were male, and the subject matter of interest to the male establishment was not always the same as that of the woman poet. Jennings was largely unaware of the disability of gender she carried. She did not share in a community of women poets, and had no language with which to critique her situation. When awareness of the constraints of gender became more obvious beginning in the 1970s, she was preoccupied with her psychic life and financial survival.

These external factors negatively influenced her life, as did the internal fear of what she called "the inward agony of self alone."[11] In order to be whole, Jennings believed she needed to be in love, but she was convinced that love constrained her freedom. She wrote constantly about her desire for non-possessive love, which would allow her to be both whole and free. She was caught in a vise of these two competing desires whose resolution remained elusive.

Jennings' commitment to a poetic vocation demanded solitude to write, but that solitude also terrified her. During the day she countered this terror by sitting in Oxford's pubs and cafés chatting up random customers. At night she would return to her cluttered room where she wrote poetry in order to push back the darkness. Poverty also challenged her poetic vocation. As a full-time, self-supporting poet she was constantly scrambling to bring in money. This clearly created anxiety in her life.

It was within this web of external and internal forces that Elizabeth Jennings lived out her poetic vocation. The probability was great that she would fail; in fact, she did not.

There were three major turning points in Jennings' life: her discovery of poetry, her sojourn to Rome, and her mental breakdown. These occurred against a background of a troubled family life and her experience of being a clumsy, sickly second child, who believed she was unwanted because she was a girl. A difficult family life was compounded by traumatizing experiences in a Catholic primary school, denigration by a priest, and the impact of a guilt-ridden religion, all of which led to what she referred to as a breakdown. Her matriculation at the Oxford High School brought some relief, especially when she was introduced to poetry. She entered that magical world and was besotted. After completing her secondary schooling and enrolling at St. Anne's she began to meet fellow poets and have initial success at publication. For eight years she worked in the Oxford City Library, continuing to live with her parents, write poetry, and mentor aspiring university student poets. In 1957, having won the Somerset Maugham Award, she was off to Rome, a sojourn which changed her life. While there she met an older Dominican priest, who became an important friend and encouraged her as a poet. Her experience in Rome powerfully strengthened her vocational resolve.[12]

The felicitous decision to devote her life to poetry had its underside. Overworked and exhausted she began to develop physical maladies. She soon learned that her parents would be moving, leaving her to live alone, and her new Dominican spiritual director, who had provided solace and intimacy, was abruptly transferred. Her terror of loneliness was made worse by this double loss and her physical exhaustion. These were the immediate causes of her *cri de coeur*, the three attempts at suicide which brought her to the Warneford Hospital and shocked those who knew her as a quiet and mild woman. She was institutionalized but never adequately diagnosed. Another Dominican served as a counselor and traveling companion, and when he died she was devastated, now being without anyone to love. Although her mental instability was brought under control, it was never completely cured. Her paranoia, depression, and acute anxiety continued.

Jennings' mental breakdown and institutionalization shaped her life, even though she wanted to minimize, even deny, they had an impact on her poetry. If these events had any positive consequence for her creativity, it would be that they prompted her to enter more fully into the suffering of others. Using "imagined experience," she wrote touchingly and bravely in the first person about society's unwanted: the homeless, the ill, the mentally deranged, the criminal, the child, the unwed mother, and even the suffering Christ. In these "persona poems" she captured the grief of the unwanted, making their suffering her own.

For fifteen years after the death of her Dominican counselor she was sustained by her friendship with the well-known historian, C. (Cicely) V. (Veronica) Wedgwood, who became her patron and principal psychological mainstay. When Wedgwood was afflicted with Alzheimer's disease and withdrew from their intimate friendship, Jennings was devastated and inconsolable. Yet she continued to write, and toward the end of her life she received further recognition: the W. H. Smith Award, inclusion in the A-Level syllabus, the Paul Hamlyn Award, and an honorary doctorate from Durham University.

The complexity of Jennings' life might be unlocked if her driving intention, what Yeats called a person's myth, is understood. Poetry was for her a means to overcome her "strange homesickness," her longing for a lost childhood, an Edenic world of delight, wonder, order, and bliss. Although that timeless world was gone, it could be restored through poetry, what she called "creation's hopefulness." The major themes of her poetry—childhood, friendship, nature, religion, time, and love—were related to her intention. She heard sounds of that world in the sea, saw its glinting in the stars, and encountered it in love. It was a world characterized by order, meaning, and freedom. For Jennings the chief function of poetry was to discover order and hence hope amid chaos and despair.[13] She insisted that "in the large flights of imagination / I see for one crammed second, order so / Explicit that I need no more persuasion."[14]

For Jennings poetry was first "communication" and "communion;" it was not confession or therapy. Its powers were vast and various. She believed it could heal the lonely and lost, haunt the reader, and speak across continents. It was a gift of kindness, a help in grappling with fear. It brought contrition, fostered justice, and served as a harbinger of peace. It was, she insisted, "an arc of good."[15] Poetry was a kind of "secular sacrament."[16]

The phenomena of religion and poetry were inextricably linked in her mind. Religion was "a way of looking," of seeing and understanding the world. The poem was a meeting place of the human and divine. She wrote "It is...in my poetry / I meet my God. He's a familiar there."[17] She analogized the poem to dervish dancing which strips away the veil and lets "God / Step out of his own inventions."[18] Creative imagination, central to both poetry and religion, produced metaphor, simile, and images, and these offered distinctive ways to conceptualize religious understanding and hence to ease religious doubt. In her unsystematic and scattered writing on poetics Jennings recognizes that poetry offers evidence of an alternative and lived expression of religious faith.

Since her verse is inspired by a longing for a timeless, blissful past, it may seem anachronistic, yet its popularity speaks to the importance of this longing in her contemporaries. She must be credited not only with linking back to an earlier incarnational tradition in English poetry, but with extending that tradition into her own time. Furthermore, her poems continue to resonate because when belief is fraught and no vision is evident she offers reminders of the desire for a world of wholeness and freedom. When considering her legacy one remembers the assertion of one of her favorite poets, Wallace Stevens, that "After one has abandoned a belief in God, poetry is the essence which takes its place as life's redemption."[19] It may be that in an areligious age Jennings' work will stand as recognition that poetry sustains a universal longing for "...truth and / Mystery, a way of being."[20]

This biography is offered as evidence of how a life is actually lived in response to both inner and outer forces and how the creative process is carried out. It puts the lie to the separation of life and work. Jennings' life made her work possible, and her work made her life memorable. The two were inevitably intertwined. Following Michael Holroyd's suggestion, in these pages a hand has been stretched out to Elizabeth Jennings to write one more work posthumously and in collaboration. May it promote understanding of her life, her work, and the woman herself.

I

Bliss

An Eden is
> Our long desire.[1]
> > "From Light to Dark"

Finding the elusive Elizabeth Jennings begins in the Edenic world of childhood, recreated by her from memory and imagination and recorded in poetry and autobiographical writing. Her "long desire" to restore this idyllic world became her lifelong ambition and her raison d'être. Here the child became a poet. Here was bliss.

Jennings insisted her recollections of her childhood world were potent, accurate, and linked to early sensual experiences: the pungent smell of honeysuckle and bonfires; the sound of birdsong, the taste of sea salt; the unbroken sight of the sky with its jewel-like stars, the feel of grass under her feet.[2] Here was "a childhood taste of heaven," an unchanging, timeless world of order and grace.[3] Trust was taken for granted,[4] protection assured. Here there were no nightmares, fear, guilt, no talk of sin. In this place she was innocent, whole.[5] As she wrote subsequently, "here I became me."[6]

The locus of her memories was the place of her birth, Boston in Lincolnshire, a flat and treeless plain from which one could see into the heart of England and to the nearby North Sea with its tides and pounding rhythms.[7] It was remote from worldliness, some 125 miles from both London and Oxford. In the 1920s Boston was home to 4,000 people who lived from the sea or worked the land growing sugar beet or acres of tulips, earning the town the appellation "Holland." Its only uniqueness was its "Stump Church" with its tall tower, a beacon for seafarers and those who traveled through the fenlands surrounding the town.

Her birth on July 18, 1926 was in most respects ordinary. Her parents, Henry Cecil Jennings and Mary Helen (Madge) Turner Jennings, had one child, Aileen, who was two when Betty, as she was known in childhood, arrived. They had hoped this second child would be a boy, and this disappointment plus the fact that an inebriated doctor caused a difficult birth convinced Mrs. Jennings she wanted no more children.[8] Three weeks after her birth Elizabeth Joan was brought to St. Mary's Catholic Church to be baptized by Father J. Gallie. Francis and Margaret (Kitty) Turner Davey, her uncle and aunt, served as godparents.[9]

According to Jennings, her family was dominated by Cecil Jennings, a small, wiry, impatient man, who was completely indulged by Madge (Figure 1.1).[10] Born in 1893 in Edmonton, Middlesex, he was ten years her senior. Their marriage in 1923 was a bonding of opposites. Intellectually ambitious and scientifically inclined, Cecil Jennings served in the British Navy in the First World War as Surgeon Lieutenant on the Royal Sovereign, and then trained as a doctor at Great St. Thomas' Hospital, London, an institution where his own father had been chief pharmacist.[11] In Boston Dr. Jennings worked as Medical Officer of Health. He loved the sea, studied art, photography, and geology, and was a fan of cricket. Years before his marriage he converted to Roman Catholicism. Madge Turner was born in 1903 in Banbury, Oxfordshire, the youngest child in a large Catholic family of nine. Her father, a gentle soul who loved to paint and fish, became the manager of the Bristol Main Midland Bank. Her mother was a beautiful woman of great vivacity. Madge herself was very pretty with lovely blue eyes and a retiring personality. If she had opinions, she rarely expressed them. Gentle, soft-spoken, generous, and imaginative, she was an able wife with a virginal innocence about her. Later Betty learned from her father that for the first month of their marriage he had to coax his wife to have sex.[12]

During their earliest childhood Betty and Aileen saw little of either of their parents except on vacations or weekends. They were remote, and although the girls longed to know them better, the most important people in their lives were their nannies, who oversaw their daily activities.[13] Betty claimed to love all her nannies and remembered them in white uniforms smelling clean and fresh.

Since Dr. Jennings made a substantial salary the family lived well and had adequate help—a gardener, a part-time charwoman, and several nannies who rotated in and out of employment.[14] Their brick house,

Figure 1.1. Cecil and Madge Jennings. Courtesy of Mark Albrow

"The Bungalow," on Tower Road in Skibeck, a suburb of Boston, had a long beautiful garden where the children loved to play. She remembered the garden as her first kingdom. There was a greenhouse, pear and apple trees, planting beds and rockeries filled with roses, lilies of the valley, and hollyhocks. There she spent many hours with the gardener,

Old Cram, from whom she learned about nature and country life.[15] If not in the garden, Aileen and Betty lived in the day or night nurseries where their play was supervised, and their sleep monitored by their nannies. The day nursery was painted white, with a white chest of drawers, table and chairs, rows of shelves for their small tin toys and a rocking horse which she rode for hours. There were frequent celebrations. Since the sisters shared July birthdays they had parties together with many friends attending. Christmas was a special occasion with decorations and stockings bulging with gifts. It was on one of those magical Christmases that Betty received her beloved rocking horse. Another memorable gift was a box of chocolates given her by Old Cram. She immediately wanted to share this gift with others. Later she would interpret this moment as an early awakening of a moral sensibility,[16] a dawning awareness of something outside herself giving purpose, value, and a sense of right and wrong.[17]

Another remembered event was her first experience of compassion, elicited by her paternal grandmother, a fearsome and difficult woman, who after the death of her husband opened an antiques shop in Felixstowe to support herself. During a holiday visit Betty was asked to accompany her grandmother on a walk, but reluctant to be alone with her, she declined the invitation, which hurt her grandmother's feelings. Although still young, Betty recognized for the first time what it was to be unwanted. It was, she claimed, her first experience of compassion for another.[18]

These early experiences of generosity and compassion did not always extend to her sister, for whom Betty harbored jealousy. Constantly trailing behind Aileen and begging to be included in her activities, Betty became known in the family as "And Me." Aileen was considered attractive, agile, and physically able. Betty, on the other hand, was prone to accidents. She recalls falling down the nursery stairs at age two and hitting her head on the stone floor of the pantry. Another fall occurred at age four or five when she came rushing into a room and hit a chair. The result was a head injury requiring stitches.[19] This was only the beginning of a series of accidents which defined her in negative ways.

As she became aware of her clumsiness, Betty also began to believe herself to be a disappointment to her parents, who had wanted a boy. Hoping to fulfill their wish, she remembered casting off her dresses for trousers, refusing to play with dolls, and trying to make her voice sound deep,[20] in short to be a boy. It is unknown whether this experience was causative of her creating an imaginary four-year-old brother named Jack Baycock, but this invention happened at about the same time. What is known is that Jack became a close companion, with whom Betty communicated with a toy telephone connected to the greenhouse where this imaginary sibling reputedly lived with his crotchety mother, Mrs. Baycock. If Jack was not a surrogate brother, he nonetheless gave entrance into a boundlessly imaginative world as well as a relief from loneliness. Several years later when the family moved Jack went with them.[21]

Irrespective of these childhood experiences of ordinary discontent, Elizabeth Jennings remembered these earliest years as the happiest time in her life.[22] She rode her tricycle, played Ludo in the nursery, and made merry with the many children who visited her home. She went to Brenner's Bazaar, where she found penny-priced treasures and tasted sweet biscuits at Mabelson's grocery.[23] All the while her imaginative life was fed by the shapes of the moon, the majesty of stars, the rhythms of the sea. She was a child who loved ritual and invented it at any provocation. When Peter, her yellow canary, was captured and killed by her black and white cat, she processed to the garden weeping and carrying the dead bird in a cardboard container for a proper burial. She later recalled this ceremonial occasion with its ordered movement and ancient repetition, with "the sky singing" and "the trees still waving farewell."[24] This ritual, this engagement with nature, gave meaning to her child's heart.

At age four she began attending a "dame school" run by a Miss Pilcher. She was happy there as well, collecting frogs and lizards, drawing pictures from the Old Testament, jumping on her pogo stick, and playing the cymbals or the triangle in a little percussion band. She was nurtured by the nursery rhymes and stories read to her, although she did not learn to read until several years later. Betty was a slow learner, showing no signs of intellectual precociousness.[25]

This idyllic life came to an end when Dr. Jennings decided to leave Boston ostensibly to provide his daughters greater educational opportunity. He accepted a position as County Medical Officer for Oxfordshire, even though his new salary would be considerably less than what he earned in Boston. When in late 1931 Dr. and Mrs. Jennings went to Oxford to scout out housing, Aileen and Betty were brought to Bristol to stay with their maternal grandparents, who as people of means lived in a large stone house near the Bristol Downs.[26] Their visit with these Turner relatives opened new worlds for the Jennings girls. This was their first occasion to be away from home for any length of time, and it offered them the chance to bond as sisters. Since five aunts and uncles still lived at the Turner home, there was ample possibility for interaction and fun. One incident recalled from this visit was Grandmother Turner telling Aileen that she was to have lots of babies. Betty's scornful response was that she would not have babies but would rather have lambs and calves and kittens.[27] This comment might have been recalled by Elizabeth Jennings either as an expression of a six-year-old child's love of the natural world or as a portent of her later rejection of a maternal role.

If Betty was fond of Grandmother Turner, she was even fonder of her grandfather. Although a man of considerable financial acumen, he was also a visual artist of some ability, as was his father. Tall and slender, with a rugged face and a military bearing, Grandfather Turner was peaceful and calm, a strong contrast to the quick-tempered Dr. Jennings. Always patient and never condescending, her grandfather took her on long walks along the cliffs and the downs,[28] deepening her love of the sea.

Betty and Aileen spent Christmas 1931 with their grandparents, but soon after the holiday their parents arrived to collect their daughters and return to Boston where they packed up their belongings, bid their household staff goodbye, and headed to Oxford and their new home. Betty wept as she left, particularly saddened to leave behind a nanny whom she especially loved.

Boston would remain an idyllic place in Elizabeth Jennings' imagination. It was for her a touchstone, a talisman, of all that was good and pure. There she experienced "endlessness" untouched by time and decay. There she was at one with the world. What stayed in her memory and imagination were visual images, especially of the stars. In her young mind, God the Father, who lived beyond the stars keeping order in the universe,[29] had scattered these jewels across the sky for her. Glimpsing them, she experienced awe and wonder. Later she wrote: "And they came and lifted me up and told me the name / Of the near and the far stars, / And so my first love was."[30] The stars offered a first glint of love and the first experience that her spirit and flesh were one.[31] Throughout her life she reimagined their magical powers:

> The child stares at the stars...
> Time halts for him
> And he is standing on the earth's far rim
> As all the sky surrenders its bright show.

He will not feel like this again until
He falls in love. He will not be possessed
By dispossession till he has caressed
A face and in its eyes seen stars stand still.[32]

If her childhood in Boston brought her to equate the stars with love,[33] it also grounded her recollections of the sea as an uplifting, repetitive, pulsating sound. For her the sea was an expansive space eliciting her inward praise.[34] She would compose numerous poems about the sea which, "reminds us of so many things . . . / Perhaps love most of all. / The pull and thrust and then the gentle / Subsidence of wave / To a clear, cool wash / A foam on the sand, / A sudden stillness."[35]

Boston was a timeless place of half-remembered bliss. Years later she wrote:

I watched as a child the slow
Leaves turning and taking the sun, and the Autumn bonfires,
The whips of wind blowing a landscape away.
Always it was the half-seen, the just-heard which enthralled—

I am wanting still to record some of the themes
Of the music heard before I understood it,
The books read to me long before I could read . . .[36]

Elizabeth Jennings never returned to the place of her birth, preferring to keep her memories intact, but her "long desire" for that lost world of innocence haunted her for the rest of life. Her recollections of childhood explain how she became a poet and came to illustrate her early experiences of euphoria. Her "[s]ickness for Eden was so strong"[37] that in her imagination she would revisit this "childhood taste of heaven," recapturing it in words that became poems.

2

Oxford

We are people of place,
Each fits his own and finds
His happiness
... hidden in space.[1]

"Spirit of Place."

If Boston was the "place" where Elizabeth Jennings' imagination was nurtured, Oxford was where her intellect was cultivated. She came to the foggy valley of the Thames as a child and would make it the center of her life. She claimed its rivers were in her veins and its meadows and squares were her playground. Here among a welter of spires, cobbled streets, sounding bells and green mist, she wrote that wisdom flowered, learning was handed down, prayers were offered, and foreign tongues mingled, and great men walked the streets. For her, Oxford was a "magical magnet" and "trusted teacher." One wonders whether she could have ever moved elsewhere. She never did.

It was early 1932 when the Jennings' family arrived in Oxford. Dr. Jennings had purchased a large, newly-built stucco house at 431 Banbury Road which was about 3 miles from the city center and a short distance from Oxford's largest cemetery, Wolvercote. Set back from the street, the house had a high-pitched roof with several gables, and narrow but ample windows. The location was suburban, just beyond the leafy streets of north Oxford with its Victorian houses and private schools and just outside the ring road. The city was close at hand, yet the open fields with poplar and willow trees surrounding the house gave a sense of the proximity of the natural world. Although this is the place where Elizabeth Jennings would live for the next thirty years, she describes nothing of the building itself. In keeping with her interests she comments only on its outdoor environment and its long garden, which Mrs. Jennings would tend, and two smaller gardens to be cared for by Aileen and her.

Betty soon acclimatized to her new home. She and Aileen shared a room, and at night they would read Beatrix Potter stories hiding under the sheets. Betty liked Alcott's *Little Women* and resonated with the second-born Jo, who was a tomboy, had a temper, and loved to write.[2] In the summer she cultivated a little garden of radishes and Virginia stock, and she and Aileen would play in the surrounding fields of poppies, shepherd's purse, and cow-parsley. When the hay was cut and mounded they would build little igloos.[3] They rode their bicycles to the River Cherwell and went swimming, fashioned bow and arrows from willow branches, or took the bus into town to shop. Betty particularly liked to visit the de la Mare Toy Shop, which sold china dolls, miniature dolls' house furniture, and music boxes. There she began a hobby of collecting knick-knacks, a diversion which persisted and grew throughout her life.[4]

Betty's youth was not without happiness, but the dominant memory of her early Oxford childhood was of turmoil.[5] She claimed the causes of her suffering were her relationship with her father, her early schooling, and her religious education.

The Jennings family appeared normal, but Betty would come to describe it as "blighted." Mrs. Jennings was always tender toward Betty, perhaps in reaction to her husband's partiality toward Aileen, his "snooks." Practical, clever, confident, and sturdy, Aileen did well in school, won awards, and excelled in games. Although she was bossy toward her younger sister, she would also defend her against their father's complaints. Betty's relationship with her father was the most problematic. As she saw it, her father was restless and thwarted. Although his interest was in anatomy, he settled on a degree in medicine. He nurtured his scientific interests by obtaining a second degree in geology; one of Betty's few memorable experiences of him was fossil hunting together in quarries. In general, she recalls her father as aloof and remote, a perfectionist who craved order and was easily angered. She remembers that once when a piece of the mahjong set was lost he flew into a rage and gave all the pieces to a friend. Another time he tore up the Sunday paper because she looked at it before he did. Although she felt her father showed her almost no affection,[6] she did recall a time at age six when he took her on a ride at the fairground and held her tight. It was, she said, the physically closest they had ever been.[7] But it was her father's nagging and embarrassing her in front of friends that left scars and made her recoil from him.[8] To her mind her father was someone to please, placate, and fear. On the positive side, she could depend on him, knowing that if she were ever in serious trouble he would help her. He taught his daughters to love order and inculcated a desire to excel.[9] He was loyal to his family and expected loyalty from them as well.

In her family Betty became known as "the plain one." She was sickly, awkward, thin, and jumpy. She would not eat and had nightmares. This was an irritant to her father who admired the healthy and physically perfect. When she was nine she had a severe accident, crashing her bicycle into a tree and losing consciousness. Her convalescence was long, and she had to stay in the dark for three weeks.[10] The monotony of her recuperation was made bearable by visits and overnight stays from her neighborhood friend Priscilla (Prisca) Tolkien. By the time she was ten she had had six severe blows to her head. In addition to being accident-prone, Betty's maladies included insomnia, lung congestion, pneumonia, tonsillitis, and nightmares. As a result she was rewarded with wounding nicknames, including "member of the awkward squad," "Awkwardness," and "horizontal child." To most people she appeared to be a shy, quiet, and clumsy second child who disliked both sports and parties. It was only later at university that she would jettison the self-image of an "ugly duckling," one who was graceless, fearful, and burdensome to parents and others. Nonetheless, even at age fifty she continued to portray her childhood self in this way—pitiful to one and all.[11]

Recollections of her childhood also reveal that she was frequently disillusioned, a characteristic she carried into adulthood. Reality did not live up to her expectations. She recalled a visit to London in her youth as evidence of what she called a life of "broken hopes." Expecting that Piccadilly and Oxford Circuses were real circuses, she found them to be what they were, merely busy city intersections. Rather than learn from this experience, she allowed it to fuel her belief that life will disappoint.[12] This negativity was accompanied by worrisome behavior of lying, stealing, and outbursts of anger which led her mother to lament that she feared her daughter would grow up to be a delinquent, a "murderer."[13] This only confirmed Betty's belief that she was "alien," an odd child not like others.[14]

About this same time Betty became inquisitive about the birth process. She admitted that as a small child she experienced infant sexuality, but her query now came from an inquisitive mind which wanted to know about sex.[15] She asked her mother to explain, but Madge Jennings, who was never at ease with an embarrassing question, put her off, fearful that her daughter was too sensitive and might become upset by her response. She suggested she would know when she was older. Therefore, Betty found furtive ways of finding information, reading women's magazines and parts of the Bible, and consulting her father's medical books.[16] From an early age, sex became a preoccupation; it would haunt her for the rest of her life.

Problems at home were exacerbated by problems at school. Soon after arriving in Oxford, Aileen and Betty were enrolled in the newly-opened Rye St. Antony School, an independent Catholic school housed initially in central Oxford, but afterwards in a large, rambling redbrick building in Headington. They remained there for four years. The school was unique in that it was founded not by a religious order of nuns, but by two lay women, Elizabeth Rendell and Ivy King, who remained in charge for thirty years. At the time of the girls' matriculation the school's enrollment was tiny, which may have contributed to Betty's negative experience there. Ironically, Aileen and playmate Prisca both flourished at the school, but Betty did not. She recalled it as a "prison house" where one's behavior was constantly monitored and guilt was instilled. An Old Testament wrathful God was always watching and ready to punish. As a student learner Betty did not do well in school and came to think of herself as stupid, a moron, and a "complete savage." She fell into the habit of cheating and lying which resulted in a traumatic experience involving her homework which she would again and again revisit. Since mathematics was particularly difficult for her, she enlisted Aileen's help in completing her homework, but when the homework was checked and found without error the teacher was suspicious and asked Betty if she had solicited help. Prevaricating, she said, no. When Aileen was queried, she admitted she had helped her sister. This childhood peccadillo was blown out of all proportion. Aileen was marched off to confession, but because Betty was under age she was brought to church by her teacher, who first kissed her in forgiveness, and then made her beg pardon at the altar. While another child might have forgotten this event, Betty never did. She condemned it as an "outrage" and an assault on her spirit.[17] She considered this the first injustice done to her, and it was from this moment her persistent sense of guilt emerged. This early education at Rye St. Antony was emblazoned in her memory as a "Chamber of Horrors" which altered her and made it impossible for her to imagine a God of compassion.[18] She began to dread school.

The Catholicism Betty inherited shaped her in profound ways. As a young girl she absorbed her religious understanding from her parents, her school, and her parish church, St. Gregory and St. Augustine on the Woodstock Road. During this period prior to the Second Vatican Council, the Jennings, like so many other Catholics, were doctrinally orthodox, obedient, and observant, but not particularly self-reflective. Unlike her father, Betty was a cradle Catholic, as she later put it, "[c]hristened to Catholic Christianity, oiled and marked, / With the name of Rome on my lips."[19] As an English Catholic she claimed to be a "cross-breed," one with allegiance to Rome and to England. But as such, she inherited a dicey history of exclusion which contributed to her sense of oddness, of being a person apart.[20] Nonetheless it was easier to be a Catholic in Oxford than in other cities. The city's history and monuments, numerous religious orders, Dominicans, Capuchins, Greyfriars, and Jesuits, memories of John Henry Newman, and the living presence of famous men who went "over to Rome," all gave luster to Oxford's Catholic heritage.

Aside from her family, Betty's most immediate education in Catholicism came from her parish church. Early in the twentieth century this small, white stucco building with a cupola began as a mission but it came to serve as the parish church for the Catholic professional and academic middle-class families of North Oxford. The Jennings family would worship there each Sunday and Dr. Jennings might well have been a member of the Catenians, an association of Catholic laymen dedicated to strengthening friendship, family, and faith. Sitting across the aisle in church from the Jennings was the family of J. R. R. and Edith Tolkien. Tolkien was then professor of Anglo-Saxon at Pembroke College and his family lived near the Jennings family. The children of both families would visit back and forth, and Prisca, the Tolkiens' only daughter, became Betty's loyal and lifelong friend (Figure 2.1). She often visited the Jennings household, and during the summer of 1936 Mrs. Tolkien and her daughter accompanied the Jennings family on a holiday to Felixstowe. Like Prisca who was three years younger, Betty also played with a younger friend, Jane Pinches, another Catholic who lived nearby.

Figure 2.1. Elizabeth Jennings and Priscilla Tolkien. Courtesy of Priscilla Tolkien

Betty made her first confession and communion at St. Gregory's when she was seven. Even then she experienced Catholicism as a "dark" religion dominated by an angry God.[21] In her first confession she revealed her thefts, and what was supposed to be a healing sacrament was experienced as hurtful, offering neither freedom nor solace. She wrote that "I think my childhood ceased on that day."[22] She hated confession and often refused to go. She was afraid of her sins and afraid of God. On the other hand, she was inspired by the Latin sung mass and especially the Elevation of the Host. Along with Aileen and Prisca she would often "play" mass using a toy stove as the tabernacle, crayons in egg cups as candles, and paper Hosts. The ritual was carried out in an invented jumble of words in imitation of the Latin service. What was important was not creed but a ritual of adoration[23] and transformation.[24] What was distinctive in Betty's response to religion was not her reaction to fear-inducing Catholicism, which was common enough at this time, but the fact that this was juxtaposed with her exultant experience of the mass with its music, ritual, and beauty (Figure 2.2).

Figure 2.2. Betty Jennings. Courtesy of Mark Albrow

Her other experience of exultation was in the natural world. At age ten she recalled walking out into the night and beholding the stars, as if they were "diamonds on receding velvet." At that moment she felt ecstatic, that her spirit and flesh were one. She never forgot this experience of wandering among the stars[25] and the sense of wholeness it engendered. But even this exaltation could not obscure the fact that fear began to engulf her. She described it as an obsession, of animals waiting for the dark in order to attack. Fear of her father and God the Father dominated her psyche.

Relief from her myriad anxieties came when Dr. Jennings decided to take his daughters out of the Rye St. Antony School and matriculate them briefly in the Anglican Hyde School. This was a courageous act given that he did this without seeking approval from the local Catholic bishop, which was the expectation. Later Betty would express her gratitude to her father for saving her intellectual life. A turning point occurred when she was enrolled in the junior department of the Oxford High School on Bardwell Road. Her insular and tumultuous youth was about to change. Oxford, the "kindly teacher," would now offer her a new environment where she discovered the lure of poetry and found her "voice."[26] Indeed, this ancient center of learning would prove to be a "magical" place.

3

A Saving Experience

I learnt that poetry
Is joy and wisdom
Art and prophecy,
A way to celebrate a
Chance to pray.[1]

"A Debt to a Teacher"

Betty's matriculation at the junior school of Oxford High School initiated a brief period of well-being. This was in large part due to the care and inspiration of a teacher, the energetic Miss Wilson, who loved both her pupils and the subjects she taught. Betty was indebted to her as the first teacher to draw her out, open her imagination and instill a love of learning. The result was that in Miss Wilson's classes—English, medieval history, and geography—she placed first. This teacher's attention was far-reaching. When Betty was ill for almost six weeks, first with a broken arm which kept her in bed, and then with lung congestion, Miss Wilson sent letters to cheer her and lessons for her to complete at home so that she would not fall behind her classmates.[2] As Miss Wilson's favorite pupil, Betty admitted to having "calf love" for her. Later she would memorialize this teacher as the one who liberated her and created what she claimed was a "golden world" in which she could "touch the stars."[3] "If Miss Wilson had not come into my life," she later wrote, "I would, almost certainly, have become a mixed-up kid. At the other school...[I] was showing all the classic signs of a juvenile delinquent in the making. Under the sunny sky of Miss Wilson's world I found a place. I began to love learning, especially in the form of English poetry and medieval history."[4]

If there was a sorrow in Betty's life now it came from Aileen, who announced that she was now too old to play with Betty and she wanted her to stop following her around.[5] Since Aileen had been her playmate and defender, this was a blow and the beginning of a gradual growing apart of these two sisters.[6]

After two years at the junior school, Betty moved to the senior school, housed in a Victorian brick building at 21 Banbury Road. She enrolled at the time when Violet Evelyn Stack began her long term as headmistress. Founded in 1875, this was the city's oldest girls' school. It offered a rigorous education and produced many illustrious alumnae. During her years of study there, Betty's love of poetry, initially kindled by Miss Wilson, was set ablaze. She later insisted that this was a "saving" experience which would have implications for her life's vocation.[7] Previously, she had hoped to follow in the footsteps of her father and take up a career in medicine. A drawing of the parts of a microscope included in one of her youthful notebooks from this period appears to confirm this interest.[8] But now, a new path was opening.

Most of the verse Betty had read in school—Shakespeare, Longfellow, Tennyson, and Walter de la Mare—either did not excite her or filled her with melancholy. However, when she read G. K. Chesterton's "Lepanto," the story of a sea battle in which the Ottoman Turks were defeated by Catholic Austria, a breakthrough came.[9] The poem's language was stirring and dynamic, and the energy of the event was harnessed within the form of the poem. Here nature and heroes, religion and patriotism were captured in pounding rhythms and commanding sound.

> Dim drums throbbing, in the hills half heard,
> Where only on a nameless throne a crownless prince has stirred,
> Where, risen from a doubtful seat and half attainted stall,
> The last knight of Europe takes weapons from the wall,
> The last and lingering troubadour to whom the bird has sung,
> That once went singing southward when all the world was young,
> In that enormous silence, tiny and unafraid,
> Comes up along a winding road the noise of the Crusade.

For the first time Betty experienced excitement and exaltation in reading verse. She claimed "Lepanto" opened a door for her. She was uplifted and freed, "locked into language with a golden key."[10] Her English mistress, Miss Thomas, wrote on Betty's school report that "Latterly she has developed a taste for poetry."[11] This was an understatement. Reading "Lepanto" changed everything.[12] She claimed to be "set afire by it," to be "knocked sideways,"[13] to be transported to a timeless place.[14]

The emotion stirred by this experience led her to read Coleridge's "Rhyme of the Ancient Mariner," Wordsworth's "Tintern Abbey," and Keats' letters and his "Ode on a Grecian Urn." She found Keats' writing so immediate and fresh that she could not believe he was dead.[15] With her passion for poetry ignited, she felt she "had entered into [her] own kingdom."[16] "Reading poetry became a kind of secular sacrament, a true grace, something altogether deeper than a mere blessing."[17] She began to write her own early poems, which she later would dub her "twaddle"[18] or "doggerel."[19]

One day when she was thirteen years old a poem came to her while she was standing alone waiting for a bus. She rushed home to write it down, titling it "The Call of the Sea." It was the work of a young girl, inspired by a vista of the sea, who dreamt of gallant and courageous navigators exploring new lands. It was her first poem.

> As I sit, high on the cliff-top
> Gazing out at the great wide sea,
> And as I look on the glistening ocean,
> It brings strange thoughts to me....
> But long ago lived explorers
> Who set out to find new land
> They sailed in their little, wooden ships
> And landed on new sands.[20]

"Moonlight on the Oxus," written the same year, illustrates her growing resonance with nature. She writes:

> The moon it shineth down upon the river,
> Making the water gleaming down below,
> Whilst nearby sings the last sweet nightingale,
> Warbling his last sweet song.[21]

Although her father did not encourage her new-found interest, both her mother and her Uncle Frank were supportive. Madge Jennings would send her daughter's poems off to publishers, and Frank Davey served as champion and critic. Davey was an author of a book of verse and subsequently worked as a journalist in the Ministry of Information. Betty remembered him with affection as a man who understood her desire to write, never talked down to her, and made her feel less odd.[22] In gratitude she memorialized him in an autobiographical essay.[23] When

she shared a clutch of her poems with him she was surprised that he
selected the four-line poem, "The Dead Bird" as the best of the lot.
The poem came directly from her experience and refers to Peter, her
pet canary, who died and was buried in the garden in Boston.[24] It
verged on doggerel:

> I held it in my hand
> With its little hanging head.
> It was soft and warm and whole,
> But it was dead.[25]

Although she continued to send out poems, unsurprisingly, all were
refused. Finally, after a year and a half of effort she received a rejection
from *The New English Weekly* with an attached note: "These poems
show talent."[26] She was heartened, and kept on writing.

Except for her awakening to poetry, Jennings records nothing more
about her experience at Oxford High School other than her infatuation with Nancy Waters, a tall, beautiful student in the sixth form,
who was five years her senior and served as her mentor in the Girl
Guides. Although Betty was not one to join in many school activities,
all students were assigned to one of the four houses named after the
four winds. Betty's house was East. She was extremely loyal to her
housemates who all wore an identifying yellow badge. Nancy Waters
was head of East and senior prefect, and although Betty had almost no
direct interaction which her, she claimed Nancy had a moral effect on
her, guiding her on the right path and teaching her virtue, especially
about purity of thought in word and deed. She worshipped Nancy
from a distance and insisted this love relationship provided a fleeting
glimpse of Eden.[27] Because of Betty's strong sense of secrecy, she told
no one of her feelings for Nancy. Later she wrote of this relationship:
"I know that what I was feeling, and thinking, about Nancy was perhaps
the purest form of love a human being can ever feel for another. I had no
wish to be close [to] her, let alone touch or be touched by her. I simply
was grateful if I could worship from a distance."[28] Shortly after this
experience, Betty admitted to having a crush on a handsome young
priest.[29] This would not be the last of her fascination with clergy.

Betty's relationship with Nancy Waters was the first illustration
of her proclivity toward hero-worship, a phenomenon which would
persist throughout her life. She was always in search of those who were
perfect, who could be placed on a pedestal and be the recipient of her

devotion. As a form of selfless love, untarnished by envy or desire, she claimed hero-worship altered everything.[30] She later admitted that she almost never lived without a love of some kind and that for most of her life she had someone she could worship.[31] This was no mere admiration for another. It represents some profound need to have a psychological relationship which would be free of physical implications.

As Betty developed emotionally she came to appreciate various forms of art. Her interest in theater was kindled when she saw one of her heroes, John Gielgud, in performance.[32] Her love of the visual arts was shaped by her visits to Oxford's Ashmolean Museum. Wandering among its treasures, she experienced a sense of freedom and exaltation much like that given her in writing poetry. The performing and visual arts would offer her not only inspiration but alternative resources to relieve the loneliness and pain which would plague her later in life.

Perhaps as an expression of her fascination with ritual, Betty and a friend, probably Jane Pinches, invented a bizarre religion dedicated to a god, Cochineala.[33] It was a creation complete with codes and customs, totems, libations, dances, decorations of skulls and knives, and tortures to be inflicted on friends who were unbelievers. The parish priest laughed at this, but Dr. Jennings was shocked and tried to suppress it, admonishing his daughter that for a Christian this behavior was unacceptable.[34] At the same time Betty defended traditional religious orthodoxy and engaged in fights on the playground with a group of Marxist atheist students contesting her beliefs. She had been trained to be loyal, and her religious allegiance would be strictly maintained. She admitted that, as she rebutted the arguments of these fellow students, she felt hypocritical, but she never spoke to anyone of her own religious doubts and misgivings.[35]

Although Betty's late youth gave her a reprieve from anxiety and introduced her to poetry, on the cusp of adolescence, when she was about to be confirmed,[36] she experienced a fierce inner war.[37] She wrote that it was then she entered "the country of doubt" and "everything faltered."[38] Given that she was certain she "was among the chosen lost,"[39] what she wanted most was to hide.[40] She attended mass out of fear[41] and experienced confession as painful.[42] Her anxiety was increased as the parish priest repeatedly harped on the dangers of falling into mortal sin. God was a God of dread and punishment who offered neither freedom, grace, nor love.[43] She was confused and hurting, but knew of no place to turn for help (Figure 3.1).

Figure 3.1. St. Gregory and St. Augustine Catholic Church, Woodstock Road, Oxford, in 2017. Dana Greene.

She feared her father and could not share her doubts with him. Nonetheless he was concerned about her and at some point arranged to have her meet with a Jesuit psychologist.[44] Betty arrived at the consultation thinking the priest was interested in her verse, but was surprised when he focused instead on her mental state. The poems she brought with her may have included "Ode to Death" and "An Elegy in a Church-yard," which were recorded in the notebook "Trifles and Tid-bits"[45] which dates from this period. Apparently, nothing came of this meeting. She continued to suffer alone.

Betty's doubts about religion were exacerbated by her sexual awakening. In "Whitsun Sacrament," a poem written subsequently in which she recalls the sacrament of confirmation and the anxieties she experiences:

> Where is peace now in our unrest—
> The childish questions in the throbbing mind,
> The new name, itching loins, the shaping breast?
> When we most need a tongue we only find
> Christ at his silentest.[46]

Prior to the onset of puberty at age fifteen Betty acted like a tomboy who loved to run through the fields and race on her bicycle.[47] She prided herself on her flat chest and boyish body, but that changed when menstruation, the "curse," arrived. In a poem written about this time she compares the war which the nation was enduring with her own inner war brought about by her bodily changes. She wrote: "France fell and concentration camps were filled / But all the blood I knew was now my own / Body grew strange."[48] She was thrown into psychic turmoil by these physical changes and claimed to have had a "breakdown" because of them, although she offers no evidence of what transpired.[49] From the Old Testament she learned that menstruation made one unclean and she construed that to mean a loss of innocence.[50] She convinced herself that sex was filthy and evil and something to be feared, but at the same time she was intensely interested in it.[51] She confessed later to having created a "travesty of religion," one that denied the goodness of the natural world and saw matter as bad and spirit good. She admitted to being a Manichean or Albigensian.[52]

Her repressed sexual development and conflicted religious imagination led to increasing emotional disturbance. Her school work suffered and she began to fight with her parents about religion. They told her to go to confession and this resulted in an event which she revisited for years. As she tells it, in confession she was given a very harsh penance which was reduced when she burst into tears. It is unclear what she confessed, but it appears it was religious doubt and sexual fears. Nonetheless she was admonished not to go to communion with others the following day "because of her pride." The priest's words—"All you think of is your ugly 'little self'" were burned into her memory.[53] As a result she felt afraid, unworthy, an outcast, and a nuisance to her parents and friends.[54] However, out of loyalty to her religion, she never spoke of this until years later when she wrote an unpublished poem, "Abuse of a Sacrament," in which she chronicled her feelings about this episode and the cruelty done to children in the confessional.[55] Later she admitted that this abusive priest was twisted and sick, but that she felt no lasting hatred toward him.[56]

The beginning of Betty's adolescence corresponded with the outbreak of war in 1939. In the poem, "The Second World War," she documents her initial fears at hearing the declaration of war,[57] and in "Wings of the War" she illustrates her patriotism in this *fervorino* about the Royal Air Force "beating down the Hun," keeping England strong, and righting wrongs.[58] The war offered her another hero, the handsome and celebrated Lord Mountbatten, but she attested that it was her own self-preoccupation which had the greatest emotional impact on her, not the war. "I was a child when the war began. . . . / Bombs fell beyond my city. All I knew / Of war was adolescence."[59]

As the war proceeded it began to change the city and the university. Unlike other cities, Oxford was a safe area with only one unexploded bomb falling nearby. As men went off to fight and government offices filled with women employees moved to Oxford, the city's demographics were altered. University enrollments declined and buildings were closed. Everyone including students had to engage in war work. At some point Betty worked in a nursery for a short period of time. There was severe rationing, the distribution of gas masks, and the presence of evacuees in the city, but none of this was memorable to Betty. Mrs. Jennings housed some evacuees in their home, including Uncle Frank who was a good complement to the family.[60] In addition to these temporary household members, sometime during the war Cecil Jennings' mother moved in as well and her son redesigned the house to accommodate her. Her presence was not positive, however, and she contributed to a home life which Betty described as a "battle ground."[61]

Grandfather Jennings, who died when Betty was about two years old, was reputed to have been a kind man,[62] but Grandmother Jennings was not. She was a nag and gossip, who was particularly uncaring toward her daughter-in-law Madge. According to Betty, her grandmother created a situation in which Cecil Jennings was caught between his mother and his wife. At one point Grandmother Jennings nagged Madge to the point of hysteria and Madge contemplated running away. Nonetheless, when Grandmother Jennings was injured in an accident, Madge cared for her until her death. Betty admitted to feeling no grief at her grandmother's demise.[63]

The other major change in the Jennings household was the departure of Aileen when she turned eighteen. Although she had the intellectual ability to attend university, she opted to join the Women's Auxiliary Air Force (WAAF) and was assigned to the weather office for fighter and bomber squadrons. It was 1942, and one can imagine this opportunity would have appeal; home life was not happy and war work was adventurous as well as patriotic. However, when Aileen found herself pregnant by a married bomber pilot, a family crisis occurred. Aileen wanted to keep the baby, but Mrs. Jennings urged her to immediately give up the boy for adoption. The matter was kept secret and Betty learned about it only years later.[64]

Aileen's leaving home meant that from the age of fifteen and a half Betty was the only daughter in the house. She continued to attend Oxford High School (Figure 3.2) and to write poetry, the only thing that gave her pleasure. She fell under the spell of T. S. Eliot and began to compose long turgid confessional poems expressing her misery and her secret thoughts. Hoping to encourage her writing, one Christmas her mother gave her a copy of Eliot's *Four Quartets*, which was first published in 1943. Although her Eliot-inspired poetry is not extant, she did admit that writing it gave her the opportunity to learn to use poetic form, metaphor, and simile, to be an "apprentice-poet."[65] Writing verse helped her find unity in herself as she confronted the tumultuous world within and around her.[66]

In February 1944, during her final year at Oxford High School, Betty took the entrance exam for St. Anne's Society for Home Students, which would later become St. Anne's College. This was the only non-boarding

Figure 3.2. Former Oxford High School. Dana Greene

college for girls in Oxford, an alternative to the more expensive Lady Margaret Hall or Somerville College. This choice may have been dictated by finances, but it suited Elizabeth, as she now insisted on being called. Her friendships had been with those younger than herself and her home life had been sheltered. She was naive and protected, even though she had not been shielded from unhappiness. Now eighteen years old she would continue to live at home, dependent on her mother, who although loving towards her did not either understand her or connect with her emotionally. With her matriculation at St. Anne's Elizabeth's adolescent turmoil was about to abate. College would expand her world, give her a new self-image, and deepen her allegiance to poetry, her "saving" work.

4

Coming up to Oxford

It starts in autumn. This ancient city opens
Its broad thick doors to youth....
The ancient books and fragrant streets, we hear
Bells sounding, see the beauty of being young
Adorning this charmed and ancient atmosphere
With eagerness, trust and song.[1]

"First Term"

Elizabeth Jennings had lived in Oxford for eight years, but in October 1944 she entered its university. Within the embrace of this "kindly teacher" she found temporary reprieve from her religious doubts and her isolation. Intellectually stimulated and socially engaged, it was here she would discover a voice of her own (Figure 4.1).[2]

Attending university meant in her case riding her bicycle or taking a short bus ride down Banbury Road to the Victorian houses which made up St. Anne's Society for Home Students.[3] In the 1940s St. Anne's enrollment was some 200 young women under the guidance of the principal, Eleanor Plummer. By 1952 it would gain full college status and later would claim as alumnae luminaries like Penelope Lively, Karen Armstrong, Wendy Beckett, and Susan Sontag.

Her initial experience at St. Anne's was challenging and she "nearly went down."[4] Her course of study was English literature—Anglo-Saxon, Middle English, and modern literature from the fifteenth through the nineteenth centuries. She read Milton, Donne, and the Metaphysical poets and then modern and contemporary ones—Eliot, Auden, Yeats, MacNeice, Day Lewis, Edwin Muir, and Graves. She studied philosophical works as well—Plato, Aquinas, Hobbes, and Berkeley. Her principal

Figure 4.1. Elizabeth Jennings. Courtesy of Mark Albrow

tutor was Miss Elaine Griffiths, but the person she remembered with most affection was Mrs. Dorothy Bednarowska, an English Catholic convert who had a distinguished reputation as a teacher and whom she credited with bringing out her unrecognized talents. While at St. Anne's she took full advantage of the intellectual offerings of the university. She attended lectures by Lord David Cecil and Professor Helen Gardner, and during her second year she participated in C. S. Lewis' Saturday morning lectures in Magdalen Hall on medieval and Renaissance literature.[5] At his suggestion, she read *Plato's Symposium* and was exalted.

University life opened a new world for her; even her nagging religious doubts were somewhat assuaged as she interacted with Catholic intellectuals. In this pre-Vatican II world, she had access to some of the best English Catholic thinkers through her participation in the Catholic chaplaincy. She heard talks by Monsignor Ronald Knox, theologian and translator of scripture, and she sought guidance from the handsome Father Martin D'Arcy, S.J., head of Campion Hall and mentor to several prominent Catholic converts.

In high school, she had been largely unengaged in social activities, but now she enthusiastically participated in various student organizations. She joined the high-powered Socratic Club and the university Film Society, which nurtured her lifelong interest in foreign films. As a foreign film aficionado, she frequently attended shows at the Scala Theatre on Walton Street on Sunday evening with Mrs. Bednarowska. Her interest in theater was spurred by participation in the university's Experimental Theatre Club where she had a minor role in Noël Coward's *Hands across the Sea* and an appearance in Keble College's production of *Much Ado about Nothing*.

The intellectual stimulation of university life was augmented by her discovery of the rich cultural resources of London. The war had precluded most travel, but at its end that changed and Elizabeth and Justine O'Sullivan, a fellow student at St. Anne's and a Londoner, began to visit the city. They attended performances of the London Ballet, the Russian Monte Carlo Ballet, Ballet Rambert, and Sadler's Wells. They made forays to the Wallace Collection and the National Gallery where Elizabeth first saw *Rembrandt's Late Self-Portrait*. It was grace, she claimed, that stopped her in her tracks in front of that painting, filling her with awe and delight[6] and assuring that experience remained in her memory. But the highlight of these London adventures was attending theatrical performances. At the Haymarket Elizabeth saw her hero, John Gielgud, in *Hamlet* and the *Duchess of Malfi*, and relished a performance of *Henry IV Part* 1 with Laurence Olivier. She was beside herself with excitement to find Gielgud, Noël Coward, Malcolm Sargent, and others in the audience all at the same time at that performance.

Although engaged in academic and social life, it is curious that during this period of savage warfare Elizabeth offers no observations on national or political events, either in her poetry or in her autobiographical writing. She does not comment on the end of war or on V.E. Day, although the nation at large was energized by victory and relieved that the devastation would cease. This lack of interest and engagement is an early illustration of what would follow. As poet, she would eschew political commentary.

By age eighteen Elizabeth Jennings' self-image as the "plain one" began to fade. Although she did nothing to enhance her appearance, she was a naturally attractive young woman, petite, and with lovely bright blue eyes. Men began to pay attention to her. During the first term at university she met Francis Muir at a party at the Catholic chaplaincy. It was Muir who gave her a first kiss and a first gin and orange. Although he expressed his love for her, she was not interested in him and their relationship went nowhere (Figure 4.2).

A more lasting relationship began at a Christmas party in 1946 where she met Stuart, whose family name she does not reveal. He was a Keble man who was seven years her senior, a former prisoner of war in Japan, a poet, and a Buddhist.[7] During the spring they spent a great deal of time together. They punted and swam in the Thames and the Cherwell and visited London, where they attended theatrical performances and Stuart introduced her to Chinese food. Although enrolled in two weekly university tutorials, she neglected most of her other academic responsibilities. After each of her exams Stuart brought her the traditional color-coordinated carnation. In the summer of 1947 she achieved Second Class Honors and the B.A. degree was conferred in October of that year. After the end of Trinity term, she spent every day with Stuart. She described this as a "summer of loving," an idyllic time which was both passionate and "innocent." Right before her twenty-first birthday in July, Stuart proposed marriage and she accepted.

Figure 4.2. Jennings family. Courtesy of Mark Albrow

Since Stuart still had to complete another year at the university, Elizabeth decided to stay on as well. Dr. Jennings agreed to pay her fees. She continued to live at home, and in the fall of 1947 she was admitted as a Probationer B. Litt. student. Her research project was to be a study of Matthew Arnold as a Romantic and Classical poet, to be supervised by Professor John Norman Bryson, a Fellow at Balliol.[8] This was an interesting choice of topic, signaling her early attempt to unify her own commitment to poetry as both rational and visionary. She shared Arnold's concern with religious doubt and the role of poetry in a world in which religion's influence was waning. Arnold's prophetic claim "... mankind will discover that we have to turn to poetry to interpret life for us, to console us, to sustain us..."[9] must have given voice to her own understanding of the future of the genre. Irrespective of her interest, she did not give much attention to her studies. She failed the preliminary exam, which was required to be admitted as a full student for the B.Litt., and decided not to present herself for a second attempt. She never completed her proposed study of Arnold, but as was the practice she was awarded the M.A. degree in June 1951.[10]

On the day she failed her examination Stuart purchased an engagement ring and presented himself to Dr. Jennings asking consent for the marriage. As Elizabeth tells it, her father was in the middle of watching a cricket match and was annoyed at this disturbance. He refused to consent, claiming such a marriage would never work.[11] But this paternal opposition did not bring an end to her relationship with Stuart.

Irrespective of academic failure, Elizabeth had had the good fortune of meeting the charming Kingsley Amis in a seminar in Elizabethan court handwriting. It was Amis who would have an important role in advancing her as a poet. Amis came up to St. John's College in the early 1940s where he met fellow students and poets Philip Larkin and John Wain. After they completed their degrees Larkin went off to work as a librarian first at Wellington, Shropshire, then at Belfast, and ultimately at the University of Hull, and Wain stayed in Oxford where he earned an advanced degree. Amis left Oxford after his first year, served in the war, and afterwards returned to the university to complete his studies. He was four years older than Elizabeth, but they got on well. She enjoyed his sense of humor, his charm, and his creativity. Together they avidly discussed poetry, listened to jazz, and attended the cinema. Most important, Amis liked her poetry.[12] Along with James Michie, Amis headed up *Oxford Poetry*, which was the organ of the Oxford Poetry

Society, founded by him, Larkin, and Wain several years before. In a 1948 issue of the magazine Amis included Jennings' poem "The Elements" which opens with this stanza: "The elements surround us, / Earth, water, air and fire, / And O my love I bring you / Those thoughts that long since found us / And quickened our desire / So this desire I sing you."[13] This was a love poem structured around the four elements of nature— earth, water, air, and fire—and as such was a portent of her future verse linking love with the natural world. In 1949 her poem "The Clock" appeared in *The Spectator* and was the first illustration of her lifelong preoccupation with the phenomenon of time. The clock "Makes me wish there were some clock within / More regular than heart, steady as rock, / That we might know / The time to end, begin, / The time for stopping love or war / Or hate…"[14] In another early poem, "Modern Poet," she illustrates her natural alignment with the spirit of that which would be called the Movement. "This is no moment now for the fine phrases," she wrote, "The inflated sentence, words cunningly spun, / For the floreate image or the relaxing pun / Or the sentimental answer that most pleases."[15] Amis was pleased with her poetry and he selected six of her poems for inclusion in another issue of *Oxford Poetry*. Later he would call Elizabeth Jennings "the star of the show, our discovery."[16]

Jennings found the university a congenial place to be a poet. Her friends were interested in her work and their criticism was helpful. Most important, she believed they cared for her.[17] During her years there she was introduced to an expansive poetic tradition. She claimed Yeats was the greatest poet of the century,[18] but she acknowledged he did not have a permanent influence on her. But there were others who shaped her poems and her poetics. From Auden she learned the use of the surprising adjective and how to turn an abstract idea into a poetic image. In the poetry of Edwin Muir she saw eloquence and intensity deepened by Christian belief and human suffering. She admired Hopkins' innovative language and especially his religious and nature poems, and resonated with the poets from whom he drew inspiration, namely Herbert and Rossetti, who like Hopkins also suffered greatly. Robert Graves' love of truth and his magnificent feel for language had an influence on her early poems as well, and she acknowledged Stephen Spender, Cecil Day-Lewis, and Louis MacNeice as poets who helped her write better verse.[19]

Oxford was an exciting place to be a poet, but English poetry was dominated by male voices. Prominent women poets were few. Vita

Sackville-West, Anne Ridler, E. J. Scovell, Ruth Pitter, and Kathleen Raine were of an earlier generation and none was an academic. The woman poet was an anomaly in the university environment. Yet it was here that Elizabeth Jennings claimed to find her poetic "voice".

Jennings' university years were intellectually invigorating and support-ive of her interests, but she was now about to leave that environment.[20] Stuart finished his studies at Oxford and enrolled in the School of Oriental and African Studies in London. Even though their relation-ship had problems, she wanted to be with him in that magical city. To that end she looked for employment and found it as a copy writer at a London advertising firm. Once employed she lived with her aunt, and she and Stuart saw each other every evening at the theater and cinema. On the weekend she would return home to Oxford. As it turned out her work, for which she earned £6 per week, consisted in writing headlines and copy for the likes of Richard Shops and Simpson's Sportswear. She was bored and miserable and was trapped in a tiny office with a temperamental older woman who demeaned her. She continued working for almost a year, but since there was not enough work to keep her busy she quit, narrowly escaping being fired. Her relationship with Stuart began to deteriorate as both were seeing other people. Elizabeth was attracted to Peter Chettle, a law student at University College, and to another ex-service man. Ultimately Stuart forced the issue, saying he wanted to get married, but she saw marriage as tedious drudgery and declined to acquiesce. Although happy to be the recipient of male attention, what she principally wanted from men was admiration for her poetry. This, plus her lingering fears about sex, limited her interest in marriage. Already she had some incipient understanding of the priority of her vocation as poet and the challenge that the entanglements of love posed. In August 1949 Stuart ended their engagement. Jennings was at that point without a job or a prospective husband.[21] With no reason to remain in London, she returned to Oxford to live with her parents.

5

Breaking into Print

Poetry's got too far away from life, become too much a parlour game
for dons and clever young men.... All the poets have retreated into
their private gardens because they didn't feel strongly enough about
the poetic world.[1]

Elizabeth Jennings to Paul West

It was humiliating to return home. Jennings felt useless, ashamed,
and very lonely. She acknowledged that the gray dampness of
Oxford contributed to her depression.[2] She was twenty-three years
old and jobless, and had to explain to those who asked why she was
not getting married. One person who was not unhappy about her
lack of a marriage partner was Cecil Jennings. He had never liked
Stuart in the first place.

During this transitional time Elizabeth continued to write poems
and to send them off to small magazines. But she was miserable. Using
her father's contacts, she finally secured a position as assistant librarian
at the Oxford City Library, a large magnificent Victorian building at
St. Aldate's in city center, now home to the Oxford Town Hall. Her
hours were long—she had to stay late three nights and work on Saturdays,
the busiest day of the week. On Thursday, her day off, she often went
into London. But her schedule was demanding and inflexible and her
salary minimal at £6 per week. Her work consisted in checking out
and shelving books and sometimes manning the reference desk. At
times, she became irritated with library patrons. Once, in a fury, she
retreated to the basement and flung a chair across the room, smashing
it to bits.[3] She admitted: "I've got an awful temper,"[4] which she claimed
to have inherited from her father.[5]

Since Aileen's marriage fell on Saturday when Elizabeth was expected to work, Dr. Jennings had to intervene with the library authorities and request that his daughter be given permission to be absent from her responsibilities. In October 1950 Aileen married Desmond Albrow, a good-natured and witty journalist who at various times would work for the *Manchester Guardian*, the *Daily* and *Sunday Telegraph*, and the *Catholic Herald* (Figure 5.1). Ultimately the Albrows would raise a large family of four children: Gillian, for whom Elizabeth would serve as godmother, Judith, Mark, and Susan.

During the first year of her employment Elizabeth records falling in love with a student named John. Again, she provides no family name. Her description of this relationship is instructive about her views on love. She admits to being obsessed with John, but she decided to banish any self-seeking on her part in their relationship. She claimed to love him with a "selfless," "maternal" love, with "disinterestedness." As a consequence she reports that her neurosis about sex took second place. When he suggested she sleep with him, she explained her "religious principles" prohibited her from doing so. In the end, she was sure he

Figure 5.1. Wedding of Aileen Jennings and Desmond Albrow, 1950. Elizabeth Jennings is third from the right. Courtesy of Mark Albrow

did not love her or admire her poems. To her mind John caused her more misery than anyone in her life,[6] and the only good thing to come of their tortured relationship was his introducing her to the future poet laureate, Cecil Day-Lewis, who would become a friend.[7]

During this time, she also made friends with Jenny Joseph and Lotte Zurndorfer, both poets who along with Elizabeth would be recognized in 1952 in *Six Women Poets*.[8] Joseph became her traveling companion as well, accompanying her on "magical" summer holidays to Italy. The sun, sand, sea, Italian architecture, and painting all appealed to Elizabeth. She visited Florence, Venice, Ravenna, Sorrento, Naples, and Rome.[9] From these journeys she claimed to have a new sense of time and landscape. She noted that the Italians lived out their history and religion in ways that the English did not.[10] These early Italian travels would remain in her imagination and have a direct influence on her subsequent life-changing decisions.

The 1950s were a fruitful time for poetry in Oxford. Although Jennings had no standing within the university, she was caught up in the poetry community that flourished among the post-war students, who tended to be conservative, cautious, earnest, and isolated from foreign influences.[11] During her second year of employment at the library she was assigned more regularly to the reference desk, which gave her ample opportunity to interact with undergraduate student poets who would greatly expand and enrich her own intellectual and social life.

As a slightly older and ambitious poet, Jennings was sought out for her counsel and advocacy. Paul West, Peter Levi, Alan Brownjohn, Anthony Thwaite, Adrian Mitchell, and Geoffrey Hill, as well as two Americans, Donald Hall and Adrienne Rich, all engaged with her, calling themselves "Elizabethans," admirers who also became friends. Their stimulating interaction was carried on in the library, at dinner, tea time, at the cinema, and through letters. This proved to be a great boon to her productivity. Although serious, self-sufficient, purposive, and dedicated to poetry, Jennings also enjoyed social life. Paul West recalls holding her out of a window while she vomited punch into the quad of Lincoln College. Apparently, it had been strongly laced with alcohol.[12]

Several of these young poets became important persons in her life. Donald Hall, the tall, burly American, arrived at Oxford with a passionate love of poetry and enthusiastically threw himself into the literary scene. It was he who introduced Jennings to the work of the American poet Richard Wilbur and deepened her knowledge of the poetry of

Robert Lowell and Wallace Stevens.[13] Anthony Thwaite was also one of her stalwarts. After he finished his studies, he went off to be professor of English at Tokyo University. Peter Levi, who met Jennings through the Indian poet and fellow Catholic Dom Moraes, was training to be a Jesuit at Campion Hall and became her longtime friend and supporter.[14] For a few years Jennings carried on a correspondence with Paul West, who finished his studies at Columbia University. She gently critiqued his poems and shared with him her concern that English poets had "lost their grip" and "got too far away from life." What she felt was needed were thoughtful poems with big subjects, a sense of personal experience, and amazing imagery rather than a small "something" in the Sunday papers.[15] Although the young American poet, Adrienne Rich, had less contact with Jennings, she considered her poetry "immensely satisfying" and her insights the most "mature" of the younger generation of English poets.[16]

After Jennings was launched as an Oxford poet by Amis in *Oxford Poetry*, new possibilities opened for her. Over the next several years her poems began to appear in prominent magazines: *London Magazine*, *Poetry Review*, *The Spectator*, *New English Weekly*, *New Statesman and Nation*, and *The Listener*. Later many of these poems would be collected and appear in her first book, *Poems*, which would be published in 1953.

Jennings' rich interaction with students, poets, publishers, and editors gave her confidence and hope, removing her earlier sense of inadequacy. Her attendance at events, readings, and parties yielded contacts. Although shy and retiring in social settings, she made acquaintance with several literati. In early 1952, she attended a London party where she met Stevie Smith, Muriel Spark, Michael Hamburger, and Wrey Gardiner. Hamburger introduced her to Janet Adam Smith, literary editor of the *New Statesman*, who accepted some of her poems for publication.[17] Stephen Spender also asked her to contribute to his new magazine, *Encounter*. She met John Lehmann, who was beginning a new literary program for the B.B.C. called *New Soundings*. It was on this program that "The Substitute," her haunting poem of "rehearsed" love by one "untutored" and "unpractised" was read.[18] Her friendship with Lehmann led also to an invitation to contribute three poems to the first issue of his new *London Magazine*. Through Lehmann she was introduced to his assistant, Barbara Cooper, who became a friend. At a party at Lehmann's house she met Edith Sitwell and the historian C. V. (Veronica) Wedgwood,[19] and at a poetry reading at the Institute of

Contemporary Arts in London she made the acquaintance of the Neo-Platonic poet Kathleen Raine, who invited her to tea at her home in Chelsea. In the end Jennings found the formidable Raine to be approachable. They shared a belief that poetry was a sacred vocation but differed about their concepts of God. On another occasion, she met the Christian poet Anne Ridler.[20] Older and a well-established poet, Ridler would soon play an important role in Jennings' success by introducing Jennings' first book of poetry. Jennings was thrilled to have met these writers, all of whom, she noted, had been kind to her.

Although known in the Oxford poetry scene as a Catholic, at this time Jennings' religious practice was perfunctory and limited to basic obligations. She remained troubled about how to reconcile sex with her religion. Her Manichean understanding of the body continued to be in conflict with her amorous desires. Jennings used the restrictions of Catholicism as a form of defense. While her relationships with men were not Platonic, they were restrained. She recorded a quip from Donald Hall: "Gee, Elizabeth, if it weren't for your religion, you'd be sleeping with Geoffrey [Hill], James [Price], and Paul [West]."[21] Hall made his own amorous advances but failed to get beyond her protect-ive shield.[22] She was "smothered by youthful admiration." Once when in Radcliffe Hospital for removal of an ovarian cyst she claimed her Oxford admirers descended en masse to cheer her.[23]

For Jennings, the highlight of the early 1950s was the publication of two collections of her poems—a small pamphlet of seven poems and a first volume of forty poems. These immeasurably increased her reputation. It was the arrival of the painter-printer Oscar Mellor in Eynsham, a village outside of Oxford, which made these publications possible. Mellor developed what was called the Fantasy Press Series, small pamphlets of seven or eight poems which sold for sixpence and were published in conjunction with the Oxford University Poetry Society. The series served to launch Oxford's poetic talent at a time when it was very difficult for young poets to get a first book published. Elizabeth Jennings' poems were featured in Fantasy Press pamphlet number one in 1952.[24] Mellor would go on to publish the poetry of Amis, Thwaite, Rich, Hall, Mitchell, Hill, and Larkin in the same format, but Jennings' poems were the first to appear. She sent a copy of the pamphlet to Edwin Muir, a poet she much admired, who wrote back commending her work.[25] Donald Hall sent a copy to Anne Ridler, who was also greatly impressed.[26] When Veronica Wedgwood received her copy, she was spurred to nominate Jennings for membership in the P.E.N. Club and to recommend her as a book reviewer for *Time and Tide*. Her first book review, a critique of *The Egotistical Sublime* by Oxford Fellow John Jones,[27] appeared in this magazine.

Based on the success of Jennings' little pamphlet, Mellor brought out her first full-length book, *Poems*, in 1953.[28] To Jennings' delight it won the Arts Council Award for the best first book of poetry published in the previous two and a half years and brought with it a subsidy of £225. Consequently, she began to receive what she called the "Star Treatment." Photographers from Oxford and London came to the library to take her photograph and interview her, the Library Committee called her in to extend congratulations, and Kathleen Raine, who also won an award that year, gave a celebratory party to which she invited the award-winning Jennings. This public acclaim gave Jennings confidence and strengthened her bold resolve to have a poem or book review published each week in one of the important London journals—*The Spectator*, *Time and Tide*, *The Listener*, or *The Times Literary Supplement*. This was an audacious aspiration.

Poems is important for the clarity of its verse, its strong, independent voice, and the themes expressed. Most of its short lyric verses are about love in various guises—false love, infatuation, love abating, and friendship. The most famous of these is the much-anthologized opening poem "Delay," in which cosmic starlight is analogized to love delayed.

> The radiance of that star that leans on me,
> Was shining years ago. . . .
>
> Love that loves now may not reach me until
> Its first desire is spent.[29]

The volume includes poems on childhood and the sea, both constant themes of her poetry. "Fishermen" was one of her best loved poems, and eight years later she included it in her anthology of her favorite poems.[30] There are also poems on travel. In "The Arrival" she compares the consequence of travel to that of love:"See how travel conveys him as love can / Out of himself,"[31] and in "The Island," she writes: "All travelers escape the mainland here. . . . Men on the shore are also islands, steer / Self to knowledge of self in the calm sea / Seekers who are their own discovery."[32] "The Island," the book's final poem, was subsequently used by Robert Conquest as the opening poem of his *New Lines* anthology.

Poems opens with an introduction by the well-connected Anne Ridler, who previously worked as Eliot's personal secretary at Faber and Faber. She commended Jennings' poetry for its clarity and exactness, noted the influence of Auden and Edwin Muir, and suggested the poems were concerned with various forms of self-knowledge arrived at by means of writing itself. Writing, Ridler said, was part of the process of discovery.[33]

Reviews of *Poems* were mixed. A *Times Literary Supplement* reviewer appreciated its rich imagery, single-minded purpose, and psychological insight and suggested that the poems contained three styles of writing— the lyrical, the metaphysical, and a synthesis of both.[34] But G. S. Fraser's critique in *New Statesman and Nation* angered her.[35] She feared Fraser's remark that he imagined Jennings putting on white gloves before beginning to write would convince readers her poems were sentimental. It gave her little solace that James Reeves wrote a positive review of *Poems* in *Time and Tide*, since she was sure no one would see it there.[36]

As a published poet Jennings began to be included in literary events. At a party at Kathleen Raine's in 1955 she met Edwin Muir, who admired her work, and at a gathering at Veronica Wedgwood's in London she encountered the American poet W. S. Merwin, who encouraged her to send her poems to American magazines. At that point, she had had only one poem published in *The New Yorker*.[37] Her P.E.N. membership led to an invitation to edit a P.E.N. anthology of verse with Stephen Spender and Dannie Abse. She accepted, and although the work was taxing, she admitted it taught her a lot about herself.[38] In 1956 she was invited to be guest poet at the 1956 Cheltenham Literary Festival, where she met the future poet laureate John Betjeman. That same year, with some trepidation she did her first radio broadcast on *Woman's Hour*.

During all this time, she was writing new poems which differed from those which appeared in *Poems*. She turned now to examine the poet's way of knowing, the relationship between appearance and the real meaning of things. Some forty of these poems were collected into her next volume, *A Way of Looking*, which was brought out in 1955 by Deutsch. These poems are lucid and restrained attempts to harmonize the intellectual and the emotional self. She asks: "How much am I then what I think, how much what I feel?"[39] Her hope was to discover the truths that underlie ordinary experience. At this point she excluded consideration of religious truth. In a letter to Paul West she wrote that for now there was much to discover and experience before she could deal with religious themes. Her present concerns were identity, the limits of self-knowledge, and the meaning underneath the surface of life. She lamented that there were so many states of mind not yet dignified by poetry.[40]

A Way of Looking contains short lyrics which use traditional verse patterns and are marked by understatement. All have a definite shape and form, and some use rhyme. Her themes are familiar ones—childhood, Italy, the seasons, the sea. In the poem "Kings" she gives the first indication of her lifelong conviction that humans need heroes, those who can be worshiped. The volume's most poignant poem is "For a Child Born Dead," written on the death of the first-born child of her sister Aileen and brother-in-law Desmond. It concludes: "Then all our consolation is / That grief can be as pure as this."[41]

Two poems from *A Way of Looking* appeared in Philip Larkin's *The Oxford Book of Twentieth-Century English Verse* published in 1973. Although it contained the work of 200 poets, only one-tenth were women. Jennings' "Song at the Beginning of Autumn," the first of her many autumnal poems, and "Answers," a poem affirming her commitment to confront large human questions, were included. In this latter poem she writes:

> I kept my answers small and kept them near
> Big questions bruised my mind but still I let
> Small answers be a bulwark to my fear.
>
> But the big answers clamoured to be moved
> Into my life. Their great audacity
> Shouted to be acknowledged and believed.[42]

A Way of Looking received critical and positive reviews. Thomas Kinsella suggested that Jennings was a competent minor poet who explored the interaction between the large themes of love, doubt, and grief, but that she created no excitement in her verse.[43] She was pleased with the review in *Time and Tide* and Philip Oakes' appraisal, but she considered Roy Fuller's review a "real Stinker."[44] Although praise for the book was muted, Jennings was elated when she received congratulatory letters from people she respected. Philip Larkin wrote that she had an uncommon gift and that he admired her sense of "ear," that she gave words space to "breathe."[45] W. S. Merwin,[46] J. R. R. Tolkien,[47] Kathleen Raine,[48] and Robert Graves[49] all wrote to congratulate her.

She was delighted when in 1956 *A Way of Looking* won the Somerset Maugham Award. It was Mrs. Jennings who had persuaded her daughter to enter the competition,[50] but Vita Sackville-West may have had something to do with her success. Before the award was made, Sackville-West inquired of Jennings her age and whether *A Way of Looking* was her first book of poems. She added that her questions were neither "frivolous nor journalistic."[51] The award carried with it the princely sum of £400 and was given to a writer under age thirty-five whose work had been published in the last year. Usually it went to a prose writer, Kingsley Amis having won it the year prior for his novel *Lucky Jim*. Jennings was only the second woman to receive the award.[52]

The Somerset Maugham Award provided support to live in a foreign country in order to study the "manners and customs of foreign people." There was no contest as to which foreign country Jennings would select. She would return to Italy, specifically to Rome, which she had visited briefly on a previous trip to Sorrento. Her plan was to secure a three-month leave without pay from the library and to depart in April 1957. But leaving would be difficult. During the last seven years she had gradually built a reputation, and greater acclaim seemed imminent. Earlier Kingsley Amis had declared she was "the star of the show." Now that star was rising.

6

The Movement

To write poems...means that one is bound, sooner or later, to come upon some of the deepest, most vital experiences of mankind. The art of poetry is an art which, of its very nature, strips away inessentials to reveal only what is important, only what will suffice. What the poem discovers—and this is its chief function—is order amid chaos, meaning in the middle of confusion, and affirmation at the heart of despair.[1]

Poetry To-Day

By the mid-1950s Jennings' star was aligned with the fortunes of a group of poets dubbed "the Movement." However, she considered this conjoining a "journalistic gimmick"[2] and that her association with it was "positively unhelpful because [she] tended to be grouped and criticized [with them] rather than grouped and praised."[3] Elizabeth Jennings did not want to be categorized and she certainly did not want to be criticized. Although her poetry did share some similarities with the work of the other Movement poets, she considered herself distinctive given that she was the only woman and Roman Catholic among them. By the time her third book, *A Sense of the World*, appeared it was evident that she had already begun to diverge from the others. At that point the Movement itself was largely defunct, each of its members having gone his separate way. If the Movement existed, and most of its members denied it did, it was short-lived.

In the history of English poetry, the Movement is considered a mid-century phenomenon. After the Second World War, there was no dominant figure in English poetry around whom other poets could align. When the poets of the 1950s emerged, they were both reacting against earlier poetry and reflecting the national desire to return to the values of a pre-war England with its unified culture. At that point the damage of the war was still evident, rationing continued, Britain's imperial power was declining, and war threatened in Korea and with the Soviet Union. An attitude of austerity and non-engagement affected the culture in general and poetry in particular. Insular and conservative, Movement poetry was shaped by and reflected the national mood.[4]

The origins of the Movement have been linked to friendships formed in the early 1940s among the Oxford poets Philip Larkin, Kingsley Amis, and John Wain, and the emergence of a clutch of magazines and publishers which made their work available to the general public. This small world of friendship was expanded ultimately to include other poets—D. J. Enright, Donald Davie, Elizabeth Jennings, Thom Gunn, John Holloway, and Robert Conquest. They were nonetheless "an accidental grouping" which was thought to embody the English soul.[5] The proximate identifying of the Movement was in an unsigned article, "In the Movement," which appeared in the October 1954 issue of *The Spectator*. It was written by the literary editor, J. D. Scott, who claimed that poetry had moved beyond the despair of the 1940s and had entered a new skeptical and ironic stage. The article stimulated discussion, which led in 1955 to D. J. Enright's publishing *Poets of the 1950s*, an anthology of poems by those who he suggested were reacting against both the political commitments of the poets of the 1930s and the neo-romanticism of the 1940s. The anthology did not have wide impact, however, since it was published in Japan where Enright was teaching. In 1956 Robert Conquest published another anthology, *New Lines*, which identified the first nine "New Liners," or Movement poets. Six of these poets were university teachers, two were librarians, and one was a civil servant. They were hailed as "University Wits," "New Liners," or "New Academics," who were grouped together because their poetry was alleged to have similar characteristics. For Conquest these poets were empirical, had a reverence for the real, used rational structure and comprehensible language, and were neither mystical nor theoretical. In short, they had a "determination to avoid bad principles."[6] *New Lines* opened with ten poems by Elizabeth Jennings, seemingly reflecting how securely she was embedded with her Movement colleagues. But she did not really belong.

The poets of the Movement have been variously appraised by critics and historians.[7] Whether they were in fact a movement at all is dubious, having never issued a manifesto or even met together as a group. The commonality they shared was their commitment to clarity, restraint, and the use of rhyme and meter. They all admired Eliot and the literary critic and poet William Empson, hence they were also called "Neo-Empsonians," and they borrowed from Graves and Auden. They respected the poets of the eighteenth and nineteenth centuries but rejected the work of Dylan Thomas with his emphasis on feeling. Their worldview was provincial, agnostic, and politically noncommittal. They were Little Englanders who were sometime crass and debunking. As boozing blokes, they made Conquest's alleged quip that Elizabeth Jennings was "like a schoolmistress" thrown together "with a bunch of drunken marines" not far off the mark.[8] Soon after the publication of *New Lines* the Movement poets each began to pursue an independent course. By the 1960s new literary groups such as the Mavericks, the Post-Movement, and The Group sprang up. Furthermore, in 1962 A. Alvarez edited *The New Poetry*, a survey of post-war English poetry, which appeared to many to be a reaction against the Movement.

Was Jennings a Movement poet? While classified with the Movement she was not fully of it. She was not ironic or satirical, she had affinities for romanticism and symbolism which were hers alone, and her interests were distinct from her Movement colleagues. Yet Amis had claimed her as the "star of the show," allying her with the others. Jennings did not seek out this alliance. Her view was that poets writing at the same time and place would of necessity share certain disciplines and characteristics. She felt that it was nearness in age rather than deep knowledge of each other that linked the Movement poets together.[9] Her lack of contact with these poets is confirmed by the fact that she only knew Amis, Wain, and Conquest. She met Gunn only briefly at a poetry reading, Holloway at a party in 1956, and as late as 1958 she had not yet met Larkin. She did not recall having met Davie, and she was acquainted with Enright only superficially.[10] She was not alone in this since Larkin too claimed not to have met Gunn or Holloway until after the Movement had crested (Figure 6.1).[11]

Jennings reflects on her relationship with these poetic colleagues in three discrete places: *Let's Have Some Poetry*, *Poetry To-Day*, and "Ten Years After: The Making of the Movement."[12] In these writings, she claims the Movement was not a literary movement because its poets did not deliberately ally themselves with one another, did not announce their aims, had no particular message like the poets of the 1930s, and used no similar technique, as did the Beats. The only values affirmed by all Movement poets were clarity, honesty, and formal perfection, but these, she insisted, were required of any good poetry.

Figure 6.1. Elizabeth Jennings. Courtesy of Mark Albrow

Her final evaluation of the Movement was that in the turmoil of the twenty years between 1940 and 1960 "[p]oetry has become a gesture of defiance, a plea for order in a universe of confusion and man–made chaos."[13] As such, poetry took on some of the work of philosophy or metaphysics, searching with honesty for the motives behind human actions and their meaning. Since the Movement poets assisted in this she considered them "humanists," contending that the best of them would outlive the artificial grouping in which they had been placed.[14]

Whatever estrangement Jennings might have felt from the Movement, it seems clear that alliance with it, at least initially in her career, garnered her affection and prominence which she probably could not have gained on her own as a young woman poet. However, she was marginalized within the Movement and then disapproved for deviating from it. The consequence was criticism which pained her greatly.

Jennings believed that the poem was part of the poet, that she was inside the poem and hence to criticize her poems was to criticize her.[15] Convinced that a bad first review of a book meant that no one would buy her work, she suffered in "pure agony" when one appeared. She insisted she was not opposed to criticism, but that much of it, particularly by anonymous reviewers, was malicious. Criticism which was helpful should be given by friends in private. But that too was painful, bringing her to tears.[16] Even positive reviews gave her pause. "They encourage me and often I look at them and wonder if they are true. The bad ones always make me feel doleful, and I feel *sure* they are true."[17] Her aversion to disapproval was profound, debilitating, and lifelong. But the critics' rejection of or tepid response to her verse did not diminish its growing popularity with the public.

The earliest extended expression of Jennings' poetics is found in *Let's Have Some Poetry*, published in 1960 and dedicated to "Jonathan."[18] In these unsystematic reflections[19] she defines poetry as communication about every kind of subject matter. For her the poem is a complex mixture of feeling, thought, language, imagery, music, and design. A successful poem balances form and content. Rhyme, through repetition, gives delight, and rhythm brings vividness to language. Although poetry has intellectual content, it does not attempt to prove anything. Rather by using language and imagery it creates an emotion which reaches toward truth. It makes something real, and as such it casts light on reality itself. For Jennings poetry does not substitute for religion, but it satisfies the religious instinct, inspiring awe and offering beauty. When it confronts tragedy, its genius is that it helps the reader both experience grief and accept it as part of some larger reality.

Jennings sees a special role for poets in helping to restore meaning and order in the chaos of a post-Eden world. In a later poem, she writes:

> We shape, we cut, we steal, we wrap, and we are
> Makers of order where there wasn't one. ...
> We lost liberty
> Of one kind but we've fashioned others. Now
> In our wild world of misrule we insist
> On shapeliness and balance. ...
> O we exist
> To make new order since our Eden loss.[20]

For Jennings poets, more than others, are aware of the meaning of things and the relationships between them. Their writing is never separate from the life they lead. Theirs "is a way of living, and of living fully and completely. It is a way of knowing and exploring as well as a way of feeling. To a poet, nothing is boring and nothing insignificant."[21] In addition to these positive reflections on the work of the poet, Jennings offers other darker comments which point to her own coming troubles. She claims that insanity has nothing to do with being a poet, and that the excessive writing and publishing of poems is a temptation the poet must resist.[22] The former was surely a belief she hoped was true, and the latter an early warning to herself.

Jennings' method of writing poems remains consistent throughout her life. Usually a single word or an opening line came quickly and she felt great excitement. She resonated with Coleridge's description of making a poem, namely that the poet experiences "a more than usual sense of excitement with a more than usual sense of order."[23] She did not mull over the words, but wrote immediately with a Biro or pencil, with almost no revisions. If a title did not come rapidly, she set the poem aside.[24] Therefore, her poetic output was prolific and her subject matter frequently repetitive, both of which were to become major criticisms of her work.

Jennings acknowledged a contradiction in English poetry at mid-century. While there were publishers, patrons, anthologies, readings, and reviews of poetry, she felt something was amiss. She explained that the English were ill at ease with the arts because the Puritan tradition casts a shadow over all pleasure and therefore over all art. The sense of the sacred had vanished from modern life, and poetry, once a communal art, had become equated with oddity. The conundrum facing the poet was that her work is intensely private, but it needed to be communicated. Furthermore, the poet was not given the freedom to follow her own development, but was immediately categorized and caged. Unlike in Italy and France, the English poet was pressured to continually improve her work. A second book was expected to be different from the first. If it was not, it was a disappointment. If it was like the first, it was condemned as repetitive. In short, the poet was doomed to criticism.[25] While Jennings acknowledged these difficulties as constraining, she saw them as external and unrelated to the real poetic struggle that was internal.[26]

As each of the Movement poets went their separate ways, so too did Jennings. This becomes obvious in her third volume, *A Sense of the World*, which appeared in 1958 and was dedicated to her parents. It contained forty-six poems and was published with a £50 advance by Deutsch in England and Rinehart in America. The book's title derived from a line from Thomas Traherne—"It becometh you to retain a glorious sense of the world." Donald Hall would include several of its poems in his important *New Poets of England and America*, but when Jennings reviewed this anthology she was highly critical, claiming that although Hall was acutely intelligent and had impeccable taste, his introduction was pontifical and didactic.[27] Ironically only three years earlier she had dedicated her second book of poems, *A Way of Looking*, to him, D.A.H.

A Sense of the World represents Jennings' experiment in innovating her technique—she included some prose poems and widened her subject matter. Her previous collections, *Poems* and *A Way of Looking*, focused on themes of place and self-analysis. This new volume, while continuing to treat subjects such as nature and children, also includes poems on Italy, portraits of individuals, and religious subjects. This last category clearly marked her off from her religiously allergic Movement colleagues.

What is notable in *A Sense of the World* is that for the first time Jennings dedicates poems to certain individuals who are identified only by a single initial. Whether this resulted from a desire to conceal or protect, it allowed her to keep their identity secret, a practice which would increase as Jennings continued to write.

Several poems in the volume illustrate her new direction. Her obvious interest in philosophical issues is evident in "Fountain," her favorite poem, in which she explores the relationship between powerful energy and calm control, polarities which haunt her for the rest of her life. She writes:

> It is the elegance here, it is the taming,
> The keeping fast in a thousand flowering sprays,
> That builds this energy up but lets the watchers
> See in that stress an image of utter calm,
> A stillness there.[28]

Of the several religious poems "Annunciation" is the most potent. In this poem about Mary, Jennings enunciates her conviction that one comes to God through love of the human:

> So from her ecstasy she moves
> And turns to human things at last. ...
> It is a human child she loves
> Though a God stirs beneath her breast
> And great salvations grip her side.[29]

The most emotionally evocative poem in the collection is "A Fear."
It expresses the crippling power of fear and shame, themes which will
become more prominent in Jennings' subsequent poetry. In this dream
poem, she writes:

> Always to keep it in and never spare
> Even a hint of pain, . . .
> And all the masks I carry on my face,
> The smile for you, the grave considered air
> For you and for another some calm grace
> When still within I carry an old fear
> A child could never speak about, disgrace
> That no confession could assuage or clear.[30]

Many of the reviews of *A Sense of the World* were positive; Jennings
remarked that they were "pleasant."[31] She especially liked Anthony
Thwaite's comment in *The Spectator* that this was her best book, "the
flowering of an outstanding talent."[32] But there was also criticism. Alan
Ross, writing in *The Times Literary Supplement*, claimed that these poems
were technically accomplished, sensitive, intelligent, and clear, but they
lacked immediacy, were drab and unexciting. The implication was that
Jennings needed to free herself from religiosity. John Heath-Stubbs
wrote that the poems were flat and muted in tone, and Larkin, writing
in *The Guardian*, acknowledged that Jennings "is still an explainer rather
than a describer, and still loves to invent preposterous explanations for
simple happenings." What is new here, he wrote, are the religious poems,
and he mused: Perhaps these are "signposts to the road Miss Jennings
is taking."[33]

What appeared to be new to Larkin was in fact a link between
religion and poetry which Jennings had already intuited. She wrote
later: "My poetry has, to me, always been a development of my religion,
even though I have only occasionally written specifically 'religious'
poems."[34] For her, poetry and religion were inseparable. *A Sense of
the World* gives early hints of the new "road" she was taking. However,
it was her sojourn to Rome in 1957, courtesy of the Somerset Maugham
Award, which had made this conjoining evident. Her journey to the
Eternal City was life changing. She insisted it was the happiest time in
her adult life.[35]

7

Rome

...Here was
Faith made easy. All the doubts I'd known
Vanished here. Belief rose up in stone
And marble.[1]

"Three Months in Rome"

Jennings' stay in Rome was of inestimable importance. She claimed that these three months, in addition to being the happiest time of her adult life, were also the most worthwhile.[2] There she rediscovered faith, confirmed her vocation as poet, and linked her religion to her craft. Rome changed her life.

As she boarded the plane at Heathrow airport in April 1957 she anticipated none of this. Weeping and full of anxiety, she bade her mother goodbye. She was thirty years old, and although she had visited Europe before, she had never been away for more than two weeks and had never traveled alone. She was haunted by the thought that if she were to die in Italy, no one would care. She carried with her a small suitcase, her typewriter, a grip, and letters of introduction from her publisher, André Deutsch. Her mood was reflected by the bleak and rainy weather when the plane landed at the Ciampino airport. She made her way to Pensione Wacker on Via XX Settembre near Santa Maria Maggiore, where she had stayed on a previous visit to Rome. But this time she was given a garden room with a view of St. Peter's. Her feeling improved as she soon discovered a nearby local trattoria run by Gino Sefanini and Maria Leopardi, who treated her as a part of their family. Immediately enchanted by the city, she began to explore its tourist attractions and back streets, enjoying these forays even with men ogling her. Although her command of Italian was limited, she found the Italians to be friendly, hospitable, and lovers of the arts. She felt accepted and began to think of Rome as her "second home."

During the next several weeks she walked the city with map, guide-book, and dictionary in hand, visiting Michelangelo's Sistine Chapel, the Coliseum, the Vatican Museum, Keats' house near the Spanish Steps, the National Gallery, the Piazza Navona, and Hadrian's Villa. She borrowed books from the library of the British Council, had tea at the Catholic English Center, attended public audiences with the pope, climbed the Scala Santa on her knees during Holy Week, and picnicked along the Appian Way with her friend Jenny Joseph who came to visit. She went to the opera, the beach, bars, shops, and res-taurants. She loved the fountains, piazzas, and especially the light and silence of the churches.[3] She visited Saint Paul Outside the Walls and climbed the Aventine Hill to the home of the Benedictines' Sant' Anselmo where the singing was the best in Rome. But her favorite church was Santa Maria Maggiore with its beautiful mosaics.

Jennings waited a week before she used her letters of introduction. She contacted the Duke of Pirajno, a fellow Deutsch author, who took her out to dinner, escorted her to the Villa Borghese to view sculpture, and invited her to lunch in Trastevere. Impressed as she was by celeb-rity, she was thrilled also to meet Princess Marguerite Caetani, an American and editor of the literary magazine *Botteghe Oscure*, in which a few of her poems had appeared. After lunch with the princess, she was introduced to other family members and invited for a subsequent visit to their country home in Ninfa.

The healing power of Rome would not have been as momentous for her had it not been for the intervention of a Dominican priest, Aelwin Tindal-Atkinson. Father Aelwin, as she came to call him, was born in Zurich in 1896, brought up in England, served in the First World War, and studied at Oxford where he converted from Anglicanism to Catholicism. He entered the seminary at Fribourg, joined the Dominicans, and at the beginning of the Second World War served as a military chaplain. In 1945 he was named Provincial of the English Dominicans, and then became part of the Dominican hierarchy in Rome. Because of poor health he was forced to leave that position in 1957 and took up less demanding work as a penitentiary at Santa Maria Maggiore. It was there that Jennings encountered him.

Several months prior to her departure for Rome, Jennings had decided to live her faith more seriously. For years she had only minimally carried out the religious requirements of a Catholic—weekly mass and very occasional reception of the sacraments of confession and communion. She now vowed to make a confession every two weeks. One day while admiring the mosaics in Santa Maria Maggiore she noticed rows of wooden confessionals with the names of the priests and languages spoken. Within a few days she returned and entered the confessional where Father Aelwin heard confessions in English. She was moved and uplifted by his compassion and claimed that it was there that she heard for the first time of Christ's love and experienced a glint of freedom and grace. She celebrated that experience in her poem "A Confession":

> And here...
> I could discourse of every shameful topic,
> Reveal the secret passions of a childhood,
> Speak, fumblingly, the fears of adolescence....
> Simply to speak here is to be accepted.[4]

Tindal-Atkinson, whom Jennings described as "cultivated, intuitive and humorous,"[5] loved poetry and music. They met frequently outside the confessional to discuss these topics. He introduced her to Traherne's *Centuries of Meditations*, which she read in one night, and she gave him a copy of her second book of verse, *A Way of Looking*. Together they explored the Borghese Gardens, the Villa Celimontana, and Ostia Antica, the ancient port of Rome. During a later visit they went to an Etruscan exhibit, the catacombs, Anzio, and the Dominican church of Santa Sabina. Jennings claimed the services there were superior to those of her Oxford parish of St. Gregory and St. Augustine. During these visits, she and Father Aelwin conversed of poetry and the mystic life. These conversations were memorialized in a poem she dedicated "For A":

> Suddenly to this fullness our words went
> Talking of visionaries, ...
> I sensed...
> That you had known such apprehension....
> I glimpsed a radiance where no shadows pass.[6]

Tindal-Atkinson stimulated Jennings' initial exploration of the relationship between mysticism and poetry, a theme she would later pursue and one she was learning about in her reading of the early writings of the monk Thomas Merton. Of all her experiences with this older

Dominican the most important was their visit to Ostia Antica, a place rich in history but with few visitors. It was there that Augustine and his mother Monica met and where Monica died. Their living echoes reverberated in these two visitors as they wandered through the ruins. For Jennings, Ostia Antica was the place where religion became real, where she intuited an order and meaning in creation which she had been sensing only vaguely and incompletely.[7] It was in Rome thanks to Tindal-Atkinson, other poets and priests, and the simple Italian people that "an unhappy childhood was handed back and altered, / an illuminated spell cast round me and on me" (Figure 7.1).[8]

It was not only that Rome gave Jennings an experience of forgiveness and freedom; it also showed her the beauty of faith. In "A Debt to a City" she wrote that Rome literally changed her life by giving her a joyful faith. Previously she had understood religion as a set of rules made by a remote Being who was to be feared. She was afraid of God the Father, and never learned of the Son, who was love. She held her

Figure 7.1. Elizabeth Jennings. Courtesy of Mark Albrow

teachers at Rye St. Antony responsible for this failing,[9] but she neglected to include her previous experiences with priests in the confessional and her father, who modeled a similar harshness.

Jennings' rediscovery of faith was not principally intellectual. She seemed immune to the incipient intellectual revival of theology which preceded the *aggiornamento* that would come to full flower with the elevation of John XXIII in 1958. What interested her were the existential and aesthetic aspects of religion. "Everywhere I saw a sense of purpose and my Roman Catholic religion was coming truly alive for me for the first time."[10] In Rome she encountered lived religion, faith embodied in life, ritual, and art. Rome was a way of being, a mingling of the sacred and the secular, the holy and the sinful. In her poem "The Power of Rome" she writes that the city took away her "austerity and self-important prudery" and caught her up in its spirit.[11] There she escaped the rigid Catholicism of her youth. In Rome it was easy to be a Catholic. The sense of oddness she had known as an English Catholic fell away and she took a "deep delight" in all things.

What appears central to this freedom was that her "spirit and flesh stopped battling and made peace with each other."[12] In her mind, this peace was intimately connected to the concept of indwelling, embodiment, and Incarnation. She wrote: "Flesh and spirit seemed at one and I was learning gradually the deep love and wisdom of my faith for the first time. Edwin Muir once wrote that Rome always reminded him of the Incarnation; I felt exactly the same."[13]

It was Rome that taught her about the Incarnation. The Divine was hidden but accessible in the sacrament of the Eucharist. In "Harvest and Consecration" she writes of how the material protects the spiritual.

> Until you said no one could feel such passion
> And still preserve the power of consecration....
> The seed, the simple thing must die
> If only to restore
> Our faith in fruitful, hidden things. I see
> The wine and bread protect our ecstasy.[14]

For Jennings art abhorred the abstract and searched for order in creation. By imitating and affirming that order, art illuminated the spiritual embedded in the concrete and material. It was David Jones, the artist/poet, who affirmed what Jennings vaguely understood: art was sacramental. In an essay on Jones she acknowledges that although he would never be a popular poet, his verse had a timeless quality. For him literature was a religious activity and the artist was a "shower-forth" of sacred signs and symbols, one whose task it was to reveal and praise God's creation.[15] In a poem dedicated to Jones she wrote:

> Then I remembered words that you had said
> Of art as gesture and as sacrament,
> A mountain under the calm form of paint
> Much like the Presence under wine and bread—
> Art with its largesse and its own restraint.[16]

Jennings believed Italians understood the importance of art, embedding their faith in stone, marble, and paint. Unlike in England where artists were considered odd, in Italy they were accepted as a valuable part of society. Rome taught her that it was not strange to be either a poet or a Catholic. Several years later in the poem "Cradle Catholic" she acknowledged the hazards in embracing this religion but affirmed that in Catholicism one found meaning, purpose, and a God of love. Poetry became a way for Jennings to make "a world within that greater core" of Catholicism.[17] Her time in Rome increased her confidence and validated her vocation. Religion and poetry were now linked. As poet, she would illuminate spiritual reality.

This did not mean that she saw herself as a Catholic or religious poet. She did not. Rather she defined herself as a lyric poet. Writing might be a sacred work, but when she was engaged in crafting a poem she thought of nothing but the poem itself. Because she considered all life religious, religion was in everything she did. She believed her faith would shine through her work naturally and indirectly.[18] This is not to say she excluded explicitly religious subject matter from her poems. "Resurrection," "Lazarus," and "Mantegna's Agony in the Garden," the first of her ekphrastic poems, are examples to the contrary.

While Romans took their afternoon rest Jennings pounded out poems on her typewriter and pondered new projects. She considered undertaking a translation of the sonnets of Michelangelo, began work on a prose book on the relationship between the making of poems and the nature of mystical experience, and compiled a series of unpublished Pensées, some 127 meditations on life and religion (Figure 7.2).[19] Modeled on Pascal's Pensées, these reflections illustrate her continued wrestling with questions of meaning, doubt, and art. Although her time in Rome may have been the happiest in her adult life, it was not

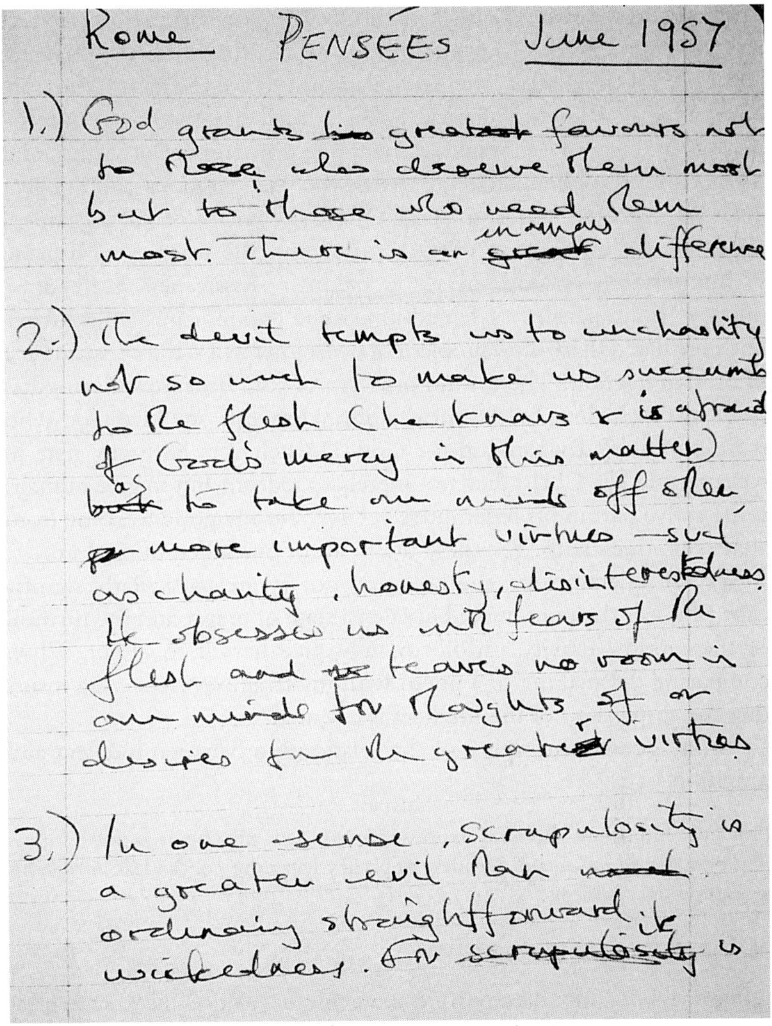

Rome   PENSÉES   June 1957

1.) God grants his greatest favours not to those who deserve them most but to those who need them most. There is an ~~great~~ *in many ways* difference

2.) The devil tempts us to unchastity not so much to make us succumb to the flesh (he knows & is afraid of God's mercy in this matter) as to take our minds off other, ~~far~~ more important virtues — such as charity, honesty, disinterestedness. He obsesses us with fears of the flesh and leaves no room in our minds for thoughts of or desires for the greater virtues

3.) In one sense, scrupulosity is a greater evil than ~~usual~~ ordinary straightforward wickedness. For scrupulosity is

Figure 7.2. Pensées by Elizabeth Jennings. Courtesy of Special Collections, Washington University

unalloyed, as the Pensées illustrate. She writes: "When the religion of one's childhood has been almost unrelieved torment one becomes almost accustomed to searching for God in agony. Strange that later when one is beginning to discover the joy in religion, even that discovery should be painful. We are not *suited* to happiness it seems."[20]

Her Pensées proceed unsystematically. Most are brief. Some reflect pre-Vatican II piety. Others are questions or admonitions to herself. Some are psychological, others moral, some refer to the nature and purpose of art, a few are theological. She acknowledges the power of scrupulosity and fear of the flesh to distract one from important virtues, and the need for the sacramental life to fuse the will, emotions, and intellect in order that one be transformed. Often, she writes of the tension of opposites and attempts to overcome dualism. She wrestles with pride vs. humility, self vs. God, success vs. failure, possessiveness vs. freedom, mind vs. body, passion vs. friendship. Some conundrums are resolved. She concluded there is no problem of evil, rather evil is the consequence of human freedom. There is no problem of pain because suffering has been made glorious by the Incarnation. How can one love God who is unknowable? By longing for God. Do believers have any part in redemption? Yes, Christ died not merely to redeem, but to give humans some active part in his redemptive act. Is there any good to come from attacks on one's faith? Yes, these draw out of one all emotionalism.

Several reflections on the poet and poetry are particularly significant. She sees the poet living between a state of prayer and the turmoil of the world's activity, unable to fully give herself to either. When comparing the making of a poem with mystical experience she insists that the suspension of the intellect is essential.

In one pensée she writes of the relationship between intellect and sensation:

However important the *ideas* expressed in a poem may be, it is not by ideas that poetry communicates. Readers of poetry learn the poet's ideas *through* his sensations and passions.[21]

She comments on great poetry:

[O]ne does not notice the words any more than one notices the paint in great pictures. The words lead on to something else...Perhaps this is why we can often remember the *atmosphere* of a poem while we forget the language used. Paradoxically, this is not a denial of precision because only the most precise poems can make the poem that lives *beyond* words.[22]

About religion and art, she writes:

The making of a work of art is never an overtly religious or moral matter...but the artist's attitude towards his subject-matter [is] a very different thing...[A] sublimely religious work of art...can appeal to and move those who neither believe in God nor in Christianity. The reason is that a truly great work of art, whether of religious or secular content, is always as deeply honest and exact on the human level as it is on the sublime.[23]

In reflections written the following year Jennings explores the peril of the artistic life. She maintains that artists have no barrier between their conscious and unconscious, and so they should be the healthiest people. However, since it is not natural to be without that barrier, they are often more neurotic than less creative personalities. The artist must maintain a delicate balance between introspection and extroversion. If too introverted, one loses the images, thoughts, and feelings given by the external world, and if too outward-looking the artist is unable to draw power from self-examination.[24]

Jennings' sojourn to Rome gave her confidence, clarity, and acceptance of who she was. As the end of her stay approached she reluctantly left Rome to visit first Assisi and then Florence. She arrived in Assisi on May 1 and found the place grim and austere, perhaps because she was staying in a French convent. Her "Letter from Assisi" speaks of the absence of sensual joy there and her desire to be flung back to the beauty of the English countryside.[25] During her ten days in Assisi, however, she grew fond of San Damiano and had the opportunity to have tea with the prolific author of religious books Nesta de Robeck. Then she journeyed on to Florence. Her visit there was more felicitous. Two English friends visited her, she had a meeting with the fascinating and antique Marchesa Trigona of Sicilian nobility, and she made the rounds of the important churches—Santa Maria Novella, Santa Croce, San Lorenzo, and the convent of San Marco. In these places, she sought out Florentine artwork. She especially loved the work of Giotto and Fra Angelico, and in a visit to the Uffizi she was entranced with Rembrandt's paintings, which she had first encountered in the National Gallery in London. Florence inspired more poems. In "Men Fishing in the Arno," she captures the calm acceptance of men who are "A little like lovers, eager but not demanding, / Waiting and hoping for a catch…"[26] After two weeks in Florence she returned to Rome where she spent her remaining days with Tindal-Atkinson. She regretted having to leave this man who had inspired and helped her in her time of need. He sent her off with the suggestion that on her return to Oxford she might seek help from a fellow Dominican, Father Sebastian Bullough, who soon would be moving to Blackfriars as a lecturer in theology.

When her departure time came she boarded the Air France flight for Orly. As prearranged she met her childhood friend Prisca Tolkien in Paris. Together they visited all the prominent tourist sites—the Louvre, where Jennings admired the paintings of Van Gogh, and the Eiffel Tower, Montmartre, Notre Dame, Saint-Sulpice, and Sacré-Coeur. Jennings was particularly taken with Chartres and Sainte-Chapelle, but she found Versailles tawdry. She constantly compared Paris and Rome; the former was always found lacking. Rome was "the world's most throbbing heart," France "a mere regret."[27] On July 3 she departed for England. She had £80 remaining from the Somerset Maugham Award and she planned to use it for a return trip to Rome, her "second home."

Jennings moved back to Banbury Road and commenced working at the library. Her reentry was abrupt, but the three and a half months of waiting passed quickly. By October she was back in Rome meeting with Tindal-Atkinson again, and on one particularly glorious day they hiked to the remote Lake Albano near Castel Gandolfo. This was a memory which lingered with her. But the most momentous event of her month-long visit happened one morning when she arose convinced that she should give up her position at the library and make her living by writing. She shared her resolve with Tindal-Atkinson, who had encouraged her to think of poetry in vocational terms.[28]

Returning to Oxford again, she apprised her father of her decision. He voiced concerns that she would be unable to support herself as a poet. Nonetheless she anxiously moved forward with her resolution, announcing to her library superiors that she would be leaving their employ in February 1958. Within the year her edited book, *The Batsford Book of Children's Verse*, would be published. It was her first foray into the world of children's poetry.[29]

To finish out her employment she was reassigned from the city library to a branch in Bury Knowle, a suburb in north-east Oxford. These last weeks of library employment passed quickly, although her religious doubts and neurosis reoccurred. While she believed only God could understand her sorrow, she was eager to revisit Rome to receive Tindal-Atkinson's psychological and spiritual guidance. She wrote that there were some "unhappinesses" that are "dark places" where nothing grows and that these could never be transformed into art.[30] By April 1958 she was once more in the eternal city.

After three months there, she returned to Oxford. She was thirty-two years old, without steady employment and feeling alone. Her psychological problems—anxiety, religious doubts, and sexual preoccupations—persisted, but having made a commitment to poetry, she dedicated herself to realizing her vocation. During the next few years a torrent of poetry, prose, anthology, and translation would pour out of her. Her productivity was remarkable, but it would come at a price.

8

Poetic Vocation

...all art is a participation in the eternal act of creation.[1]

Every Changing Shape

Elizabeth Jennings' journeys to Italy gave her psychic relief, renewed her religious commitment, and affirmed her poetic vocation, which she considered "participation in the eternal act of creation." When she returned to Oxford her literary outpouring was extraordinary. Never again would she have such concentrated output as during the two-year period of 1960 and 1961 (Figure 8.1).

Giving up her library position meant that she needed to earn a living as a writer. Therefore, she was willing to take on multiple projects. Reviewing books and writing articles were easy and resulted in immediate payment. During the next several years her reviews appeared in *The Listener, London Magazine, The Observer, Encounter, The Spectator,* and *New Statesman and Nation.* Her articles were published in *New Blackfriars, The Dublin Review, Twentieth Century,* and *The Month.*[2] Even *Vogue Magazine* commissioned her to write an essay on the city of Rome.

Two requests came in to write short books on poetics and the contemporary state of British poetry. This resulted in *Let's Have Some Poetry* (1960) and *Poetry To-day* (1961). Without realizing how much work was entailed she also agreed to edit *An Anthology of Modern Verse, 1940–1960* for Methuen. Her increasing reputation may have influenced her inclusion in a new Penguin series on modern poetry,[3] and being named a Fellow of The Royal Society of Literature. At age thirty-five she was on her way to acclaim as an important English poet. But this demanding work brought with it mental strain which would ultimately take its toll.

POETS' CORNER

18. ELIZABETH JENNINGS

Figure 8.1. Cartoon of Elizabeth Jennings by R. S. Sherriffs, *Punch* magazine, reproduced courtesy of Punch Ltd.

In 1961 Jennings published five books. The *Anthology of Modern Verse* dealt with the twenty-year post-war period which she described as "suffering," "restless," and "meaningless."[4] In the face of this chaos and confusion, the poets of the 1950s, the so-called Movement, defiantly searched for clarity, formality, and order, and sought guidance from the poets of the 1930s—William Empson, Robert Graves, W. B. Yeats, and Edwin Muir.[5] While the Movement poets faced a common situation and had similar aims, Jennings repeated her view that they should not be considered a movement in any traditional sense. However, her anthology included poems from each of these poets as well as three of her own poems—"Fountain," "Fishermen," and "A Child Born Dead." Her critique of the Movement poets was published at the same time as her own poetry was moving in a new direction.

It was the Folio Society, a publishing house which produced beautiful editions of the world's great literature, that requested her to create a new English edition of the sonnets of Michelangelo.[6] Although Jennings was not a highly experienced translator, as a poet very familiar with sonnet form, one can imagine she would have been attracted by this invitation. Michael Ayrton, who wrote the introduction to her translation, portrays Michelangelo as a conflicted genius who battled the forces of good and evil, spirit and flesh. For Jennings, he was a "noble and tormented man."While in his lifetime Michelangelo was acclaimed, he died lonely, desperate, and mad. In her translator's note Jennings reveals her own interest in his sonnets. She claims that both Michelangelo's poetry and sculpture express a "vehement energy" which was controlled by his "longing for order."[7] It was precisely such qualities of energy and order she had tried to replicate in her own poem, "Fountain."

In developing her translation, Jennings used the 1863 Italian version of the sonnets by C. Guastis, as well as the 1878 English translation by John Addington Symonds. She confessed that the work of translation was not easy because Michelangelo compressed meaning. Consequently, she found some of his sonnets baffling. However, she did try to retain both his original meaning and his rhythmic patterns. Her rendering of these sonnets remained the most popular English translation available; it had twenty-one editions, and continued to sell for the remainder of the twentieth century.

But it was *Every Changing Shape* which was Jennings' most important publication of this period. For several years she had pondered the relationship between poem-making and mystical experience, and now, given her revitalized religious interest and her clarity about her vocation, she was willing to explore it.[8]

This project began in 1959 with the publication of her articles on select mystic-poets which ultimately became the basis of *Every Changing Shape*. The book's title was borrowed from Eliot's *Portrait of a Lady* in which he claims to "borrow every changing shape / To find expression." In an age of increasing unbelief, it was a bold undertaking to write on the esoteric subject of poem-making and mysticism. Although Deutsch brought out the book in England, her American publisher, Rinehart, rejected the manuscript.

In many ways, *Every Changing Shape* can be understood as a logical extension of her poetics. In her previous poetry and her unpublished Pensées there are hints that she imagined poetry pointing beyond itself toward the numinous. *Every Changing Shape* continued that discussion. Although she did not disclose her motivation in writing this book, the fact that she had grown distant from her Movement contemporaries meant that she was in search of her own poetic tradition. Believing that poets work on and through one another, she found her affinity with certain poets and mystics ranging from early Christianity into the twentieth century. She believed these ancestors lived on, their faces shining in her poems.[9] They were her mentors; she belonged with them. Either consciously or unconsciously the laborious research and writing of this book was a means of finding a home and affirming her desire to reconcile her poetic and religious experience, a desire awakened in Italy and nurtured by Aelwin Tindal-Atkinson, to whom she dedicated the book.

To undertake this work Jennings read Catholic authors, including Dom Cuthbert Butler, Dom John Chapman, Reginald Garrigou-Lagrange, Etienne Gilson, Joseph Marechal, Conrad Pepler, and R. C. Zaehner. Although each of them discussed the subject of mysticism, none addressed in any sustained way the relationship between mysticism and poetry. It was rather from the writings of early Christian mystics and select poets that she teased out insights about her subject.

The book opens with a statement of Jennings' intention: to explore the making of poems, the nature of mysticism, and the relationship between these two. She defines poetry as the language of embodiment and enactment by which through rhythm, word order, and diction a spiritual dimension is conveyed. Citing Augustine, she claims poetry gives a kind of contact with God because "... all art is a participation in the eternal act of creation." Borrowing from Cuthbert Butler, she identifies mysticism as the study of a direct union with a personal God, established by means of love, and going beyond the senses and reason. Because poetry not only describes this relationship, but evokes it, it can be used to express mystical experience. However, unlike the poets, the mystics are not driven to communicate what they have experienced. She suggests that poetic and mystical experiences come from the same source and are similar in kind, but not in degree.

Jennings examines the writings of both mystics and poets. Among mystics she finds that Augustine uses imagery to describe truth; the author of *The Cloud of Unknowing* confirms that language and imagination can be trusted; Julian of Norwich discloses that suffering is a part of the experience of union with God; Teresa of Avila demonstrates the use of analogy and metaphor in describing mystic life; and John of the Cross reveals how poetry can be used to express mystic experience.

As for Christian poets, she suggests that George Herbert and Henry Vaughan believe that poetry can express the experience of the presence of God; Thomas Traherne conveys the belief that, since God penetrates all things, all is sacred; and Charles Peguy's poems show God reaching down to man. Gerard Manley Hopkins unites feeling and thought and uses fresh and daring language and imagery to illustrate his double vision of God within man's soul and permeating the universe. In the last section of the book Jennings addresses those she calls "secular angels," writers who are not specifically Christian but who in some way illuminate a relationship between mystical experience and writing of various sorts. She believed these poets had much in common with orthodox visionaries and mystics. Here she includes Rilke, for whom poetry is a way of life, and Simone Weil who sees a unity between prayer and poetic experience. George Bernanos, the novelist, understands the power and peril of imagination, and Edwin Muir believes that poetry demands love, honesty, and disinterestedness. She claims that T. S. Eliot's plays are about people searching for mystical experience and that his poetry has the quality of timelessness. She admires David Gascoyne for his ability both to take old symbols and make them new, and to write poetry that is radiant and truthful. Wallace Stevens is commended for acknowledging the power of imagination, and she applauds Hart Crane's insight that detaching symbols from orthodoxy renews them.

The volume's concluding chapters contain Jennings' exploration of the writings of two Dominicans, Thomas Gilby and Henri Brémond, who directly considered the relationship between poetry and mystic experience. Gilby, following the lead of Aquinas, claims that wholeness, harmony, and clarity are characteristic of both poetry and prayer. For Brémond both the poet and the mystic begin with the mind in conflict, followed by the experience of being visited by some outside force, and ultimately encountering release. In his view what separates poetic and mystical experience is that the former needs to be communicated hurriedly, and hence it is more superficial and less unifying than mystic experience which is derived through love.

Every Changing Shape was reviewed positively by Jennings' friends, Peter Levi in *Time and Tide* and Veronica Wedgwood in the *Daily Telegraph*.[10] But she was depressed by Donald Davie's criticism in the *New Statesman*[11] and devastated by Christine Brooke-Rose's assessment in

The Times Literary Supplement, which argued that the book was plodding, monotonous, trite, and unoriginal.[12] Nonetheless *Every Changing Shape* was Jennings' favorite prose book. It was composed, she said, with the intensity of poetry.[13] It was as if she had to write it.

The final publication of this period was *Song for a Birth or a Death*, a title borrowed from Eliot's poem "Journey of the Magi." Its poems were written in the second half of 1960, and the following year the book was selected as the Poetry Book Society's Summer Choice. It opens with a revealing introduction in which Jennings acknowledges that it is "an honor and responsibility to be a poet" but also "painful, precarious and deeply disturbing."[14] It is these characteristics which describe many of the poems of this volume. In reviewing this book, her Jesuit friend and poet Peter Levi suggests that these deeply personal poems were characterized by a "darkness and gravity."[15] Jennings acknowledges that the poems of *Song for a Birth or a Death* are more personal than any of her earlier work, but claims that because they were not autobiographical, they were not an embarrassment to her as the author. The fact is they were autobiographical and detail her actual experience.

The book's opening poem, "Song of a Birth or a Death," sets the haunting and unsettling tone in which a "savage world" is described as one where "cries of love are cries of fear." She writes:

> The fox's fear, the watch-dog's lust
> Know that all matings mean a kill:
> And human creatures kissed in trust
> Feel the blood throb to death until
>
> The seed is struck, the pleasure's done,…[16]

Jennings indicated this opening poem was written about a particular person.[17] Its dedication reads, "For S,"[18] and it chronicles an event which would trouble her for years.

Song for a Birth or a Death contains forty poems which are principally concerned with childhood, religion, and relationships with the people Jennings loved. The three childhood poems are congruent with her life as she discussed them in interviews and autobiographical writings. In "Family Affairs" she writes of the passing away of familiar anger into indifference and asks whether the family has cut the "umbilical" cord which connected them.[19]

In "Passage From Childhood" she relives the agonies of youth and her guilt.

> Where hell was open and the threshold crossed,
> With seven deadly torments in my head
> I walked and lived. At dark, wide-eyed I tossed
> Feeling my body feverish on the bed
> Certain I was among the chosen lost.[20]

She goes on to write that this agony taught her compassion for the suffering of others and it was this she needed to share.

One of the book's most well-crafted poems is "My Grandmother," in which Jennings recalls her father's mother who lived with the family for several years. When she died there was "no grief at all." Several other poems attest to Jennings' religious interest and turmoil. She honors John of the Cross and Catherine of Siena in two prose poems, and in "At Mass" she describes the struggle to be both artist and believer. "I struggle now with my own ideas of love / And wonder if art and religion mean dividing."[21] In the long poem "Notes for a Book of Hours" she recognizes the liturgy of monastic life as "diffused theology," and the need to create her own great book of hours.[22] Her preoccupation with religion and the necessity to clarify her own vocation is tellingly expressed in the poem "To a Friend with a Religious Vocation," which is dedicated to "C," probably her Catholic friend Charlotte, who became a Benedictine nun in 1958. In this poem Jennings directly explores her quandary over the vocation of artist. She writes that she has no desire to have children or to be a nun. Directing her comments to her friend, she writes: "Your vows enfold you. I must make my own."[23]

Another long and essentially religious poem is "The Clown," a figure Jennings will reconsider many times. The clown is "aloof" yet "strangely vulnerable." He makes himself ridiculous and seemingly uncaring. He allows himself to be laughed at and never protests. In him people see their lost innocence and their fear. Neither victim nor scapegoat, the clown is "sympathetic yet remote" like Christ on the cross.[24]

Several love poems are particularly revelatory of her suffering from unrequited love. In "World I Have Not Made" she writes that she lives in a world she has not created and suffers from trying "to love without reciprocity."[25] In "No Child" she refers to a sterile love relationship which produces "No marriage and no child."[26] In "The Instrument" she alludes to disappointed love:

> Only in our imaginations
> The act is done, for you have spoken
> Vows that can never now be broken.
>
> It is your vows that stretch between
> Us like an instrument of love . . .[27]

In "Unfulfilled" she questions "When did desire enter and / Confuse the sweetness, heat the blood? // Where does love start and friendship end?"[28]

In "Remembering Fireworks," the final poem of *Song of a Birth or a Death*, she recalls the experience of erotic pleasure:

> We, fumbling
> For words of love, remember the rockets,
> The spinning wheels, the sudden diamonds,
> And say with delight 'Yes, like that, like that.'[29]

Jennings ends the volume with this description of a moment of sexual ecstasy. Although she always maintained her poetry was not confessional[30] or autobiographical,[31] "Song for a Birth or a Death," as well as "World I Have Not Made," "No Child," "The Instrument," "Unfulfilled," and "Remembering Fireworks" are poems which are congruent with and descriptive of the events of her life.

9

The Darkness

It is the dark, the dark that draws me back
Into chaos where
Vocations, visions fail, the will grows slack . . . [1]
"To a Friend with a Religious Vocation"

Underlying this period of tremendous literary productivity was an impending crisis during which Jennings was besieged by religious doubt, anxiety, neurosis, physical illness, and exhaustion. The darkness developed slowly, beginning with her departure from the library.

After spending three months in Rome she returned to Oxford in July and was confronted with an unexpected employment opportunity proffered by Chatto & Windus, the prestigious, hundred-year-old literary publishing house in London. Initially she was ambivalent about the offer since she he had just given up one job, and to take another would mean less time for writing. But she liked the people at the firm and was impressed with the quality of their publications. Although her new spiritual director, Sebastian Bullough, urged against taking the position, she nonetheless agreed to sign on after negotiating a salary of £800 per year and a start date of October. This delayed beginning of employment meant that she could again return to Italy to be with Tindal-Atkinson, who she hoped would provide both spiritual guidance and psychotherapy. Confused and vexed, she needed his help to untangle the connections between her psychological and spiritual problems. It was during this second visit that she was introduced to Bet Davidson, a convert to Catholicism, who would soon enter a Carmelite convent. Davidson in turn introduced Jennings to two Italians friends, Cesare and Jole, who shared their warmth and rich lives of faith with her.

In October 1958, having returned from Rome, Jennings was ready to commence employment in London and she set to work finding a place to live (Figure 9.1). She finally rented a room above a convent in the Swiss Cottage district and mapped out her bus route to the Chatto & Windus office. Her assignment at the firm was to read manuscripts and determine their literary quality. Although she considered most of the manuscripts dreadful, she did find some good ones to recommend for publication, like one by her friend Paul West.

Jennings developed friendships with several people associated with the firm, especially a co-worker, Gina Pollinger, and Cecil Day-Lewis and his wife, Jill Balcon, with whom she would spend two Christmas holidays. Day-Lewis would go on to be professor of poetry at Oxford University and subsequently poet laureate. Since the Hogarth Press had now merged with Chatto & Windus, Leonard Woolf would visit

Figure 9.1.   Elizabeth Jennings, 1957. Photograph by Rollie McKenna. © Rosalie Thorne McKenna Foundation, courtesy of the Center for Creative Photography, The University of Arizona Foundation

the firm every week and Jennings got to know him as well. Through contacts at the firm, it was arranged for her to have tea with T. S. Eliot in his office, the so-called Uncle Tom's Cabin, at Faber & Faber in Russell Square. She resonated with Eliot's sense of humor, and was delighted when he showed interest in her work on the relationship between poetry and mystical experience. After their encounter Jennings wrote that she was walking on air, and that meeting Eliot was like meeting God face to face.[2] She also had the opportunity to make acquaintance with Edith Sitwell, who twice invited her to lunch. Initially, Jennings was apprehensive about this meeting, but she found Sitwell to be gentle and kind. Sitwell spoke to her about her own unhappy childhood and introduced her to her Jesuit spiritual director who had facilitated her own conversion to Catholicism.[3]

Work at Chatto & Windus was exhausting and she carried on an active social life, attending the theater, concerts, and cinema, and having dinner engagements with friends in the evenings. Through an introduction provided by Tindal-Atkinson, she met another Dominican, Father Simon Blake, who became a theater companion. Another important friendship was made with Dr. John Butterfield, professor at Guy's Hospital, and his wife Isabel.[4] The Butterfields were Catholics and great lovers of poetry. They became loyal friends, and subsequently John Butterfield invited Jennings to read her poetry to his research group.

Between work at the firm and social activity Jennings had insufficient time for writing. To ameliorate this, she petitioned to have a four-day week during which she would finish work on Fridays at 1 p.m. and return by 1 p.m. on Mondays. This allowed her to visit Oxford for the weekend where she would write and have two sessions with Sebastian Bullough. Psychological anxieties about both religious doubt and sexual neurosis continued to plague her.

Jennings had first met Bullough sometime in late 1957 when he arrived at Oxford. Competent in languages, music, and scripture, he had a notable pedigree. His father had been professor of Italian at Cambridge University and he was the grandson of the famous Italian actress, Eleonora Duse. At age forty-eight Bullough was already well known as a scholar of Hebrew scripture and an outstanding preacher. Jennings described Bullough as tall, slender, and with penetrating eyes. But what was most important to her was his pastoral gentleness. He served as her confessor, spiritual director, and psychological counselor.

This latter role was not uncommon for clergy at the time, even though their training in that area was minimal.

Concerned about her psychological fragility, she made another trip to Rome for a week in May 1959 to confer with Tindal-Atkinson. While there she attended a luncheon at Bet Davidson's, during which time hot coffee was accidentally spilled on her arm. The burn with its intense pain shocked her and she poured out her anxieties to Davidson and Tindal-Atkinson. She returned home soon after this accident, miserable, vulnerable, and needy.

What followed in the summer of 1959 would be long remembered by Jennings. Initially she saw this as an "exciting" and "magical" romantic period which lasted about a year. She describes this in her autobiography, but probably to protect the reputation of her lover, she never reveals his name but refers to him only as "B."

Quite suddenly, almost out of the air it seemed, I fell in love with B. For various reasons, I could not marry him, but this did not prevent us from having a most passionate affair. My whole body seemed to have come to life again and I was made aware of ecstasies which I had never known before. For the first time in my life, I wanted a child by the man I loved, but this was, of course, impossible. I was deeply in love and only sad that our mutual love could not reach fulfilment.[5]

Jennings' poems, "No Child," "The Instrument," "Remembering Fireworks," "Unfulfilled," "World I Have Not Made," and "Song for a Birth or a Death," this latter having been dedicated to "S," were each written in 1960. It seems clear that they relate to this love affair, whether the lover is referred to as "S" or "B."

According to Jennings this love relationship could not be consummated because of her religion and her sexual fears,[6] and his vows which could never be broken.[7] What was initially described as "exciting" and "magical" came to be referred to as sterile, making her "unhappily in love."[8] Jennings would revisit this affair again and again in the coming decades.[9] In "The Demands of Love," she wrote of this summer of passion when, still half a child, she engaged in something unknown. During the day they made love, and at night she would return to her own bed. But love, she wrote, left her, and passion drove her on to great pleasures and great loss.[10]

This passionate relationship appears to have ended abruptly, probably at the initiative of "B." Claiming to be "gifted at concealment," Jennings scrupulously never reveals his identity.[11] Whether coincidence or not, it is suggestive that sometime early in 1960 Sebastian Bullough left Oxford and was reassigned to teach at Llanarth where the Dominicans had a priory and preparatory school.[12] Shortly afterwards he moved to Cambridge where he became a lecturer in Hebrew at the Faculty of Divinity.[13] Although Jennings did not preserve photographs, either by intent or by mistake, three small photographs of an unidentified handsome young priest were included among her massive archival papers (Figure 9.2).[14]

Jennings did not speak publicly of this love affair, although it is alluded to in later poems. But it was an injurious event which increased her fragility and would contribute to an impending breakdown. Given the times, her Catholic culture, and the absence of any support, silence was required lest there be scandal. It was impossible for her to untangle the issues of power, sex, religion, and neediness at play in this affair. As a result, her anger and sense of betrayal would go within, contributing to her inner war.

Figure 9.2. Unidentified priest. Courtesy of Georgetown University

When Bullough left Oxford, he urged her to find a spiritual director from among the older Dominicans at Blackfriars. She resisted, claiming she wanted to see the Prior. And so she did. Hildebrand James, then Prior of Blackfriars, became her spiritual director.

Psychologically Jennings was becoming increasingly fragile. For no apparent reason she would break down sobbing at work or in the cinema. Later she admitted: "In short I was cracking up."[15] At the same time she began to experience intense pain across her abdomen. Probably frightened by what might be the cause, she refused to go to a physician and instead began to take pain killers and digestive tablets, but the pain persisted. She offers no explanation of her refusal to seek medical help, except the unconvincing suggestion that the children of doctors often avoid medical intervention. Given her naivety, it was more likely that she was fearful that her romantic liaison was the cause of a disastrous consequence.

This pain, her anxiety, exhaustion from her job, the demands of writing, and the strain of her relationship with "B" became unbearable. James suggested that she leave her job at Chatto & Windus, but she was reluctant to do this. She enjoyed the friendship of the firm's employees and she was afraid that if she left she might not be able to support herself. Furthermore, she was wary of what her father would say. To ease her fears, James spoke to her father privately. Ultimately, in the summer of 1960 she left Chatto & Windus. During her final months of employment she was physically ill most of the time.

In the fall of 1960 Jennings traveled yet again to Rome for a month. It was clear at that point that she would have some income since she had secured a regular reviewing position with the *Daily Telegraph*, and a British and an American publisher guaranteed her an income of £500 for three years.[16] Although eager to see Tindal-Atkinson, she regretted leaving "B," even though she now saw him only occasionally. While she missed him very much, her immediate preoccupation was her terrible abdominal pain. Tindal-Atkinson finally convinced her to see a doctor on her return to Oxford. Arriving back home in November, she was confronted with the depressing reality that Hildebrand James, who had completed six years as Prior of the Dominicans at Blackfriars, was now reassigned to Hawkeshead Priory and Spode House in Staffordshire. In January of 1961 she visited him there, staying at the adjacent Spode House. She was in terrible pain and he insisted that she see a doctor. She was admitted to the Radcliffe Hospital in Oxford in

February and was finally diagnosed with gallstones. Her case was severe, and she was given pethidine for pain. In the process of removing the gallbladder an ulcer also was discovered. During her hospital stay her spirits were lifted by visits from many friends, sometimes as many as seven at a time. After she left the hospital she convalesced at her parents' home where her recovery was slow. Visits from friends, especially the Butterfields, gave relief from the irritant of her father's nagging.

As she recuperated from surgery, she wrote many new poems which were ultimately published in *Recoveries*.[17] This book was dedicated to John and Isabel Butterfield and contained thirty-five poems and a translation of Albert Camus' prose poem, "Wedding Rites at Tipasa." Written in short lines and using scant imagery, her poems had a detached quality. The best of them is the long opening poem, "Sequence in Hospital."[18] In this she recalls that in the hospital there is no place to hide, and death is never spoken of. The dominant mood is one of fear, which becomes absolute, destroying a sense of both past and future. Thomas Kinsella, writing in *The New York Times Book Review*, panned the book, claiming she over-explained and that her verse was "verbal tedium,"[19] but Anthony Thwaite's review in *The Times Literary Supplement* commended Jennings for the vulnerability and lack of self-indulgence in her poetry.[20]

Although *Recoveries* was not one of Jennings' best volumes, it did not injure her reputation. She continued to gain acclaim. When Donald Hall's influential *New Poets of England and America* was published Jennings was the only woman to be included among the twenty-seven English poets.[21] Likewise, she must have been cheered when a reviewer of Robert Conquest's *New Lines 2*, which included several of her poems, claimed Jennings "has a gift in no way equaled by the others here for letting the music of her lines convey her mood before the sense of the word does."[22]

By June 1961 Jennings was well enough to go on holiday with Hildebrand James, the first of many she would spend with him. They visited the seaside town of Tenby in south Wales where they walked on the beach, and because both liked gambling, they bet on the horses and played the machines. Jennings confessed that gambling gave her a sense of power.[23]

Although this holiday gave temporary relief, Jennings was under increasing pressure. She was overworked, exhausted, depressed, and worried.[24] She had taken on a huge workload in part to ensure that

she could support herself as a writer. Her gallbladder operation and
an ulcer had weakened her physically, and her recent unfulfilled love
relationship with "B" contributed to her emotional fragility.[25] Now
at age thirty-five it was probably becoming clear that she would be
alone, that she would not marry but be one of the "spinsters" she would
write about.[26] By 1962 a great darkness began to engulf her.

10

Breakdown

Do not be surprised if we blink our eyes
If we stare oddly
If we hide in corners...

For everything looks strange...

And where do we come from?
Where did the pills take us,
The gas,
The water left pouring?
Limbo? Hell? Mere forgetfulness?...

We have a whole world to arrange.[1]

"Attempted Suicides"

What brought Jennings beyond the point of endurance was the news that when her father reached age seventy he would retire and he and Madge would move to the seaside resort of Eastbourne on the southern coast of England. Mrs. Jennings was eager for this move, and her husband accommodated her. Elizabeth considered Eastbourne socially and intellectually barren, and she could not consider relocating there. But the prospect of her parents' departure terrified her. Except for short stints in London and episodic forays to the Continent, Elizabeth Jennings had lived with her parents for all her thirty-seven years. Terror at her impending loneliness is not too strong a descriptor for what she felt.

The events of the early 1960s would have ramifications for her for the next twenty years, threatening her life and her vocation. Beginning in 1961 she experienced uncontrollable weeping, and in 1962 she was frequently depressed. In an unpublished poem she lamented the untimely suicide of Marilyn Monroe in August, calling the starlet a confused, distressed kid without parents, someone who wanted desperately to belong.[2] Sylvia Plath's suicide followed shortly after in early February 1963, and in another unpublished poem, "The Dead Selves," Jennings recalls the suicides of Plath, Edward Thomas, and Hart Crane and says she prays for them. She wonders if they ended their lives because they could not bear the pain.[3] In a letter to Anthony Thwaite, Jennings confides that she is upset by Plath's death, and that she is feeling depressed herself.[4] A week later when she was at Spode House visiting Hildebrand James she was overwhelmed by fear and took an overdose of Nembutal. Realizing she needed help, she told the house warden what she had done and she was rushed to Rugeley Hospital where her stomach was pumped. Full of fear, she begged to go to confession. She claimed not to know why she had taken this life-threatening action.

While in the hospital she was attended by Dr. Michael James, Hildebrand James' brother, who suggested that she might have a lesion on the brain and recommended that she go to Guy's Hospital where John Butterfield had been on staff. Within days she left for London where she stayed with the Butterfields while undergoing tests. A skull X-ray, lumbar puncture, and arteriogram were administered in hopes they would reveal some brain abnormality which would explain her fear and neurosis. Much to her disappointment they revealed nothing.[5] Dr. David Stafford-Clark, a psychiatrist, advised her to get psychotherapy and her father concurred. Like Elizabeth Jennings herself, Cecil Jennings always knew there was something wrong with his daughter. Ultimately, she did not follow through on the recommendation for psychotherapy, in part because she was afraid to do so, in part because of the expense. Rather, she returned home to Banbury Road.

Shortly after her release from hospital, probably in late winter or early spring of 1963, she and Hildebrand James headed to Tenby again for another holiday, but as they prepared to return from their vacation, for the second time Jennings took an overdose of pills, which according to her account shocked James and made him angry. He, of course, had to find a doctor, telephone her parents, and send her back to Oxford. A few years later, writing in her autobiography, Jennings admitted that James was serving as her father figure, and she described this incident as a cry for help, not a real desire to kill herself.[6]

Since her parents planned to sell their house and leave Oxford by early summer, Jennings began to search out a place to live, even though she did not want to live alone. She found two rooms at 49 Park Town, a desirable section of north Oxford off the Banbury Road. After a holiday in Tenby, she returned to her new flat, having to face sleeping there by herself. Frightened by this prospect, she went to her parents' home for the night. In the morning, while they slept, she went into the kitchen, wrote a note saying, "God will understand," and clutching her rosary beads turned on the gas and put her head in the oven. When her father awoke he found her unconscious; he immediately administered artificial respiration. She was transported to the Radcliffe Infirmary where again her stomach was pumped. As she wrote, "It seemed to me that to kill my fears, I must kill myself."[7] She begged again for a priest to hear her confession, and consumed by guilt she asked to confess a second time. She felt as if she had estranged herself from God, made her parents suffer, and lost her vocation as poet.[8] In the hospital, she overheard her father say to the doctor, this is "all too much for us."[9] In the unpublished poem "Taking Life" Jennings attributes her suicide attempts to the fact that she could not face being alone, could not bear "being simply one."[10] This sense that without another she could never be whole would haunt her for her entire life. Her fears were now compounded by her unrelenting guilt and unhappiness at being alive.

From summer 1963 until the end of 1965 Jennings was a patient in the Warneford Hospital, Oxford's major mental health center. She chronicled her time there in her autobiographies[11] and in poems of this period, especially those in *The Mind Has Mountains*.[12] What these two sources indicate is congruence between these events and her descriptions of them in her poems. Years later an interviewer asked her about the use of "I" in her poems—"Is this 'I' actually you?" She responded, "I think it is." But she went on to deny that poetry and sickness had anything to do with each other. Although she had a breakdown many years ago, she claimed that most of the poems of this period were not about her; they were not confessional.[13]

Prior to her admission to the Warneford Hospital, Jennings had been interviewed by Dr. Seymour Spencer, the Freudian psychiatrist at the Radcliffe and consultant at the mental hospital. Spencer, a Jewish convert to Catholicism, was gregarious and had an expansive personality and a wicked sense of humor which both delighted some people and irritated others. Jennings came to fear and detest him. She insisted that she did not want to be admitted to the Warneford Hospital, but Spencer informed her that she had no choice in the matter. She was admitted in July 1963; she insisted Anne Ridler and Hildebrand James be informed of her situation.

Jennings was brought to a female ward, given a physical exam, and asked to hand over her clothes, money, nail file, and mirror. She felt like a leper who needed to ring a bell to warn others of what she had done.[14] Her July birthday followed soon after; she spent it weeping and feeling miserable.[15] The first several months in the hospital were particularly devastating. She was medicated with sodium amytal for depression and paraldehyde for anxiety. Because she had lost a considerable amount of weight she was given insulin to strengthen her. When Donald Hall visited her he was dismayed at how physically changed she appeared.

Every Tuesday she would have a two-hour session of psychotherapy with Spencer. She dreaded these meetings, during which she felt that she was mocked and made to feel both useless and guilty. Uncomprehending of what was happening to her, she felt that Spencer's "sadistic" and "brutal" treatment would break her spirit. She was told that her problem—unresolved infantile anxiety and desires—was intense and deep and had been concealed for years. Spencer chastised her for a self-pitying, attention-getting, and childish attitude. She admitted that she was afraid to kiss even as a child does, and that if someone touched her she moved away.[16] Spencer urged her to go out and do what she feared.

In her published hospital poems Jennings reveals her deep animosity toward Spencer. In "Diagnosis and Protest" she writes that her lifelong habits of trying to please, offering presents to others, and accepting blame were understood by Spencer as evidence of her infantilism. She retorts that while her emotions are infantile, she has true maturity because she has known passion, has wanted a child, and is not "wholly undefiled." She speculates that her pain may be the price of art.[17] In another poem, "The Interrogator," she expresses her bitterness toward Spencer. He is the one who is always right, who always has an answer and always knows best. He is happy when she loses her temper and accuses him because this proves he is right.[18] Her attack on Spencer and his Freudian interpretations is captured in her jingle: "Ring-a, ring-a-roses / Freud is picking posies / Guess what he will use them for? / To make a sexual metaphor."[19]

At the time shock therapy was a principal treatment for many forms of mental illness, but at her insistence Jennings was only given anti-psychotic drugs. Unlike most patients she was not required to participate in occupational therapy, and her request for a quiet place to write was granted.[20] Nonetheless she persuaded John Butterfield, Hildebrand James, and her friend Vivien Greene, Catholic convert and estranged wife of Graham Greene, to meet with Spencer and to try to convince him to change his attitude and tactics in treating her. As it turned out they each came away urging her to keep on with her therapy, reassuring her that Spencer admired her intelligence and character. James suggested that Spencer needed to be harsh with her in order to release the hidden aggression which afflicted her and that she acknowledged. In the unpublished poem "Volcano," written a year or so later, Jennings describes an impending explosion in her calm exterior. She notes that seven-eighths of her is below the surface, and that although cold to the touch, she could burn.[21] In other unpublished poems, she writes of her anger, her fear of memory loss, and her inability to write. She fears the people around her; they are trying to die or to kill and they are all mad, as she is mad. She calls her depression a beast which numbs her, and she complains that her senses are deadened by her pain.[22] In her poems, she also remembers lost love. In the unpublished poem, "Surely?," written for "S," most assuredly the same "S" to whom she dedicated "Song for a Birth or a Death," she writes: "You are afraid of love as much as I / Not only love, but all emotion too, / Were it not so you would not have to try / To let me not be drawn too much to you."[23]

Although Jennings later admitted to having both "melancholy" and "high spirits,"[24] during this period she suffered severe mental dislocation. In a strange essay, "You Won't Tell Anyone Will You?,"[25] she alludes to some of her desires. She confesses that she is always looking for someone she can love and with whom she can share the "dark box of secrets" hidden inside her mind. She is terrified of touching people and catching diseases, and of committing murder. She fears madness. Although she has never shared her secret of the wild animals in her mind, she hopes she can find someone she can love so that her secret wild animals would be tamed. In unpublished poems of this period she insists that if she could be shown that she is lovable and can love, she might heal.[26] She wants two kinds of love—friendship and that which knows aching hunger and painful jealous longing.[27]

If Spencer was the bane of Jennings' existence, there were others who helped her endure her two years in the Warneford. These were friends, not family.[28] Soon after her admission to the hospital Vivien Greene came to help her. She visited Jennings frequently, often bringing some alcoholic drink. She took her out to lunch and invited her to visit her home, Grove House. There Jennings found order, pleasure, and an experience of being loved.[29] She especially enjoyed seeing Vivien's large collection of eighteenth- and nineteenth-century dolls' houses. At Christmas 1963 Jennings stayed with Mrs. Greene and her son Francis. The opportunity to be in a home, to help dress the tree, entertain guests, and receive and give presents was a great pleasure and relief for Jennings. Christmas was her favorite time of year, and throughout her life she wrote dozens of poems about the Christmas holiday.

By 1964 Jennings met two wonderful women in the Warneford who helped her both survive and heal. Rugena (Ruga) Stanley was a Jewish Czech refugee and Holocaust survivor. When Ruga arrived at the Warneford she was very ill, but she recovered quickly and was discharged before Jennings. While they were in the hospital together Ruga helped Jennings with all manner of things, from typing her poems to cleaning the wastewater sluice for twelve weeks, a task Jennings considered an indignity. After Jennings left the Warneford she went to live with Ruga, who took care of her, even though Jennings was often disagreeable toward her. Ruga remained a steadfast friend until her untimely death several years later.

Sister Ettie Synan, an Irish Catholic nun and a nurse at the Warneford, took a great interest in Jennings and her poetry. It was to Synan that Jennings attributed her healing. In the poem "Night Nurse" Jennings marvels at Synan's resilience and the purity of her vocation. She attests that she felt unsafe in the hospital until she met her, but in her care she experienced being a child again. She called Synan a "child's hope," a "savior," and seemingly without hyperbole, wrote that she would live through those hospital years again just to know her.[30] Jennings considered this compassionate nurse a counter to Spencer with his harsh treatment. When Jennings wept and cried hysterically, Synan would ease her pain and tuck her in bed. She could talk to her about their shared interest in religion, illness, poetry, horse racing, and gambling. One Christmas Synan gave Jennings a copy of the *Confessions of Saint Augustine*. When Jennings left the hospital on brief holidays she often wrote to this nun-nurse who ultimately would ease Jennings' reintegration into normal life outside the hospital. Years later Sister Synan developed a brain tumor and went to the Marian shrine of Lourdes hoping for a cure. She was killed there in a car accident.

Gradually Spencer began to change his tactics with Jennings. At first he tried to have her see another psychotherapist, a Dr. Robert Gorman, who was to serve as "Good Daddy" while he would continue to be "Nasty Daddy." But this modification did not work out. There was a temporary improvement in Jennings' relationship with Spencer when at one point, toward the end of her hospital stay, Spencer injured his foot in a cricket match and Jennings began to feel compassion for him. For Christmas 1964 she gave him a gift of her *Sonnets of Michelangelo*, but there was no long-term amelioration in her attitude toward him.

An anonymous benefactor came forward with a gift of £100, meant to provide an activity which would give Jennings some solace and relief.[31] A trip to Spain was proposed, but although Jennings longed for such an escape she had grown dependent on the hospital environment and was fearful to leave. Nevertheless in May 1964 she and Hildebrand James left on a three-week trip, first to Barcelona where they saw the sights, and then to the resort town of Sitges where they walked on the beach, swam, and shopped. After the trip she returned to the Warneford where Spencer continued to try to get at the root cause of her problem, which he believed was her terror of her father.[32]

By 1964 Jennings was sleeping at the hospital at night but returning to her Park Town flat during the day in order to write. There she edited a book on Christian poetry and another of poems for children. Her National Heath Care stipend paid part of her rent, and a special literary fund had been established to make up the difference. Her flat, what she referred to as "my nursery,"[33] like all her subsequent living quarters, was cluttered with her many belongings. She was still fearful of sleeping there alone, but gradually, with the help of Sister Synan, she made the transition. Since her drugs were dispensed at the Warneford she returned there every other day, but a change in her medication in May 1965 caused poisoning which brought her back to the hospital in a state of hysterical confusion. She writes that during these "lost weeks" she was absolutely "nuts."[34] She ran around the hospital dormitory and punched the head nurse in the jaw. She was put in a locked ward where she had wild, explicitly sexual dreams, and woke up screaming. Except for Sister Synan, she did not recognize anyone who came to visit her, even her mother. Once her medications were changed, however, she began to function normally. In "Prayer for a Sick Poet" she wrote of being grateful for her responsive senses, for poetry which was her anchor, for the gift of loving and being loved, which she claimed healed her, and for the understanding of one or two persons, namely Sister Synan and Ruga, who rescued her when she was ill.[35] In a subsequent appearance on the B.B.C. radio program *Woman's Hour*, Jennings stated that those who are mad are often very sensitive, vulnerable, and insightful. Her belief was that love, combined with skill and experience, was the only real cure for mental disorders. Every patient was a child again, one who could be healed by trust and caring.[36]

In the poem "Voices," written in late summer of 1965 after she had been discharged from the Warneford, Jennings asserts that it was the fear of a lonely life which prompted her earlier desire to die.[37] She admits that she had spent most of her time feeling guilty and wanting kindness, but what was most important now was to know what was wrong with her. Since she did not know why she had been ill, she was afraid of the future.[38] Her religion at times gave her solace, but God was often absent and remote.[39] In the poem "Prayer" she describes the forms of God she could love and worship; a fierce God, the God who appears as Host, and God as a helpless child. But it was in her experience of suffering in the mental hospital that she encountered the God who became man. There the spirit of God was near. She saw it in the guardian nurses and the gentle patients.[40] Jennings' institutionalization was a pivotal experience in her life, one formative of her future, much as her time in Rome had been. Although life in the Warneford nearly destroyed her, it brought with it an increased compassion for all those who suffered and were misunderstood. This new sensitivity would find its way into her poetry. It also deepened her religious experience.

After her discharge from the hospital Jennings gave up her Park Town flat, and in late 1965 moved to 8 St. Andrew's Lane, Old Headington, where she lived with Ruga. The house they occupied was owned by Michael Wheeler-Booth, son of Angela Wheeler-Booth, who was Ruga's friend. It was there that Ruga dutifully took care of Jennings, feeding her and typing her poems. Jennings continued to vacillate between being grateful for this care and being disagreeable toward her caregiver.

Depressed, Jennings regularly medicated herself with alcohol. She occasionally saw Spencer, and in a letter to him confessed that she was still terrified of her father. But, fearful of Spencer's Freudian interpretations, she kept silent about other aspects of her life.[41]

What she wanted now was to be re-integrated into the literary world. She had lunches with Veronica Wedgwood, Cecil and Jill Day-Lewis, and Kevin Crossley-Holland. She also returned to Sitges with James where they saw flamenco dancing and went to bullfights. Jennings was "thrilled" by the matador and his elegance, and saw his death-defying contests as a celebration of life.[42] Living now outside the hospital, she was constantly in need of money and was not shy about asking friends for loans or outright gifts. She must have been relieved to learn that thanks to John Wain and Kevin Crossley-Holland she had been awarded in 1965 an Arts Council Bursary of £750.

During this entire period of institutionalization Jennings continued to write. She served as a reviewer for *The Listener*, and was author or editor of *Christianity and Poetry*, *Frost*, *The Mind Has Mountains*, and *The Secret Brother and Other Poems for Children*, all of which were published between 1964 and 1966. Jennings wrote because she needed to earn money, but also to survive psychologically. On both levels writing made life possible. Or at least almost possible. She would go on writing, understanding full well that her life was precarious.

II

Writing in the Dark

Writing poetry is never separate from the life one leads.[1]

Let's Have Some Poetry

Poetry was Elizabeth Jennings' life. Her poems came from her life. In crafting them her life was sustained as she offered them to the reader as a source of life-giving inspiration. This intimate connection between life and art was clearly expressed in her writing in the years 1963–6.

During her period of institutionalization Jennings produced two volumes of poetry: *The Mind Has Mountains* and *The Secret Brother and Other Poems for Children*, the former being the more substantial of the two.[2] She was now published by Macmillan and proud of it. *The Mind Has Mountains* was dedicated to Jennings' "savior," Sister Synan, and its title derived from words in Hopkins' poem: "No worst, there is none. Pitched past pitch of grief." *The Mind Has Mountains* won the Richard Hillary Memorial Prize, garnering her a much needed £400. The fact that her friend Peter Levi was on the Hillary Prize selection committee may have helped secure this win. The book's most important poems were those about her experience in the hospital and her relationships with doctors, nurses, and patients.

Although in "Diagnosis and Protest" she speaks of her own pain and fear,[3] generally her hospital poems have a cool, detached quality about them. In them she is not self-pitying, but is focused principally on describing what she sees in her environment and the suffering of those around her. She describes meaninglessness, hysteria, blankness, suicide, and anguish. In a hospital sitting-room

> Too many people cry, too many hide
> And stare into themselves.
>
> The only hope is visitors will come
> And talk of other things than our disease...
> So much is stagnant and yet nothing dies.[4]

Reviews of the volume were mixed. Seamus Heaney commended her for her lack of sensationalism and the "restrained treatment of this personal hell."[5] However, others were disappointed, claiming the poems did not reveal Jennings' skill or her voice.[6] Later, to protect her reputation and to guard against being defined as a confessional poet, only a few of these hospital poems were included in the volumes of her collected verse.

Next to poetry Jennings' favorite art was painting, and she wrote many poems in the ekphrastic tradition. In *The Mind Has Mountains* she includes poems about Van Gogh, Caravaggio, Samuel Palmer, and Marc Chagall. Van Gogh is conceived of as a kindred spirit who painted "wild, surging art" which tormented him but gave pleasure to the viewer.[7] In a poem about Caravaggio she explored his search for meaning in his "Narcissus."[8] Palmer and Chagall are considered visionary painters who lived at different times but who shared a sense of truth and integrity which made "the wildest, darkest dream serene."[9]

In her several love poems she recalls the first sweetness of love and then its pain, but she reiterates that through its many stages love is always kind. In another love poem she remembers the freedom of not having to please another, but then the ache of the flesh returning.[10] One of her most popular love poems, "One Flesh," is about her parents, whose hunger for the flesh abated as they grew old. She submits that all of life is a preparation for this chastity of old age, when the fire goes cold.[11]

Publication of *The Secret Brother*, the other volume produced during this period, may have been made possible by the fact that Jennings' friend, Kevin Crossley-Holland, was children's editor at Macmillan. The book's title was taken from its opening poem about her imaginary brother, Jack Baycock. Initially she planned to dedicate the book to Ruga, but she changed her mind, offering it instead to the memory of Angela Wheeler-Booth, who had been kind to both Ruga and herself. Its poems are written in a rhyming pattern about all kinds of youthful interests—kites and cats, hamsters and dogs—and include several about

Jennings' own childhood. One telling ditty is about friendship and the desire to possess and to not share a friend with others.[12] Although this reflects a child's narcissistic sensibility, the poem mirrors Jennings' own adult expectation of friendship—a desire for complete possession.

Jennings' institutionalization in the Warneford did not mean her productivity abated. Although she sometimes feared she might lose her inspiration, she wrote prodigiously, sometimes composing eight or nine poems a day. Only a minuscule portion of her total output was ever published. A feeling of excitement preceded her starting to compose.[13] Then she wrote quickly and revised little, claiming that if a poem were good, it gave itself a title.[14]

Preoccupied with her mental state, she nonetheless took on two prose writing projects: a biography of Robert Frost and a history of English Christian poetry. Apparently, she wrote the biography because she both admired Frost and wanted to take on his critics. It was published in England in 1964 by Oliver & Boyd in its series of short critical studies, each with a biographical chapter, and in the United States by Barnes & Noble.[15] And although about Frost, this biography can be read as a defense, albeit an indirect one, of Jennings' own poetry, poetics, and person.

As she saw it, Frost's poetry was highly respected and popular because it was subtle and original, as well as simple, honest, clear, and direct. His poems, which she considered a search for order and an attempt to hold back chaos, began with the particular and then moved to the general without ever becoming abstract. According to Jennings Frost was *sui generis*; he distrusted the academy and was never part of a literary movement. As an inward poet who guarded his privacy and did not write autobiographically, he aimed to separate his poetry from his own dark interior life. The biography concludes with a consideration of each of Frost's critics and a refutation of their arguments. Although it was published on both sides of the Atlantic and had many editions, it was a flawed life narrative at least in part because of the obvious conflating of Frost's life concerns with Jennings' own.

If the Frost biography required energy and focus, *Christianity and Poetry* did so even more.[16] In this eclectic and personal book Jennings tracks the history of Christian poetry in England from the seventh through the twentieth century, examining each period through the lens of a few select poets. Her announced purpose is to interest Christians in poetry, not poets in Christianity. In the introduction she examines what makes a poem "good," namely its integrity, truth, and technical competence, not its subject matter. Neither does subject matter make a poem Christian. Rather it was the sensibility of the author who is grounded in the Incarnation which determines a poem's religious character. She begins *Christianity and Poetry* with a consideration of seventh-century Anglo-Saxon poetry which first met these criteria.

In the English Renaissance she recognizes Shakespeare as the humanist who understood the human condition, but his inclusive charity also earned him a place among Christian poets. In the Reformation Christendom was divided and religion became more psychological and individualistic, more cautious and private. The seventeenth century was the richest period of English religious poetry, almost all of which was written by Protestant poets, Herbert being the greatest of them. By the eighteenth century, poetry had become a vehicle for the expression of philosophical ideas and moral values; however, the best writing of this period was not poetry, but prose. The Romantic poets of the early nineteenth century expressed an unorthodox Christianity while later more orthodox Catholic poets—Newman, Patmore, and Thompson— were merely minor versifiers. In this case, Hopkins was the exception. The great Christian poets of the twentieth century—Eliot, Auden, and Thomas, were Anglicans; the Catholic convert David Jones was the only religious poet in their league. Jennings believed that in the materialistic and technological twentieth century, Christian poets confronted great difficulties, and the greater the poet, the greater the conflict. Since they must neither conceal their faith nor preach it, the options were either to interpret the world from a Christian point of view or to rebel against their own culture. In sum, for Jennings art which was true and appealed to what was deepest in man's mind and heart was, in fact, Christian. The work of the poet was to be a spokesperson for that truth.

In reviewing *Christianity and Poetry* G. S. Fraser lauded Jennings as a fine poet and commended her for dismissing Christian verse makers like Chesterton and Belloc. However, he pointed out that Christian poets were out of sync with their age, and that the Christian church no longer was interested in mystical or visionary poetry, but rather in morals and practical fellowship.[17]

Jennings' occasional use of religious subject matter, the publication of *Christianity and Poetry*, and her later editions of *The Batsford Book of Religious Verse* and *In Praise of Our Lady* confirmed her as a religious poet in the public imagination, but she explicitly rejected that designation, defining herself rather as a lyrical poet who tried to express in her work what she felt, thought and understood. If all of life was religious, she argued, then everything one did was religious, but religion entered indirectly and naturally and was not defined by the subject matter one used.[18] She did not deny the importance of religion in her life and work, however. When interviewed she said, "My Roman Catholic religion and my poems are the most important things in my life."[19] Her language was that of Catholic sacramental and liturgical life, and her emphasis on suffering and yearning for the numinous reflect Catholic preoccupations.[20] Poetry reputedly "saved" Jennings' life, and there is no doubt that Catholicism was an important impetus for her poetic vocation.

If Jennings recognized the import of religion in her poetry, she was less conscious of how gender shaped her artistic life. But she did hint at the conundrum of the woman poet. In an article on Emily Dickinson she acknowledged Dickinson's poetic skill, personal honesty, and ability to write fresh and passionate poems, which she attributed to her rich interior life. Jennings acknowledged that as a female poet Dickinson lived a life apart, enduring loneliness and suffering.[21] She considered Dickinson a major American poet and thought it inappropriate to refer to her as a "domestic" or a "woman" poet.[22]

A more direct commentary on the woman poet was included in a commemorative article Jennings wrote for *The Spectator* on the death of Edith Sitwell in 1964. In this she admitted that social expectations inevitably enter an evaluation of a woman's artistic contributions. As a consequence women poets respond in various ways. They become recluses, like Dickinson, Charlotte Mew, or Emily Brontë, or they hide what they really feel behind an elaborate, absurd, or sublime persona, which was the recourse of Sitwell. Although Sitwell's eccentricities both irritated and charmed, Jennings found her to be a gentle and compassionate woman. She noted Sitwell's suffering as a child, her fervent commitment to poetry, the importance of Catholicism in her life, and her willingness to contest whenever she was attacked.

Jennings made a few additional comments about the woman poet in another interview that same year. As she saw it, there was a dearth of women poets first because most women expressed their creative urge in marriage and children, which left little time for other forms of creative expression. She believed poetry was essentially virile and masculine, and it demanded a "ruthlessness and wholeheartedness."[23] Hence women poets remained unmarried and led lonely lives. Jennings believed that there were not many important women poets, but she offered the exceptions of Elizabeth Bishop, Marianne Moore, and Sylvia Plath, Americans who, she thought, had an easier time of it than women poets did in England.[24]

The publication of Simone de Beauvoir's *The Second Sex* (1961) and Betty Friedan's *The Feminine Mystique* (1963) seems to have had no impact on Jennings. Toward the end of her life she stated emphatically that she was not a feminist, that the equality of women was long ago achieved by the likes of Mrs. Pankhurst, and that the issue of gender-neutral language was ridiculous.[25] These views may be explained in part by the fact that Jennings was born in the mid-1920s into a traditional English Catholic family in which she sought the approval of males, her father, priests, and male poets. She had a few older women poet acquaintances—Raine, Sitwell, Ridler, Pitter—and some contemporaries—Joseph, Zurndorfer, and Rich—but none of these women was a longtime poet-friend who might have encouraged a sense of female solidarity. By the mid-1970s when feminism became an issue in public discourse, Jennings was fifty years old and preoccupied with her psychic and financial survival. Rather than embrace feminism she would unconsciously adopt one of the strategies available to earlier women poets like Edith Sitwell. As a lonely spinster Jennings would take on an eccentric demeanor and unconventional dress.[26] The tension between being a woman and a poet was never completely resolved by her. Nonetheless she did benefit from the opportunities which gradually began to be opened to women in the arts beginning in the mid-1970s.[27] She continued to publish her work, and have it reviewed, anthologized, and offered to the public through readings and radio broadcasts. Increasingly she gained acclaim.

Jennings' years of institutionalization would affect her for a lifetime. After leaving the sheltered world of the Warneford, she worked to regain an emotional and social equilibrium. While continuing to be depressed and longing to be a child again,[28] she nevertheless wrote unrelentingly and prolifically. The next few years would be ones of stock-taking, regrouping, and attempting to re-establish herself in the literary world.

12

"As I Am"

This is my life—to find poems anywhere...[1]
"An Impertinent Interviewer"

During years of mental illness Elizabeth Jennings created poems which gave her disordered, fearful mind an anchor and a means to overcome her great loneliness. Now, having returned to the world outside the hospital, she had plans. She set to work on several projects—preparing a manuscript of her collected poems, writing an autobiography, producing a brief biography of T. S. Eliot, readying a new book of poems, *The Animals' Arrival*, and writing three introductions to forthcoming books. This Herculean task was completed between 1966 and 1969.

In the midst of this prodigious writing Jennings was concerned about her father's deteriorating health. "Thinking of My Father's Future Death," and "To My Father,"[2] two unpublished poems, illustrate her unresolved difficulties with their relationship. She confessed that he dominated her psyche even more than her unrequited love affair. They had not seen each other in a long time and she was anxious about visiting him. She had changed, but she feared he had not.

In 1966 Cecil Jennings was diagnosed with kidney cancer and underwent an operation. Madge cared for him for eighteen months, but ultimately he was transferred to a nursing home. When his death seemed imminent, Aileen prompted Elizabeth to visit. Arriving two days before he died, Elizabeth hoped she could meet him without distress or tears.[3] She found him shrunken, and when she kissed him, something she had not done for years, her hatred and fear of him receded.[4] Although he was glad to see her, she could not bring herself to thank him for her birth or his rescuing her from her attempted suicide. To her mind he was full of anger which she attributed to his being thwarted from following his true inclination. This had made their home a place of great conflict. When he died in November 1967 at age seventy-four she felt no grief, but rather regret for the wasted years when there was no love between them.[5] Elizabeth Jennings wanted to please her father, but the "dreadful truth" was that she did not love him.[6] There is no indication she attended his funeral.

In an unpublished poem of this period, "The Known Thing," she recalled that she was the son her father wanted but never had, and he was the father she wanted but never knew. There was a world of misunderstanding between them,[7] and their blighted relationship continued to haunt her for many years. She admitted that she cared for him in a "twisted way," but that both of them were afflicted with "guilt, ambition and envy."[8] Ten years after his death she wrote a poem about an imagined experience of their reconciliation in order "[t]o dare our differences and to respond / To love we both once lacked."[9] But she never overcame her conflicted emotions about their relationship. In "Apology to My Dead Father" she writes that he understood her and helped her grow,[10] but in an undated essay she admitted she was like him, and she could not love him deeply. She laid out his limitations and attributed them to his being unloved in childhood.[11]

After Cecil Jennings' death Madge Jennings moved to a small flat in Eastbourne. Elizabeth admired her mother's courage and claimed to be concerned about her, but she recognized that they were very different from each other.[12] As a consequence she rarely visited her in her new home.

Another death a few months earlier in 1967 ended one more conflicted relationship. Sebastian Bullough died in a freak motorcycle accident on July 30, 1967. Jennings never publicly or directly commented on their relationship or on his death, but in a letter to her friend Barbara Cooper, apparently referring to Bullough's death, Jennings admits that the circumstances of the death were dreadful and the death itself appalling. She was stricken, could write nothing, and would think about the death for a long time, perhaps always.[13] Nonetheless she would continue to write unpublished poems about the event, recalling a summer when childlike she entered the unknown and was taken over by passion. This love lasted a year. When her lover departed, she was left in a prison, the "spirit on the body's rack."[14]

The deaths of her father and of Bullough in 1967 were destabilizing, but in the same year a boost was given to her literary reputation with the publication of *Collected Poems*, a compendium of her verse written over a fourteen-year period.[15] The volume was dedicated to Hildebrand James, O.P., and contained 207 of her 243 poems published previously in book form. The excluded poems came principally from *Recoveries* and *The Mind Has Mountains.* Eleven new poems were added.

Jennings must have been delighted to have this retrospective of her work appear at this particular time since it would re-establish her as a leading poet after the tepid reception of her two previous books. She also might have wanted to ensure that she not be dismissed as a "confessional poet," a designation especially unappreciated in England at the time. The gathering of a substantial body of work into one volume and the exclusion of her hospital poems could renew critical interest in her poetry. Also, she now had a prestigious publisher, Macmillan, and the issuing of a hefty volume with that publisher could be lucrative. Rather than being a "swan-song,"[16] *Collected Poems* might have been conceived of as a new start.

Clearly *Collected Poems* was also an attempt to establish Jennings as a poet deeply indebted to the English poetical tradition. In the book's introduction she writes that in creating this volume she became aware of the influence of former poets—Graves, Auden, Eliot, Yeats, and Muir—and the development of her own personal subject matter and style. She briefly reviews how she began to write poetry and how it became for her both "the creation of a world and a way of know-ledge." Writing poetry was a "way of discovery of the truth, both in myself and in the world around me." She concludes that every poem in the book contained "part of my own essential self," and hence was precious to her.[17]

This first retrospective of Jennings' work was reviewed widely and positively. Her friend Anthony Thwaite wrote that the collection showed "a steady and persistent contemplative gift, rational but open to mystery, tender but on the whole unsentimental, expressed in forms and words that were almost always pure, clear, gravely lyrical and com-mitted to a sense of hard-won order out of chaos."[18] An anonymous reviewer writing in the *Times Literary Supplement* pointed to the poems' paradoxes. They were reserved yet open and confessional, abstract yet concrete, lyrical but with strong didacticism. He judged the volume to be "substantial" and "impressive," and conceded that G. S. Fraser's earlier canard that he imagined Jennings putting on white gloves before writing expressed something of the purity of these poems.[19] Julian Symons, reviewing in the *New Statesman*, praised Jennings' ingenuity, and while he saw little stylistic development in her work, there was a change in her subject matter. Pointing out the "cool firmness" of her poems, he commented that no one has "written less hysterically about hysteria."[20] The "restraint," "candour," and "deep sensibility" of these poems was lauded by Edmund Blunden, who stated that Jennings used traditional form with authority. He acknowledged that form was a necessity for her, helping her to discover order.[21] A common criticism of Jennings, this time leveled by Edward Lucie-Smith, was that she wrote too much and thereby muffled her good poems.[22] Jennings did write too much. And more was to come.

The publication of *Collected Poems* was not without its problems. Jennings believed that, because her earliest book, *Poems*, was out of print, its rights reverted to her. Macmillan and her agent, David Higham, blamed each other for what appeared to be a breach of contract with the original publisher, Oscar Mellor. At one point Jennings thought she might be financially responsible, a worrisome notion for a woman who was constantly anxious about money.[23] But the worst did not happen.

Collected Poems served as a retrospective of Jennings' work. With that completed, she turned to writing an autobiography. The origin of this project is unknown, but perhaps her book review, "Women's Autobiographies," stimulated her to consider writing about her own life. In doing so she might have been guided by her prescient insight that autobiography should capture the character of a person and be more than facts about a life.[24] Lamentably, she did not follow her own advice.

Whatever its origins, writing an autobiography was a curious under-taking given that Jennings was only forty-one years old, a person who considered herself to be shy, reticent, not self-promoting, and one who understood that autobiography demanded the author present herself "in the distorted mirror of self-regard."[25] There were certain reasons, however, which might explain why she would want an autobiography, and why she might want it at this time. After several years of hospital-ization Jennings was now reintegrating herself into literary society and an autobiography would establish her place in that world. As well, after the closure given by the deaths of her father and Bullough she was freer to reflect on her life, to make sense of what had been years of tumult. An autobiography was her opportunity to tell her story and to tell it as she wanted. She did just that. This was her story, her "myth," of how poetry became her life (Figure 12.1).

It appears that Jennings might have begun her handwritten auto-biography prior to her father's death since that event is not mentioned in the first draft. She titled her work "The Inward War,"[26] words taken from Marianne Moore's poem "In Distress of Merits"—"There never was a war that was not inward." The manuscript is brief and proceeds

Figure 12.1. Elizabeth Jennings. Courtesy of Special Collections, Washington University

chronologically, following Jennings' major life events beginning in Boston and then in Oxford, describing her family life, her schooling, and university experience. She discusses her love life, her work at the Oxford City Library, and her interaction with poets both young and established. She chronicles her life-changing experience in Rome, and briefly acknowledges her breakdown, but her emphasis is clearly on her blissful early development. Sometime later, probably in 1968, she expands the manuscript, producing some 200 handwritten pages and entitling it simply "An Autobiography."[27] In this iteration Jennings augments the content by including a section on her breakdown, hospitalization and her father's death. Her concluding chapter entitled "Freedom" is meant to convince the reader that, although her past has been difficult, she has emerged free of resentment, with a stronger religious faith, a continuing desire to learn, and an intention to help people love poetry. She acknowledges that her illness has been a powerful force in her life for many years, but maintains that only infrequently was she cut off from poetry, the vital work of her life. If "An Autobiography" has an overarching theme it is that Elizabeth Jennings had a lifelong, almost inevitable vocation to be a poet and that nothing had tempered that commitment.

Writing her autobiography was a project in myth-making, but if it had a defining characteristic it was Jennings' immaturity and naivety. As poet and person Jennings comes across as both childlike and childish. It is interesting that in an unpublished poem written about this same time she describes analogies between the child and the poet. Both are alike in their emotional reactions, their delight in the senses, and their closeness to nature and other children. Although they are aware of the pain of others and want to heal them, in themselves poets and children are confused and unhappy. They believe in a love that can never happen or in the wonder that it can.[28]

The third iteration of Jennings' autobiography was completed no later than 1969. Its title, "As I Am," refers to how Jennings believed her friends saw and accepted her—as she was.[29] This typed draft follows very closely the earlier draft of "An Autobiography." The change in title from "The Inward War" to "As I Am" appears to reflect Jennings' greater self-confidence.

In these autobiographical writings Jennings alludes to her difficult family life, her religious shame, guilt and doubt, her fears, and her sexual fantasies, but none of these issues is examined directly or fully.

She offers abundant detail about her life, but her character is hidden and elusive. She is a master of indirection and concealment. In a telling unpublished poem of this period, "Nobody Knows," she writes that no one knows what she is thinking or dreaming, that she has a secret place which no one can see; it is hidden far behind her face.[30] Certainly, by the criterion laid out in "Women's Autobiographies" her own autobiography is a failure. It does not reveal Elizabeth Jennings. As much as she might have wanted to do so, Jennings was incapable of self-revelation, and in order to "find her" one must search beyond her autobiographical writing.

Jennings was determined to publish her autobiography and sent a manuscript off to an American publisher, who was pleased with the first chapter but in the end declined to publish it.[31] When her friend Veronica Wedgwood read the manuscript she urged against publication. Since Jennings was incapable of hearing criticism of her work, Wedgwood's critique was gentle. She suggested the autobiography was "fascinating" and "very moving," but because the genre of autobiography had changed, Jennings' work might be misunderstood and poorly reviewed. She concluded, however, that it was a "touching" work which was valuable and may have been valuable for Jennings to write. She recommended that Jennings wait, and that in a few more years she might be able to speak more freely about her father and reveal more than she did now in this draft.[32] Jennings subsequently wrote the poem "To One Who Read My Rejected Autobiography" and dedicated it to Wedgwood.[33] In this she praises Wedgwood for seeing the egotism and naivety of the autobiography and for understanding that she was not lying or deceiving but only striving toward the truth. She admitted she could not say all she wanted about her father because she was haunted by their relationship. She thanked the reader for her care, which gave her solace and relief.

It is unclear whether Jennings sent a draft of the autobiography off to other publishers, but as late as 1986 she submitted a sixty-five-page manuscript of the autobiography to the Celandine Press.[34] It too was never published. And in the early 1990s she would write a new autobiography entitled "Without Whom."[35] Elizabeth Jennings wanted her life story told, and told by her.

As if work on the autobiography were not enough, Jennings undertook other writing projects. In 1969 she published a new book of poems, *The Animals' Arrival*, which contained forty poems, only four of which would be included in her later collections.[36] Although not widely reviewed, it was commended by Michael Mott, who cited Jennings' courage in seeking out order in a disordered world. He added that if Jennings had previously been convicted of "tameness," the poems in this volume were almost "shrill" and concerned with a "harrowing vision."[37] Jennings dedicated *The Animals' Arrival* to the poet and Roman Catholic priest Peter Levi, who worked with junkies and the suicidal. She had known Levi for many years, during which time they supported each other as poets and reviewed each other's work.[38] She admired his poetry, which she claimed was written in graceful and sensuous language and was concerned with timeless themes.[39] The most memorable poem of *The Animals' Arrival* is a paean to Levi in which she compares his pale face to an icon and sees a "fragility" and "a steel-like strength" emanating from within him. "A Letter to Peter Levi" is one of Jennings' important poems on friendship, a theme she returned to again and again.[40]

Why Jennings decided to write *A Brief Study of Eliot and His Life* is unclear.[41] Previously she had written about the mystical element in Eliot's plays and his *Four Quartets*, and she had fond memories of meeting him when she worked at Chatto & Windus and having tea in his small office with its many books and photographs of Groucho Marx and Virginia Woolf. She recalled him as tall, slightly stooped, distinguished looking, modest, gentle, and understanding. Perhaps it was this personal memory which inspired her to write her study, or perhaps because Eliot had died only a few years earlier she thought such a book might have currency and would produce income. Or perhaps, since she had recently produced a study of Frost, she felt confident to take on this titan of British literature. She was soon to find out, however, that Eliot's widow was unwilling to cooperate with anyone writing about her husband. Consequently, Jennings' study of Eliot was not only brief but thin. It was never published.

The format of the study was chronological. But as was often the case, Jennings found elements of her subject's life and character which she admired and therefore emphasized. In this case she focused on Eliot's "toughness," his lack of self-pity, and his refusal to be defeated. She claimed that he, like all poets, did his best work when he was not altogether happy. His deep mystical faith informed all his work, and while he had mystical experiences, he spoke of them only indirectly. When her manuscript was rejected, and the publisher asked her to return the advance, Jennings was deeply depressed. Wedgwood wrote saying that she should have no doubts about the manuscript,[42] and even Seymour Spencer offered supportive suggestions.[43]

In the summer of 1969 Jennings was particularly depressed, in part because of the rejection of the Eliot book, but also because of her continuing psychological maladies. For solace she relied on Wedgwood. In their correspondence Wedgwood suggested that every creative writer loses faith in her work and therefore experiences the sin of acedia. She commended Jennings as a very good writer, but explained that diminishing self-confidence was caused by aging, which makes one more self-critical.[44] When Jennings indicated that she was reluctant to pour out her troubles to her, Wedgwood encouraged her to do so. Her response to her beleaguered friend gives some sense of the nature of Jennings' anxiety. Wedgwood wrote: "Of course I don't get upset by your telling me these things. We all have these distressing secrets—either more or less troublesome to us. It is part of the human condition—the fearful antagonism between man as spirit & man as animal, very few people fully resolve it. The most sensitive and imaginative suffer most."[45]

Jennings' depression must have been lifted when she received notice from her old friend John Wain announcing that he had written "Green Fingers" and dedicated it to her.[46] Wain's poem concludes with these lines: "I see your colors and I catch me [sic] breath, / For joy that once again you have come through. // Your art will save your life, Elizabeth."[47] Tenderness, praise, and fellow feeling are evident in these lines written by one who would soon be appointed professor of poetry at Oxford.

Jennings' art had saved her; she had "come through." In addition to *Collected Poems*, *The Animals' Arrival*, her autobiography, and the study of Eliot, she also took on some smaller projects, all of which were of interest and certainly would produce income. In 1970 Faber & Faber brought out a selection of Christina Rossetti's poetry[48] for which Jennings received £100 plus royalties for selecting the poems and writing an introduction.[49] There had been a flurry of interest in Rossetti subsequent to her death in 1894 and for a few years afterwards, but Jennings' work was one of the first to revive interest in her in the middle of the twentieth century. In her introductory essay to Rossetti's poems Jennings picked out aspects of the poet's life which uncannily paralleled her own. Like Jennings, Rossetti wrote romantic and children's poems; she was melancholic, had a mental breakdown, was deeply religious, highly productive, and refused marriage after two semi-amorous affairs. Jennings pointed out how fortunate Rossetti was to live in a family which encouraged the arts, and how much Rossetti, like Dickinson and Mew, was drawn to "broken things." Although she appreciated Rossetti's flawless sense of sound, she considered her work dated and her subject matter narrow. In her estimation, Rossetti did not have the necessary "scope, the depth, the variety" and hence she was only a minor poet. Jennings ended her introductory essay with a criticism of a recent biography of Rossetti by Lona Mosk Packer, who examined Rossetti's abortive love affairs. In Jennings' mind these had nothing to add to an understanding of Rossetti's work; her poems spoke for themselves. Jennings continued to have interest in Rossetti and as late as 1997 she wrote an unpublished essay about her in which she praised her poetry as both delicate and tough, and acknowledged that she was a poet confident in her feelings and in control of her craft. She denied, however, as she did with Dickinson, that Rossetti was a "woman's poet."[50]

Writing two other book introductions occupied Jennings during this four-year period. Although differing in subject matter, these essays are linked in their exploration of visionary experience. In 1968 Jennings' publisher Macmillan brought out *The Story of My Heart*, the autobiography of Richard Jefferies, a nineteenth-century nature writer.[51] Jennings wrote the introduction, in which she claimed that Jefferies' autobiography was his record of visionary occurrences. Like Wordsworth or Traherne in his closeness to nature, Jefferies was neither religious nor Christian, but he conceived of all of reality as supernatural.

Jennings' final project, an introduction to *Wuthering Heights and Select Poems*, was an edition of Emily Brontë's novel and some of her poetry.[52] In this Jennings argues that juxtaposing Brontë's prose and her lyric poetry is appropriate because both are part of a unified vision of mind and heart in which Brontë elevates her prose to the point where it meets poetry. She describes *Wuthering Heights* as "rugged," "bleak," "passionate," "wildly lyrical," "a work of contradiction" which is made possible because of the author's vision. Brontë's lyric poetry, she allows, was self-revealing and concerned with the inner life.

Jennings' post-hospital years were immensely productive but she remained fragile. She was fortunate to be sustained by two friends, Veronica Wedgwood and Michael Schmidt. Wedgwood was sixteen years Jennings' senior, a well-regarded scholar, a recipient of many honors and awards, a defender of poetry and the poetic nature of historical writing, and a homosexual with a long-time partner in Jacqueline Hope-Wallace. Wedgwood was much lionized in literary and artistic circles and in 1969 she became only the third woman to receive the Order of Merit. Although Jennings met Wedgwood in the 1950s their friendship did not blossom until the late 1960s. Remarkably, Wedgwood became Jennings' advocate, offering psychological, practical, and professional help. She made contacts for her, typed her poems, gave her financial support, and provided stimulating intellectual friendship. She literally took care of Jennings.

Jennings' relationship with Michael Schmidt was equally felicitous. Jennings and Schmidt first met in 1968 when he was an undergraduate at Wadham College and editor of the student-run magazine *Carcanet*. The young Schmidt along with another Wadham student, Grevel Lindop, would visit her in her flat at 31 Polstead Road. Schmidt and Jennings kept up their weekly meetings for four years until 1972 when Schmidt moved to Manchester. Ultimately *Carcanet* became *Poetry Nation* and later *PN Review*, which Schmidt continued to edit. He would later establish Carcanet Press in Manchester and become Jennings' publisher.

In the years after her release from the Warneford, Jennings seemed to have closed an earlier chapter of her life, made an attempt at self-revelation in her autobiographies, and positioned herself for a comeback. But no immediate comeback was to be. The early 1970s were years of mediocre achievement accompanied by yet more tragedy.

13

The Interim

When my broken heart
Mended, the gift, by using
All that loss
    Hammered it into art.[1]

       "Drying Up"

Retrospectively Jennings thought of the early years of the 1970s as an interim between the publication of her *Collected Poems* in 1967 and the release in 1975 of *Growing-Points*, a book hailed as a new beginning.[2] During this time she lost a dear friend and gained another, and by writing another biography, this time of Gerard Manley Hopkins, she began to clarify the issues of her own "inward war." By using her "gift" she hammered her losses into art.

Jennings was needy, both physically and emotionally; she wanted to return to childhood, to be taken care of, to be dependent. Her friends attempted to meet her needs, but their intervention was never enough. Mild, gracious, and obviously troubled, she elicited the sympathy of acquaintances. She would talk with kindly neighbors for hours, sometimes even visiting them during the middle of the night when she was particularly worried. She was continuously anxious, especially about her financial situation. Her friends—Priscilla Tolkien, Wedgwood, the Butterfields, John Gielgud, Roger Pringle (director of the Shakespeare Birthplace Trust), Desmond Albrow, and others—gave her monetary gifts or loans. However, she did not deny herself what she wanted. She traveled, shopped, and regularly attended the cinema and theater.

She was endlessly preoccupied with her living arrangements and began a pattern of moving from one flat to another in north Oxford. In the space of three years she moved from 31 Polstead Road, a place she called "The Shack," to 11 Fyfield Road, where she complained that no one spoke to her, to Fairfield House, a residential home at 115 Banbury Road, to 11 Winchester Road where she lived miserably off and on for many years. Sometimes when she was particularly beleaguered by her fellow lodgers or landladies, she would move in with friends for a few days or weeks and then return to her room to have the process begin again.

In an effort to find consolation and make a home she would purchase items which reminded her of childhood. Her lodgings were crammed with books, reproductions of Old Masters, dolls' houses, music boxes, wooden toys, bird cages, and stuffed animals. She especially loved the concentrated energy and craftsmanship of miniature objects. Buying knick-knacks was empowering, as was giving them to others, which she did occasionally. She wrote that to give things away with joy was to have these gifts "glow with the giver's gaze."[3] These were "unnecessary things," but there was glamour in having them. She was not ashamed of the clutter in her living quarters and delighted in laying out her treasures to see patterns and links between objects where others saw only randomness. She would become angry when a visitor misplaced or reordered anything. This disarray not only perplexed her friends, but forced her to take to her bed to write, notebook on her knees, since there was no clear space available on table or chair. Her possessions were precious to her and she immortalized this detritus in several poems.[4] She wanted her room to be her domain, a haven, a place of protection, but during the day it was not. Since she craved interaction with others she would take the bus into town, sit in cafés for hours, attend the cinema, and in the evening return to her room.

Jennings' depression returned, and in 1970 John Butterfield arranged for her to have counseling sessions again with Seymour Spencer; Veronica Wedgwood paid the bill.[5] She also paid for Jennings' phone calls, and for a time half her rent. As a consequence of her mental distress, Jennings wrote poems of fear, dread, and death; she revisited her past with all its hurts. She was paranoid and suspicious, especially of those who meant the most to her, and felt betrayed by the thoughtlessness of others. Bereft, she wanted someone to look at her with longing, but then she had lustful thoughts and experienced guilt.[6] "I am left over / I am a second child," she wrote, "I am singing to a vague tune / I am afraid of men // I am lonely, lonely // I am afraid, afraid . . . "[7] When she was particularly depressed she would write frenetically and her ordinary loopy handwriting was replaced by a tiny script. In late summer of 1973 in thirty days she wrote 192 poems.

Jennings must have had some relief from her depression when she and Hildebrand James went on their five-month-long holiday to Sitges, even though they quarreled some of the time. Jennings had also proposed that she and Wedgwood take a trip to Rome but Wedgwood begged off with a variety of excuses: obligations to care for her mother, too much work, and that she was too moody, selfish, and solitary to be a good traveling companion. She believed Elizabeth thought too highly of her. Furthermore, she argued that their friendship was balanced now with daily telephone calls and weekly lunches.[8] Even though no trip materialized Jennings was grateful to Wedgwood for all she had done for her, and consequently she dedicated her new book, *Lucidities*, to her.[9] Wedgwood claimed it was a healing book of poems, Jennings' most beautiful work.[10]

Critics were not as impressed. Terry Eagleton, writing in *The Times Literary Supplement*, said the poems were fragmentary and the emotions were not controlled.[11] Roy Fuller, commenting in a later review of *Growing-Points*, said that there were enough naiveties in *Lucidities* to trouble even sympathetic readers.[12] Presenting a more nuanced critique, Margaret Byers wrote that some of Jennings' recent poems were "sentimental simplifications rather than lucidities but the best of them are her finest work to date." She defined Jennings' poems in general as "moving always closer and closer to bedrock."[13] Perhaps the most telling poem in *Lucidities* was "Vocations," which was dedicated to "H," presumably Hildebrand James. She writes that he knows human love, but not "the pleasure reaching to the bone" because he has a "call." As for herself, she averred love is a "constant strain / I have the urge to reach, to touch / And feel the ecstasy again . . . "[14]

In June 1971 catastrophe happened. While Jennings and James were vacationing together on Guernsey in the Channel Islands, James fell ill and died of a heart attack. He was sixty-nine years old. They had been quarreling for a day or two before the attack, and when the police arrived on the scene Jennings blurted out that she had killed him. They declined to arrest her when they realized her verbal quarrel with James was the reason for her confession. Devastated and in shock,

Jennings was consoled by a Dominican from Blackfriars, Osmund Lewry, and by the calming presence of Veronica Wedgwood.

Hildebrand James had been Jennings' closest confidant after Sebastian Bullough left Oxford. Prior to James' death she wrote the poem "A Decision," which concludes with "I think we must be chaste yet loving still / And only thus shall you and I endure."[15] At his death, she claimed to have lost her greatest friend. Years later in her poem "A New Elegy for a Friend Dead Seven Years," she wrote that she was not prepared for the "beast passion" taking her over. It was passion for its own sake and she knew because of his promise, it had to stop.[16]

At James' death she entered a great darkness, wanting to cling to him and longing for his human warmth. She too wanted to die. She acknowledged, however, that her love for him was "a mixture of childish need and lovers' play."[17] Although not ascribed to him, she wrote many unpublished poems about their relationship, admitting they had been happy together, but that there was a strong undercurrent of tension in their love because it could not be fulfilled. She concluded that God had wanted his death; that it was a blessing. For the next twenty years she lamented his demise, remembering his gentle, hopeful, patient personality which never scolded or upbraided her. She regretted the angry and cruel words she spoke to him during his last days. Places like the English Channel, which once reminded her of joy, were now places of darkness. She vowed to remember him always.[18] In "After a Time," one of the few published poems about his death, Jennings calmly recognizes his passing. However, this is an exception. Her unpublished work did not reflect this serenity.[19] Later, in summarizing her loves, Jennings wrote of "romantic dalliances, one engagement and several deep though *not* permissive love affairs."[20] These later love affairs were most assuredly with "B" and Hildebrand James.

Even as Jennings mourned James' death she was confident that another love would come into her life. She maintained that since childhood some person always emerged who would be her "sun and moon." This person would just appear; there was no need for a search.[21]

A clue about that next person to be her "sun and moon" is evident in her unpublished poem "O Goodness," written in 1973, two years after James' death. In it she writes that she has met two people of complete goodness, each of whom was whole and a healer. One had died two years ago; the other was a well-known living woman writer,[22] the unnamed Wedgwood, who shared many intellectual interests with her.

Wedgwood was a great advocate of poetry and the visual arts, a trustee of the National Gallery, on the Council of the Victoria and Albert Museum, and a member of the Arts Council. Jennings appreciated her craft as a historian and saw similarities between their chosen genres. In her mind the historian and the poet both enter into the experience of others and have a commitment to style. Both create "magic."[23] Over the course of the next several decades Jennings wrote some hundred unpublished poems about her relationship with this prominent woman.

Wedgwood was in fact an immense help to Jennings psychologically and professionally. She selected which of Jennings' poems would be sent to magazines and publishers, handled much of her correspondence, and petitioned granting agencies to award Jennings money.[24] If Jennings' attitude toward Wedgwood was adulation, Wedgwood's was one of care-taking. In letters to Michael Schmidt, Wedgwood expressed her concern for Jennings' increasing dependence on her. In the fall of 1971, she queried him about where Jennings should spend Christmas, her favorite holiday. Since Wedgwood was convinced Jennings should not be left alone, she wondered whether Ruga or John Wain would take her.[25] When asked, Vivien Greene declined to invite her, and Wedgwood admitted she understood her reluctance. "Elizabeth, alas, is a problem,"[26] she wrote. Wedgwood's view was that Jennings always anticipated the ideal Christmas; she expected too much and then inevitably was disappointed.

Wedgwood complained to Schmidt that Jennings was increasingly jealous and quarrelsome about her forty-year relationship with Jacqueline Hope-Wallace. It was her surmise that Jennings, like many depressives, had a dangerous self-hatred. She concluded that when Jennings did not like something she built up a wall and fenced herself behind it. For instance, if it were suggested that she rewrite a poem, she would threaten to tear it up. In Wedgwood's estimation, Jennings always saw the dark side of things and she would be better off if she had to fend more for herself, which she certainly could do.[27] Like so many others, Wedgwood expressed her irritation that Jennings would phone her in the middle of the night.[28]

Through the turmoil of James' death Jennings continued to write, hoping for greater critical appreciation. To her mind, the state of poetry in the early 1970s was healthy. Public interest in the genre was high, as evident in poetry readings and the publication of poems in weekly and monthly magazines.[29] In her case *Relationships*, her next book of poetry, published in 1972, was named a Poetry Book Society Choice and sold thousands of copies.[30] Public expectations for the book must have been great, given the earlier success of her 1967 *Collected Poems*. But overall the poems of *Relationships* were not compelling.

Surprisingly, given its title, there are few poems in this volume which examine relationships. The one relationship explored is friendship, with its qualities of humility, trust, respect, and awe. Other poems illustrate Jennings' attentiveness to the suffering of others. There is a long sequence on the seven deadly sins in which she calls lust the kindliest one because it produces happiness. Pride is the worst of sins because it wishes to possess and own. As a whole, critics considered the poems of *Relationships* to be lackluster. Alasdair Maclean in his review in *The Listener* calls her language colorless, stilted, awkward, and didactic, and notes her "catastrophic" decline.[31] Only four poems from this volume would find their way into subsequent volumes of her collected verse. *Relationships* was dedicated to Michael Schmidt, who was now on the cusp of creating Carcanet, which would become Jennings' publisher.

The year 1973 brought moments of sadness when Jennings learned of Auden's death—her response was to laud him in "Elegy for W. H. Auden"[32]—and joy too when Larkin's *Oxford Book of Twentieth-Century English Verse* appeared, containing five of her poems. She also finished a project which she had been mulling for some time: a biography of Gerard Manley Hopkins. She undertook this writing even though she had been largely unsuccessful with her previous attempts at biography and autobiography. Initially this 400-page manuscript biography was accepted by an American publisher with the expectation that Bodley Head would bring it out in England. But it was never published on either side of the Atlantic. This may be explained in part by the fact that Jennings was fearful that the book might lose money since two different agents were involved, and each could claim a portion of sales.[33]

Jennings titled the Hopkins biography "The Inward War,"[34] the same title she used for the first iteration of her own autobiography. This repetition of title suggests the connections she perceived between Hopkins' life and her own. She considered Hopkins to be a man of strong passions who lived within the constraints of poetic and celibate priestly vocations. The result was internal conflict,[35] an experience not distant from her own.

Like Hopkins she was a poet who understood her own vocation as priestly. As a child she played priest at mass and she saw the training of poet and priest as having certain correspondences.[36] She believed poetry, like the priestly act of communion, was a sacrament. Both priest and poet were transformers, who offered bread and words which gave access to a supra-rational reality.

Jennings expressed her admiration for Hopkins in the poem, "Hopkins in Wales."[37] Later she would include several of his poems in her *Batsford Book of Religious Verse* and in *In Praise of Our Lady*. Previously she dedicated an entire chapter to him in *Every Changing Shape*. There she claimed: "No other poet, religious or secular, has ever before used poetry as a means whereby men may encounter one another's inmost being unprotected by masks or veils."[38] For her, Hopkins was a great poet because of his artistry, craftsmanship, and discipline. His self-mastery, simplicity, and ability to endure suffering gave him a "toughness" which helped him hold together his double vocation as priest and poet. What Jennings admired most about him was not his language but the wholeness of his vision, in which there was no separation of thought and feeling, a unity which derived from his understanding of the Incarnation. Hopkins believed that art was not for art's sake or life's sake, but for God's sake. To create was to praise God and participate in the great act of creation itself. Influenced by Duns Scotus, Hopkins believed that the Incarnation was more than a means of redemption; it was a glorification of the material world. God was in all things, all things were in God, and all manifestations of human love reflected God's love. For Jennings, Hopkins was a companion of both fascination and solace.[39]

To write this biography she mined Hopkins' sermons and especially his poetry, which she claimed reveal the man and his inward war. She writes that in a quite literal sense the poems are the man.[40] This is a curious statement given her own insistence that her poems were autonomous entities and not autobiographical,[41] that the poem was not the poet.

"The Inward War" was an admiring biography undertaken to emphasize the importance of religion and the Jesuit order in Hopkins' life. In it she traces his youth, family, travels, and university life, the influence of J. H. Newman, his conversion to Roman Catholicism, his entrance into the Jesuit order, his various priestly assignments, his ill health, and the suffering which accompanied each phase of his life. She calls him a hero-worshipper and idealist and points out his affinities with Matthew Arnold, Herbert, Rossetti, and Augustine, all of whom

Jennings appreciated herself. Throughout she stresses Hopkins' physical suffering and the lack of understanding of him by contemporaries and friends. Her thesis is that Hopkins cannot be understood independent of the myriad forms of suffering he endured. She considered suffering essential to the poetic life and laments that Hopkins never received psychiatric help, which would have been available if he had lived in the second half of the twentieth century.

Jennings suggests that Hopkins, like all great artists, had an androgynous nature. But she dismisses what she considered an overblown claim that he had homosexual inclinations. She argues that his innocence and purity, as expressed in his love of nature and children, were the strongest argument against this claim and adds that no one suggested that he "practiced" this "perversion."

In concluding the biography Jennings takes on each of Hopkins' critics and offers arguments against them. She asserts his genius is demonstrated by the depth and breadth of his poems and the fact that they have endured.

The early 1970s were difficult years for Jennings. She lost her cherished friend, Hildebrand James, and the psychological stability he offered. Her two publications, *Lucidities* and *Relationships*, were not well received, and her biography of her beloved Hopkins remained unpublished. Nonetheless she was aware that she was growing and that some new beginning was at hand. This would come in the form of a new publication and a deepening friendship with Veronica Wedgwood.

14

Revival

I think it has returned
Though I scarcely dare say it.
I am speaking of the gift of verse.

Now, perhaps, I can give back again
A little of what I owe to so many.[1]

"Revival"

J ennings' "gift of verse" was reviving. The summer of 1974 was
glorious as she wrote poems which would be published a year later
in *Growing-Points*, the title of which was particularly apt. She was
growing, and this would be her first book to appear under the Carcanet
imprint, a publishing firm she thought of as a young Faber & Faber.[2]
During these next two years she would be invited to America to
lecture and would produce a prose book, *Seven Men of Vision*. She was
forty-nine years old and in a new place. "You are no longer young,"
she wrote. "Nor are you very old. // This is a time to begin / Your life.
It could be new."[3]

By early 1974 Jennings moved to 18 Winchester Road, a short distance
from St. Anne's College. Off and on for the next eighteen years she
would be ensconced there. She spent the first part of the year preparing a lecture to be given at Barnard College in New York City. This
would require her to make her first and only trip across the Atlantic.
As the Gildersleeve Professor for Women From Abroad her charge was
to present a lecture and interact with students and faculty. She stayed
in New York for about a week, taking time to visit art galleries and
attend Broadway plays. While she experienced the city as exciting and

Americans as friendly, she was convinced she could never live there. For her the place was all speed and ambition. It was unnerving, people were constantly rushing, there was no quiet, and being still was considered "a disgrace." There were numbered streets without names, suicidal skyscrapers, and cab drivers who were afraid of being robbed at gunpoint. Nothing was built to last, everything was brand new, nothing was green. The experience in New York brought back to her how much she loved England with its flowers and old churches.[4]

The subject of her Barnard lecture was David Jones, a fellow Catholic poet whom she admired. Her presentation would be reworked and subsequently appear as a chapter entitled "David Jones: A Vision of War" in her forthcoming book, *Seven Men of Vision*.[5] That chapter, and an undated essay on Jones, summarize her esteem for him.[6] She admitted Jones would never be a popular poet since his poetry was complex and dealt with the large issues of creation and God, topics which are not fashionable. Nonetheless his work had a timeless quality which would give him a lasting place in literature. She saw Jones as a religious writer who through his work participated in God's act of creation. In his epic poem, *In Parenthesis*, Jones illustrated how in the Great War moments of comradeship and tranquility transformed the experience of the war's horror, futility, and dread. A few months after Jennings returned to England, David Jones died. To commemorate his life and work she wrote an "Elegy for David Jones."[7]

During the summer of 1974 she was happier than she had been in many years. She spent several months writing poems, and in August participated in the Edinburgh Arts Festival. Then in September, thanks to Wedgwood who purchased the tickets, she holidayed in Greece and Sicily where she delighted in being near the sea. In early December, she received news that her dear friend Aelwin Tindal-Atkinson, who had lived in Rome since 1956 and had just returned to London, had been killed in an automobile accident. She considered it a "grace" to have known him. It was he who brought her from a religion of fear to one of joy and helped her see the Incarnation not only as redemption but as a blessing of the material world. As a "cradle Catholic" with his help, she was able to embrace her birth-right Catholicism and affirm her vocation.[8] When she experienced doubt she could petition Christ: "O Take my unlove and despair / and what they lack let faith repair."[9]

The publication of *Growing-Points*, Jennings' twelfth book of poetry, was the highlight of 1975. It was first offered to Macmillan, her current publisher, but was rejected because the firm was curtailing its poetry line. However, there is some reason to believe that Jennings' requirement of a large advance and a paperback edition may have contributed to this rebuff.[10] Initially Michael Schmidt was reluctant to take Jennings on as an author because of the financial instability of Carcanet and Jennings' need for royalties. But the appearance of *Growing-Points* marked the beginning of their long publishing relationship. As was her custom Jennings sent Schmidt her poems in spiral notebooks with her preferences for publication indicated by one or two stars. From the welter of more than 1,000 poems submitted for *Growing-Points*, he selected eighty-six. As it turned out, *Growing-Points* sold well, had sixteen editions, and was translated into three languages. Almost all its poems would be included in Jennings' next compilation of collected poems, published a decade later.

Growing-Points was dedicated to "O. B.," Oliver Bernard, poet, Catholic convert, and translator of the poems of Arthur Rimbaud. This dedication, like some of her others, appears random, except in this case six poems by or after Rimbaud had been translated or authored by Jennings, and included in *Lucidities*. This dedication was an expression of her gratitude to Bernard.

It was widely recognized by critics that *Growing-Points* was an improvement on her two previous volumes and that she was now substantially separated from the Movement. Her poems on Greek mythology— Orpheus, Persephone, and the Minotaur—Chinese culture, and various religious subjects clearly set her apart from them, as did her elegiac poems honoring Mozart, her favorite composer, Rembrandt, her favorite painter, and other poems on Aquinas, Hopkins, Auden, and Mondrian. These poems lauded the arts. Of painting, she writes: "to paint's to breathe, / And all the darknesses are dared;" of music:"God gave [man] art / And God is proved in every note . . . ;" and poetry is power "that dreads away the darks, the doubt."[11] The poems of *Growing-Points* showed great technical command and were expansive, and written with longer lines. The collection represented a new style which Jennings insisted was arrived at unconsciously.[12] She attributed her burst of new poetry to the fact that in the early 1970s she broke from her "psycho" psychiatrist, Seymour Spencer.[13] *Growing-Points* proved to be her favorite book of verse because, she claimed, "I" was used less frequently.[14]

Critics also agreed that the book marked a new beginning, although some complained that Jennings was still capable of writing "vague" poems. The most exuberant reviewer was Veronica Wedgwood, who called the book "remarkable" and "astonishing" in its richness and variety, and "exhilarating" compared with much contemporary poetry. She suggested that it was the technical skills developed by Jennings in her last two volumes which gave her the confidence to explore new forms.[15] Roy Fuller, former professor of poetry at Oxford University, writing in *The Times Literary Supplement*, commended Jennings' vigorous vocabulary and indicated that she was developing a new direction.[16] Her old friend Alan Brownjohn attested that with this new publication she was leaving behind a "lean" period. These poems were evidence of a broader scope and richness and a real improvement in the ordering and freshness of ideas. Admitting that some of her verse was weak, Brownjohn nonetheless saw the good poems dominating.[17] Like others, Edmund Levy pointed out a linguistic freshness, a greater range of subject matter, and a compassionate understanding of suffering.[18] Other reviewers were more circumspect. John Matthias made the perennial complaint that Jennings wrote too many poems and as a consequence the reader was required to do substantial "weeding." He agreed that there were good poems in the book, but others were sentimental and lacked energy.[19]

One of the most striking aspects of *Growing-Points* was the inclusion of ten poems with explicitly religious subject matter. One among them, "Christ on the Cross," became a model for much of Jennings' poetry, particularly her unpublished Christ poems which number more than 150.[20] These persona poems reveal Jennings' confrontation and struggle with the world's myriad evils. In them Christ speaks in the first person to God the Father about issues pertinent to his humanity including: evil, sadism, war, madness, heresy, death, suffering, lust, doubt, betrayal, freedom, fear, free will, terror, treachery, and anger—issues pertinent to Jennings as well. What was important to her was the human Christ, who suffered like all of humanity. She quotes Pascal: " 'God made himself man in order to unite himself with us.' "[21] Jennings admitted to being in awe of the Holy Ghost and fearful of God the Father.[22] The person of the Trinity who was accessible to her was God the Son. It was his suffering which revealed why the Father could allow suffering to exist.[23]

In the late 1970s she wrote several poems using the motif of the clown as an alternate persona for herself. In an earlier poem, she wrote that the clown reminded her of Christ on the cross. Both were innocent, submissive, meek, and humble, and allowed themselves to be laughed at.[24] But in these poems the clown is more complex. In "The Awkward One" Jennings draws on her own childhood nickname and confesses that she shares the clown's sadness. In a bit of self-advice, she commends all who do not "fit in" to learn from him.[25] In "The Clown" she describes this "fool" as uncaring of what others think of him, but nonetheless selfless, one who pleads the cause of those who suffer.[26] In other poems, she distinguishes the clown with his multiple personalities from other misfits. He is laughed and shouted at, but he also carries away one's fears, making one feel free like a child. But the truth is the clown is a tragic hero who laughs at the beholder, calling him a fool. The clown has a dark sense of cruelty.[27]

Jennings' ability to enter into the suffering of others was born of her own vulnerability and strengthened by her religious commitment. She wrote of women who were single or infertile or who had miscarriages or abortions, adopted children, the elderly, the poor, the sick, prisoners, and even murderers. Her capacity to resonate with them was one of the unique qualities of her poetry and in part explains its popularity. In order to write in the first person about the shattered lives of outcasts Jennings needed artistry, craftsmanship, and a talent for "imagined experience."[28]

Although Jennings was never entirely free of fear and anxiety during this period, there were moments of joy and exhilaration, first of which must have been the success in sales and positive reviews of *Growing-Points*. Another was the publication of *Seven Men of Vision*. This was an immensely positive study of diverse twentieth-century poets who offered a vision of hope for their own anxious times. Cognizant that her selection was personal and that these authors came from different nations and backgrounds, Jennings argues that each nonetheless offers a vision of truth born of personal suffering. In every case what they have in common is humility, charity, and wonder. Prophet-like, each provides a vision of hope and a way into the future. Jennings describes Yeats as creating a vision of joy arising from his own anguish. D. H. Lawrence is identified with a vision of the natural world which is based on love of life. Lawrence Durrell suggests a vision of an observer who marries mind and the senses. The man of affairs, St-John Perse, sees a vision of a sacred material world. David Jones proposes a vision in which fear in war is transformed by camaraderie and bravery; Antoine de Saint-Exupéry's vision of space describes man at one with the vast universe, and Boris Pasternak presents a vision from prison. Neither bitter nor desperate, Pasternak manages to see the light in the darkness and to affirm that human love carries the divine within. Seldom had Jennings written anything as optimistic and uplifting as this book. Like *Every Changing Shape*, *Seven Men of Vision* is her attempt to acknowledge a poetic tradition to which she could belong.

Other joys of the mid-1970s were travel and weekly attendance at the cinema or theater. She was particularly fond of Shakespeare's plays and "needed" to hear them for restoration and revitalization.[29] Frequently she took the bus to Stratford where she would attend a play and visit friends. One of these friends was Roger Pringle and his wife, Marion, who often entertained her as a house guest and supported her in a multitude of ways. Jennings was always responsive to the generosity of others and sometimes extended her gratitude by dedicating one of her books to benefactors. The Pringles would be recipients of one of her dedications. As a staff member, and later director of the Shakespeare Birthplace Trust, Roger Pringle arranged to have Jennings read at the 1975 Stratford Poetry Festival. He invited her to return twice more, even though she shuffled her papers and appeared nervous in front of a crowd.

Poetry readings were a way to sell books, and as she became increasingly concerned about her finances, she did more of them. However, unless the audience was appreciative, she did not enjoy these events. In "The Poetry Reading" she explains why. There are certain types who always appear: those who sit in the front row, have not read the poems, and want to talk about something other than poetry; women who know something about poetry, but come to get out of the house; middle-aged men who want to talk about sex; bored married men who are dragged there by their wives; and culture hunters, who are well informed and will buy books. She confesses that sometimes she is bored by her own reading, and wonders why she participates in these affairs since they are analogous to a public striptease.[30]

In general, poetry readings in the 1970s were attended by more men than women. In fact male poetry readers outnumbered females two to one with male academics and teachers making up the single largest group, followed by white-collar men, and then by housewives.[31] Obviously, Jennings' readers included both males and females and Catholics, who although a minority group, added to her supporters.

The joy of the previous two years came to a halt in January 1976 when Jennings was admitted to Holyrood House in South Leigh. It was called a "nerve hospital," but in fact it was also an alcohol detox clinic. For most of her adult life Jennings used alcohol to ease her anxieties; the situation had now reached a crisis point. She was hysterical for part of the time she was in the clinic, and she refused to actively participate in group therapy sessions. In a letter to Michael Schmidt she admitted that she had never been unhappier in her life.[32] She left after three weeks, but she was not well enough to live alone. By February she was a resident of Freeland House, a care center in the village of Freeland, 11 miles outside Oxford. She would remain there until 1979, leaving episodically to travel and give readings.[33] While there she wrote several poems about living in Oxfordshire, being in touch with the pulse of life and appreciating the beauty of the English landscape.[34] But generally, particularly in the beginning, she was miserable and very lonely. In a letter to Schmidt she complained that he did not realize how near she was "to cracking up."[35] Freeland House was a home for the elderly, and at age fifty Jennings was by far the youngest person in residence. She called it a place for the "deaf, dotty, and dying," an "expensive slum."[36] There men were no longer men and women no longer women; all were children. The past and the future were shut out and death was everywhere.[37] During this time, she was grateful she could write,[38] and did so incessantly. In one twelve-day period she wrote sixty poems. She produced unpublished poems about Christ, death, and fear. Some poems were written in a male voice. In one poem she analogizes herself to a Russian doll, with one small doll inside the other, each with a blight on it.[39] In "Ugly Duckling" she calls herself a parody of a person whose parents look on her with pity, who is a burden to others, and whose sister is beautiful and clever.[40] In "Fear" she writes that obsession begins early in life when a child is slapped by a parent or is told she will become a murderer. Fear feels like animals waiting in the dark to attack.[41] She writes of the "Classic Fear" in which parents want a son and therefore the daughter always tries to please the father.[42]

While at Freeland House Jennings was diagnosed with coeliac disease, which causes anemia, blackouts, and nausea.[43] She also had episodic manifestations of psychological fragility expressed in a variety of ways—anxiety, fearfulness, loneliness, and paranoia. Her excessive writing, alcohol consumption, gambling, overspending, and inability to sleep worried friends. Her discursive conversation, the inability to stay on topic, was one difficulty she acknowledged. In an unpublished poem of this period, "Attempt to Stop Over-Working," she writes that her mind is a "roundabout," "a spinning top," "a train whose brake won't work."[44] In a later interview she confessed: "I do tend to run off at tangents. . . . I don't do it deliberately to be evasive;" she said she just enjoyed it.[45]

During her years at Freeland House, Jennings continued to be highly productive. Writing poems gave her pleasure, but it was also an "absolute emotional necessity."[46] Nonetheless her excessive poetic output and its increasingly religious and artistic subject matter were seen as detrimental to her reputation. In late 1976 John Betjeman, poet laureate, a Jennings fan, and a nominator for the Queen's Medal for Poetry for 1977, inquired of Philip Larkin whether he thought Jennings should be recommended for the award.[47] Since its inception only two of the forty-three recipients had been female, Ruth Pitter and Stevie Smith. Larkin opined that while Jennings was a serious and worthy contender she wrote too much and churned out "acres of meaningless pieties." He considered her most recent work emphasizing art and religion to be inferior. The medal was awarded to Norman Nicholson. The revival portended by *Growing-Points* only two years earlier had faltered and would not recur for another decade.

15

Grief's Surgery

I have come into the hour of white healing.
Grief's surgery is over and I wear
The scar of my remorse and of my feeling.

I have come
Into the time when grief begins to flower
Into a new love.[1]

"Into the Hour"

While living in Freeland House for the three-year period 1977 through 1979, Jennings experienced both extraordinary productivity and physical and psychological illness. She feared an impending mental breakdown.

Her notebooks of this period are filled with thousands of poems, only a limited number of which would be published in *Consequently I Rejoice*, *After the Ark*, *Moments of Grace*, *Winter Wind*, and *Selected Poems*. This last collection proved to be her most popular book; it sold out in two weeks and ultimately 50,000 copies were purchased. She was proud to be a Carcanet author. Although her success as a poet was evident, her inner life was in turmoil again. She was increasingly paranoid and needy. But by the end of these three years, after a return to Italy and a deepening friendship with Veronica Wedgwood, her inward war appeared to abate.

On the surface Jennings carried on her normal life of traveling, connecting with friends, working with her publisher, and giving readings, all the while living in the care center. In 1977 she traveled again to Sicily and to Sitges, the "Eden" where she had shared many joys with

Hildebrand James. She was drawn to the Spaniards who, living between two seas, were Spartan-like, loving the extremes of the mystic and the bullfighter.[2] She would later visit Torquay in Devon with her longtime friend and fellow Catholic Leila "Tommy"Tomlinson, a retired school inspector. In 1979 she would return to Tuscany.

Her relationships with family, friends, and acquaintances preoccupied her. She wanted to draw closer to her mother who was now seventy-three and becoming frail. While recognizing that they were very different from one another, and each was needy, Jennings nonetheless wanted to please Madge. She feared for her mother's death, noting that as a daughter she desired "the warmth of the womb."[3] She spent a week visiting her in Eastbourne, but during the visit she became angry, insisting that her mother treated her like a child.[4] There does not appear to have been much subsequent interaction between the two of them, although Mrs. Jennings lived on for more than a decade. Elizabeth also experienced estrangement from her sister and mourned the loss of the sisterly love she knew in childhood.[5] Although the sisters exchanged courtesies, they did not visit each other often, and according to Elizabeth, Aileen did not answer her letters.

Jennings was also concerned about her friends and acquaintances. When Peter Levi left the priesthood without laicization and married soon after, Jennings was "shocked," but in a letter to him she empathized with his decision and wished him happiness.[6] However, in the unpublished poem "A Priest Abandons His Office," written at about the same time,[7] she speculates that perhaps the priest no longer believes, and she fears that he might never rid himself of the shame of abandoning his vows. Levi went on to become professor of poetry at Oxford University, and remained a friend who continued to praise Jennings' work. For her part, Jennings was convinced that his intensely personal poetry with its timeless themes would endure. Although a remote acquaintance of Robert Lowell—Jennings met him only once— she admired his work and empathized with him on account of his severe mental illness. When he died in the fall of 1977 she wrote that she was "crushed." In a poem written in his memory she comments that, although he had bouts of mental illness, he died of a heart attack, not suicide.[8]

These preoccupations did not deter her from carrying on with her writing and participating in poetry readings. She read in Stratford, Essex, London, Bristol, Hampstead, Florence, and even at Freeland House, and gave a radio reading in Oxford with Anne Stevenson. Her work was also included in exhibits. One of her poems appeared in a display of Oxford writers sponsored by the Bodleian Library and was published subsequently in *Six Oxford Poets*.[9] A year later Roger Pringle curated "Poets of Our Time," an exhibit of ten poets who had established their reputations during the last twenty-five years. Her work was included among the likes of Larkin, Plath, Hughes, Hill, Heaney, and others. She was also widely anthologized, her poems appearing in the *Penguin Book of Women Poets*, *The Anthology of Contemporary Poetry: Post War to the Present*, *An Introduction to Fifty Modern British Poets*, and *Eleven British Poets*.[10]

These activities brought recognition and money which she needed. Other sources of income were her royalties, stipends for reviewing books, gifts from friends, and awards. In 1979 she was given the Southern Arts Literature Bursary of £1,250. The arrival of this gift was fortunate given that she had received a doctor's notice that she was "not incapable of work" and hence her sickness benefit would cease. She wrote Schmidt that, given this support was ending, she needed additional work such as translation, editing, or poetry readings.[11] Unexpectedly, and as a happy circumstance, she was informed in early 1980 that her previous Civil List pension of £700 would be supplemented by an additional £150.[12] It is estimated that all these sources of income, many of which fluctuated, would yield approximately £11,000 per year for living expenses.[13]

Jennings continued to use her money for things like travel, which gave her pleasure. She was reluctant to return to Boston because she had memories of the place and wanted those memories "shut."[14] She was also hesitant to revisit Italy,[15] but in 1979 she returned there, first spending two weeks in the little town of Bibbiena near Arezzo in Tuscany and then visiting Rome. While in Bibbiena she wrote more than eighty poems, many expressing her joy in having come back to a place where she felt accepted, where her "English shyness" disappeared, where it was not strange to be English or a Catholic, and where her life seemed to have a plan. In Italy, she encountered no Puritanical instincts. Rather the Incarnation, which blessed all creation, dominated life. It was a "healing" and "entrancing" place, a country of a million prayers, full of saints and persons of lust and greed. There was no rift between flesh and soul, but a happy integration.[16] She was glad to be there, and the effect of the visit was such that when she returned to England her dread subsided. She claimed now that she looked outward rather than inward.[17]

During this period much of her published poetry contained specifically religious themes. This development was prepared for in *Growing-Points*, but in *Consequently I Rejoice* and *Moments of Grace*, religious poems represent a major portion of each volume. *Consequently I Rejoice* took its title from Eliot's poem "Ash Wednesday," which was appropriate given that its poems both acknowledged despair and offered hope of redemption. Initially, she wanted to dedicate the book to Michael Schmidt, but because he was now her editor such a dedication would be viewed as unsuitable. The dedication read simply "For M."

The eighty-eight poems of *Consequently I Rejoice* are brief, the vocabulary simple, and the tone uniform. Included are poems about family, nature, and tributes to her favorite writers and visual artists—Aldous Huxley, Tolstoy, D. H. Lawrence, Klee, Turner, Cézanne, Woolf, and Edward Thomas, whose poetry she particularly admired. About a third of the poems of this twelfth book of verse have a specific religious content, which was a brave undertaking given the lack of interest in religion in England in the late 1970s. The most distinctive of them is a series of meditations on Christian faith, including eight monologues by Christ and four by Mary. In these, Christ addresses questions to his Father about his loneliness, temptations, and agony. In other poems Jennings reveals her Catholic understanding that both creation and ordinary life give access to the divine. She sees the world as sacramental and her poetic vocation to reveal the divine. Although she includes poems on doubt, suffering, and death, there are none on shame or guilt, illustrating how much her views on religion had changed since her early years. Her focus in these poems is on the intersection of the ordinary and the divine, the visible and the invisible. Her popularity as a poet, at least among religious people, must have been explained in part by her much more affirmative understanding of faith.

Reception of *Consequently I Rejoice* was positive. Reviewers in the *Daily Telegraph*, *PN Review*, and *The Times Literary Supplement* all cheered her on. *The Tablet* reviewer claimed her poems were "radiant" with meditative meaning,[18] and Anne Stevenson, writing for *The Listener*, said the book was "a brave and appropriate new collection" in times of self-indulgent poetry.[19]

Moments of Grace, her other major book, appeared two years later in 1979. It was briefer than *Consequently I Rejoice*, and its subject matter, focusing as it did on awe and wonder, was more contemplative than religious. It was reviewed by *The Spectator*, *The Tablet*, and *The Times*

Literary Supplement. The latter noted the predominance of religious poems and the absence of poems about mental illness.[20] Its dedication to actors Richard Pasco and Barbara Leigh-Hunt illustrates Jennings' eagerness to express gratitude to anyone who showed interest in her work, especially celebrities. Pasco and Leigh-Hunt had attended one of Jennings' readings, bought a signed copy of *Growing-Points*, and gave her a front-row seat to *The Merry Wives*, in which Barbara Leigh-Hunt appeared. Jennings' desire to attach herself to notables is evident also in her correspondence with the acclaimed actors Sir Alec Guinness[21] and Sir John Gielgud, who both graciously responded to her. She claimed that Gielgud was a man without malice or envy.[22] He occasionally sent her money, and she dedicated two books of poetry to him. They never met, but he was her "pin-up." On the walls of her room she had photographs of him, Pope John Paul II, and Lord Mountbatten. She confessed that since childhood she loved those who were most successful—the winners and heroes; they stirred her heart and made her feel as if she were fit to be with people who were wise and great.[23]

The poems of *Moments of Grace* affirm that ordinary life gives access to grace, even if it comes infrequently. Included are poems about animals, the seasons, and the sea. In "An Education" she recalls her childhood and the moment she looked at the stars. She writes: "I am a wanderer still among those stars."[24] But in other poems she chronicles times of despair, doubt, and frustration. In "Beseeching" she begs to have hearts moved and doubt taken away.[25] In "The Whole Bestiary" she shows the splendor of creation, but claims this world is "maimed" and "shadowed," perhaps by a brooding creator.[26] Although she almost never wrote about contemporary social issues, she includes a poem on euthanasia. The topic was obviously germane, given that she was living in a care home for the elderly, and although euthanasia was illegal in Britain, there was much public discussion of the topic. This obviously struck fear into her and her housemates.[27] Unique to this volume also was a very long poem, "Christmas Suite in Five Movements."[28] Christmas, the celebration of the Incarnation, was always a magical time for Jennings.

Moments of Grace was a testament to Jennings' poetic vocation. In "I Count the Moments" her dedication to poetry is made clear. For her poetry is not therapy, but it does heal the reader and open closed minds. It is both "pain as well as passion" and in it she finds order.[29] Writing poems was a moment of grace for Jennings; it gave her fleeting contact with the divine.[30]

In two years Jennings published these two major volumes of poetry and two smaller ones—a chapbook, *Winter Wind*,[31] and *After the Ark*, a slim book of children's poems.[32] Although the former contained only eight poems and had a print run of only 220 copies, the latter book of twenty-seven poems sold well, after some initial bungling by Oxford University Press. Given that she lived in a care home Jennings missed children and as a consequence writing these poems for young people gave her great pleasure. Each poem is written in the voice of a domestic or wild animal which tells of creation's diversity and urges humans to respect every creature. *After the Ark* was a sustained illustration of her use of "imagined experience." In earlier poems, she had spoken in the voice of the clown, Christ, Mary, the beggar, the homeless, and the prisoner. In this book, she gives voice to nature's many creatures.

Jennings' years in Freeland House were capped by the publication of her immensely successful *Selected Poems*. This was an easy book to assemble given that it was a collection of 103 poems arranged chronologically from all her poetry published between 1953 and 1972. Most of the poems were from her earliest work; few were retained from *Recoveries* and *The Mind Has Mountains*. *Selected Poems* was reviewed by *Encounter*, *The Listener*, *The Tablet*, *The Spectator*, and *The Times Literary Supplement*. It sold well.

As poem after poem appeared in print, thousands more remained unpublished in Jennings' notebooks. Wedgwood complained to Schmidt that she was "appalled" by the number of poems Jennings wrote each day.[33] For example, in less than two months in spring 1977 she produced 486 poems. These poems document her inner life and her wrestling with questions of meaning. They were shared with no one.

Jennings' extraordinary productivity was carried out all the while she was both physically and mentally fragile. Although never in the best of health, at this point she was worn down by a poor diet, lack of sleep, and general anxiety. She suffered from stomach ailments, anemia, low blood pressure, and blackouts. In 1978 she spent four and a half weeks in the Radcliffe Hospital, receiving blood transfusions and having other tests. Her diagnosis of coeliac disease was finally determined to be incorrect, and she could be freed from the dreadful diet she had followed for two years.[34] Jennings' physical maladies had an obvious impact on her visage, and when combined with a lack of attention to her clothing and insistence on toting five or six carrier bags, she made an odd-looking appearance.

Her psychic life was very delicate and was characterized by anger, possessiveness, and paranoia. In an earlier unpublished poem, "The Paranoid," she acknowledged that she was suspicious and expected the worst from others.[35] According to Wedgwood, Seymour Spencer claimed Jennings' paranoia was incurable,[36] and she questioned whether Jennings could live alone. Jennings attributes her anger and rage to her "blighted" family, in which both she and her father could be envious, ambitious, cruel, and guilt-ridden, neither loving the other.[37]

Jennings wrote frequently about her loneliness and believed a remedy for this was her ferocious loyalty to friends. While admitting that others might conceive of this as a "childish" quality, she wrote that she did not care what others thought; her friends were never wrong.[38] Seemingly without hyperbole, she allowed that if the devil himself were her close friend, God would be her enemy.[39] Her speculation was that her idealism about some people derived from the fact that as a child she was dominated by guilt and sin and that this led her to seek the perfect, the hero.[40] But she also saw the human need to adore someone, be it God or man.[41] Hierarchies were necessary, as was hero-worship; she considered this latter the purest kind of love, given it caused one to forget the self.[42] Such loyalty and fidelity was the "twin" of love.[43] Hero-worship, adoration, loyalty, and the various forms of love were remedies for loneliness.[44] These, in addition to poetry and religion, gave life meaning.

The principal psychic issue Jennings wrestled with during this period was how to love. She considered the need for love a part of the human condition which demanded that one be in relationship with another. But love raised the problem of possession, both being possessed and possessing.[45]

Jennings knew the perils of passion. She called love a "torture, rope and rack,"[46] which brought out her worst qualities, her selfishness, and a degrading passion for the flesh.[47] She claimed that throughout her life she always had someone to love. At one time passion took her over and she was obsessed, almost reaching lunacy. Broken in heart and mind, finally her anguish abated when another love took over.[48] In another poem she recalls her wandering hand in hand with the unnamed Hildebrand in the Eden of Spain and his shocking death. She felt sure he would be glad that now new love had come to claim her.[49] She wrote many poems about her desire to cast off lust and embrace friendship, which would allow her to be free.[50] Since it was Christ who could love without desire or possession, she took him as a model.

For Jennings, the issue was not merely how to love someone purely, but how to love both God and another human.[51] She writes that God is a jealous God and she has been both loyal and unfaithful to him. She confesses that she cannot give up on human love, she could not "shut her heart's door" to her latest love which was a relationship of sympathy and compassion.[52] This latest love was with Wedgwood, who Jennings contended taught her the difference between love and lust.[53] Even though when Wedgwood was away Jennings missed her "violently,"[54] she remained grateful to Wedgwood, who found good in her, and under whose "tutelage" she discovered a new sense of herself.[55]

Although Jennings met Wedgwood decades earlier, their relationship began in earnest right after James' death. According to Jennings their love was of a rare kind. Their exchanges were kind, delicate, and full of understanding; their hugging and kissing had no sexual passion.[56] Over the years Jennings became increasingly reliant on Wedgwood, but she was also aware of this dependency, of her unreasonable demands, and how she annoyed Wedgwood and others.[57] In 1979, while in Tuscany, Jennings pondered all her former loves: the right and wrong ones, the unwise, the unjust. She concluded only one love remained, one friend, who had become the love of her life, her "rock of gold," her "coin in fountains," her "ark in the storm," her "sky"[58]—Wedgwood.

Jennings claimed she was happy not to have a husband or family, but that she was lonely and longed for "shelter."[59] Friendship with Wedgwood provided that shelter, as well as shared intellectual life and mutual interests in poetry and the visual arts. The fact that they both had July birthdays was an added delight. As a descendant of an important family, a highly esteemed historian, and a recipient of many awards Wedgwood was a friend whom Jennings respected and admired. For Jennings, their friendship unraveled the conundrum of love, allowing her to be free, whole, and fully herself. Her loneliness appeared to be diminishing.

Because Jennings had the "gift of concealment," and Wedgwood's side of the friendship is largely undocumented, it is difficult to determine the exact nature of their relationship. What is clear is that Wedgwood, a lesbian who lived for decades with Jacqueline Hope-Wallace, had other homosexual liaisons, and was a public supporter of decriminalizing private homosexual acts, assumed the role of Jennings' caretaker. For her part, Jennings was besotted with Wedgwood. Over the next two decades she would write scores of poems about her.

In 1979 Jennings experienced healing from the torment of the last several years. She wrote that new-found peace resulted when judgment of her former loves was put aside[60] and when her faith and her poetry were fused as one.[61] Italy had once again provided the locus for that freedom. The other cause of healing was friendship with Wedgwood, the greatest love of her life. She had "come into the hour of white healing. / Grief's surgery [was] over...," but as was so often the case, this sense of well-being was only temporary, only a brief reprieve.

16

Reprieve

...I gave up but felt a great power pull
Me back and now I see why and am glad,
...Call that power God,
As I do, call it fortune. I have found
Some use in all those shadows. They have told
Me of the terror that makes dying bold
But now I hear its soft retreating sound.[1]

"Rescued"

The shadows which had terrorized Jennings for decades appeared to be retreating and she entered the 1980s happy and full of energy. For the first time in many years she admitted to feeling mostly peaceful.[2] She cherished her experience in Italy where she was accepted both as a poet and as a Catholic, and relished her friendship with Veronica Wedgwood which made her feel whole.

True to form she remained immensely productive, publishing *Celebrations and Elegies*, *A Dream of Spring*, *Italian Light and Other Poems*, and two anthologies, *The Batsford Book of Religious Verse* and *In Praise of Our Lady*, all in a period of two years.

After having lived in the countryside for several years, Jennings left Freeland House and returned to Oxford where she stayed with "Tommy" Tomlinson for a few months. She was delighted to return to the bustle of urban life with its bookshops, libraries, and access to newspapers.[3] But she was tired of relocating, having lived in five different residences in the prior fifteen years. She considered herself "a parcel" sent to and fro, stamped with "not known here."[4] She began residing at 11 Winchester Road but the place was less than ideal. The manager did not make timely repairs, there was too much noise, and she was constantly annoyed by the "yobbos" she had as housemates. When she felt particularly oppressed and persecuted she would escape again to "Tommy's" or to the Pringles in Stratford, or to a hotel where Wedgwood would pay the bill. But most days she followed a similar routine, spending her time out and about in Oxford's city center. She usually rose late, had a cup of coffee, and then took the bus to one of her favorite eateries—the Emperor's Wine Bar, Café Beau Champs, The Grapes, the Randolph Hotel, Old Orleans, or Yates's Wine Bar (Figure 16.1). She would spread out her books and papers and spend the day there, chatting up other customers. As she was a regular patron, people called her by name. She would read *The Guardian*, do crossword puzzles, and write letters and book reviews. She might go for a walk, eat a meal, visit a bookshop, or get ice cream at the Häagen-Dazs parlor. She went to see films several times a week at the Walton Street Cinema (Figure 16.2). Occasionally she would go to the theater, visit the Ashmolean, play Scrabble, or watch televised snooker.[5] When she returned to her room around 6 or 7 p.m., she would eat cold, watch the 10 p.m. news, and climb into bed where she would read and write poetry. Since she could write poems only when it was quiet, she would finally retire at 3 or 4 a.m., usually having churned out several poems.[6]

Figure 16.1. Elizabeth Jennings in a wine bar, 1980. Courtesy of Clay Perry, photographer

Figure 16.2. Former Walton Street Cinema. Dana Greene

Although her *Selected Poems* continued to sell well, Jennings fretted over lack of reviews or her exclusion from anthologies. She was miffed when D. J. Enright, who had included her in his *Poets of the 1950s*, had not done so in his newly-released *Oxford Book of Contemporary Verse, 1945–1980*. Of the forty poets included, only three were women—Patricia Beer, Stevie Smith, and Elizabeth Bishop. She was miffed further when she learned that Enright had received the 1981 Queen's Medal for Poetry, an honor she had been denied.[7] She was "furious" when Thwaite rejected two of her poems for publication in *Encounter*,[8] and dispirited when *The Times Literary Supplement* called *Celebrations and Elegies* a "disappointment."[9] Schmidt always admonished her to stop worrying about the critique of the literary world, reassuring her that she had an audience.[10] He also urged her not to play down her religious poems—something she might have worried was an impediment to her success.[11]

Although Jennings often felt excluded by the literary establishment, she remained generous toward other poets. She was grateful to John Betjeman as an admirer of her poetry and one who resonated with her themes of love, religion, and doubt, and she must have been delighted to contribute to *A Garland for the Laureate: Poems Presented to Sir John Betjeman on His 75th Birthday.*[12] She also wrote congratulatory letters to John Wain on his receiving the CBE,[13] and to Philip Larkin when he won the W. H. Smith Award.[14]

The diminishment of her inner turmoil had implications for her unpublished notebook poems, which for the first time chronicled her engagement with political issues. These express her desire to help a world in pain and her hope that her poems might give consolation.[15] Nonetheless this poetry was simplistic and politically naive.[16] If her political position were to be characterized, it was probably left of center, although she was socially conservative. In the 1979 election she supported Margaret Thatcher,[17] but she ultimately came to abhor her politics, probably because of Thatcher's lack of support for social programs and the arts. She wrote of the prime minister: "Number 10 is a house / of ill-fame / Its keeper one Thatcher / by name. / She misleads and / lies / But she can't terrorize / The many who've / rumbled her game."[18]

Jennings wrote political poems in response to events which touched her. When in 1981 an assassination attempt was made on Pope John Paul II she wrote several poems expressing her shock. This man of peace and love was now experiencing his "Calvary."[19] When martial law was established in Poland that same year and the Poles took to the streets, she lauded the resisters who both marched and prayed.[20] She wrote other poems about refugee children, war in Northern Ireland, the earthquake in Assisi, and the buildup of nuclear weapons.[21] She also wrote five poems on abortion, which are written in both the first and third person.[22] In these she expresses a variety of views: of a woman encouraged to have an abortion, a man accepting pregnancy as proof of passion, a woman complicit with an abortion, and another woman who refuses it.

The event to which she gave most attention, however, was the Falklands Conflict of 1982. In her unpublished poems, she recognizes that there is no glory in war, except for the courage of men who learned that war is a waste and that it begets more war.[23] However, in her only published statement on the conflict she is more ambiguous and patriotic.[24] Along with more than a hundred other authors Jennings offered her argument that no foreign power has the right to invade another, and therefore when the Argentines invaded the Falklands, Britain had to respond. All the Services were victorious, but at a terrible price. Her ironic conclusion was that the bitter lesson of the conflict was that Britain needed a large and totally modern navy. Jennings was first and always a patriot who would defend the nation at war, even though she claimed that seeing Remarque's film *All Quiet on the Western Front* had made her a pacifist for life.[25]

If Jennings' poetry demonstrated a new interest in world events, it also illustrated her continuing interest in religion. She was clear: she adhered to Christianity because it offered a God who became man, and knew torture, evil, and death. As such it provided the best explanation of suffering, allowing her to apprehend glory and order amid darkness and dread.[26]

The public acknowledged Jennings as a "religious" poet and she was included as one of the twenty-six twentieth-century poets in *The New Oxford Book of Christian Verse*.[27] She probably took on the work of editing two anthologies, *The Batsford Book of Religious Verse* and *In Praise of Our Lady*, released in 1981 and 1982 respectively, in order to earn money, but she was a likely candidate for these editorships. Her previously articulated definition of religious poetry was congruent with what she set out as the criteria for selection of poems in these anthologies. Her brief introduction to *The Batsford Book* states that verse must be good poetry rather than merely a devotional aid, and that the purpose of the volume is to give pleasure and excitement rather than to teach or convert. In this anthology her scope is broad, including poems of doubt and poems by agnostics like Matthew Arnold. She gives greatest emphasis to the poetry of the seventeenth century and much less to that of the twentieth century with its preoccupation with anxiety and materialism. But she does include six contemporary poets "crying in the wilderness" who offer light amid the twentieth century's unbelief and fear.[28] *The Spectator* acknowledged that while the book was a personal selection and not historically comprehensive, it was "intelligent" and "literate," something only a pedant would reject.[29]

As a Catholic and a poet, Jennings was also a likely editor of *In Praise of Our Lady*.[30] The book carried a foreword by Cardinal Basil Hume, Archbishop of Westminster, and several beautiful illustrations and paintings of Mary. In her introduction Jennings points out that the pre-Reformation period produced numerous poems, prayers, and hymns about Mary, but that fewer were written in subsequent centuries. Only in the twentieth century had Catholics and Anglicans begun to write Marian poetry again. Among those she includes is Karol Wojtyla, then Pope John Paul II, whose two poems are translated by the Polish Catholic poet Jerzy Peterkiewicz.

Jennings own poems offer ample evidence of her religious interests. *A Dream of Spring* is a small, illustrated book containing only seventeen poems, most of which are about springtime, but two poems, "From Light to Dark" and "A Way of a Creed" illustrate her increasing clarity about the role of religion in her life.[31] In the former she announces, "An Eden is / Our long desire," and speaks of a "strange homesickness" for a "lost home."[32] In "A Way of a Creed" she attests that her struggle between loyalty to God and to poetry is resolved; the two have now have become one.[33] In *Italian Light and Other Poems* she brings together twelve previously published poems from her 1957 Italian trip with new poems about that blessed landscape.[34]

Her major book of this period *Celebrations and Elegies* was dedicated to her sister and brother-in-law, Aileen and Desmond Albrow, and contained forty-two poems focused on nature and love. Some poems recall her past or her recent holiday in Bibbiena, others explore prayer, liturgy, crucifixion, Lent, and Easter, and many others are linked by the language of light. Light is "a sign // of peace and benediction,"[35] "Light...candles us / Through the labyrinth where we go."[36] While these poems contain echoes of Jennings' suffering, overall they are remarkably positive. She writes: "Innocence...is closing in again"[37] and "Surely when we gather the good about us / The dark is cancelled out."[38]

Although Jennings may have gathered the good around her, the poems of *Celebrations and Elegies* were not her best verse. As the *Times'* reviewer indicated, they did not compare to the lucidity and control of her earliest work. Many were sentimental, and written using flat language and contrived rhythms.[39] Less prestigious newspapers responded more kindly. *The Daily Telegraph* carried Wedgwood's review which praised *Celebrations and Elegies* as Jennings' best and most varied work thus far,[40] and the *Glasgow Herald*'s reviewer wrote that "the outstanding thing about Jennings' poetry is its wisdom, hard-earned from grief and religious faith."[41]

Although Jennings never wrote a systematic poetics, her early views on poetry were recorded in *Let's Have Some Poetry* and *Poetry To-day*. Later reflections on the craft are found embedded in her voluminous unpublished notebook poems of this period. To her mind poetry leads away from the self, and hence is not self-expression or self-pity. It is not autobiographical, nor is it meant to solve a person's distress, although it can do that because it reminds one that pain is bearable and that it will pass. Like all art, poetry is not a means of escape from one's own life or from a violent world; rather it is an escape into a greater reality. It civilizes and ennobles and gives a sense of justice. Poetry is an onward drive forward toward truth and mystery; at its best, it is celebration. It enlarges what one sees, takes one beyond what the senses provide, and releases one from the quotidian, which is self-regarding. But she warns, apparently unaware of how personally apt her words were, the poem, much like the preacher's sermon, can surpass the poet's character and virtue.[42]

For Jennings, poetry is close to religion. It is like Eucharist in that a simple element is offered, words are spoken, and transformation takes place. When given, poetry, like the Host, becomes "yeast" in those who partake. Poetry could also be a form of prayer. She allowed that poetry was her way of reaching God.

Jennings' unpublished notebook poems are also a source for her mid-life reflections on her life. At this point she is fifty-eight years old and attempting to bring closure and acceptance to difficult aspects of her past. She remembers herself as a helpless, awkward, shy, lonely, and diffident child who thought no one cared for her.[43] As far back as she could remember she felt set apart, a child who was "alien" and "odd," one who hated parties and craved recognition. Moods of ecstatic joy shaped her. She was moved by the mass but hated the confessional.[44] Her earliest love affairs were first with a girl whom she worshipped, then with an older boy to whom she did not "lose her heart," and finally with one with whom she enjoyed the golden summer of love, a love which ended in death. These unnamed loves were Nancy, Stuart, and "B." There were days and nights of passion when she entered sleep with her senses tingling, when overpowering passion took away the gentleness of her first love-making. In this case love was abused, turned bad, spoiling early love and becoming a sickness; it was passion seeking its own satisfaction.[45] She recalls that in these "romantic dalliances" there was tension between her need for love and her love of art, and at times the former was victorious.[46] Nonetheless she regrets none of these love relationships because they taught her compassion, understanding, and virtues which helped her conquer fear.[47]

She remembers death as well; that of a "great nurse," the unnamed Ettie Synan, who was her healer in the Warneford,[48] and of her friend the unnamed Hildebrand James, whom she recalls in two poems, "After a Death" and "Who Forgives Who?" In the former poem she asks: After months of holidaying in distant places, why did she let herself love so totally, allow herself to be possessed and to possess?[49] In the revelatory latter poem, she admits she cannot forgive herself; she was the deceiver who blamed the affair on him. Driven by passion they both suffered, but it was a relationship which could never be because he was committed elsewhere. Only death could end it. Now ten years after his death she still did not understand their affair, and so could not accept his death. She queries: What will "untie our raveled knot?"[50]

In other unpublished poems of this period she reflects on forms of love. She sees marriage as a flawed institution and considers domestic bliss a contradiction in terms. Her conclusion is that in marriage love must die or at least die down.[51] On the other hand she lauds friendship, a relationship in which the wills of two who have shared interests become one, and desire and possession have no part. Friendship's greatest qualities are trust, compassion, and the power to heal grief and hurt. She writes that as a union of respect and loyalty, there is nothing equivalent to friendship.[52]

Familial love was another matter altogether. During these years Jennings' relationship with her family, although never very positive, continued to deteriorate. Madge Jennings, after having lived in Eastbourne for many years, in 1984 moved to Mayfield House, a retirement home in Walton-on-Thames, near Aileen. Jennings' visits with her mother were "tense" and she called their love "disfigured." There was anxiety too when she visited her sister and brother-in-law. She would assume the role of guest and expected to be waited on by Aileen. Animated conversation between Liz and Desmond, who was a Tory, would mean that Aileen was excluded. For her part, Liz lamented that she grew up in her sister's shadow and envied Aileen for her confidence.[53] Aileen, on the other hand, was probably jealous of her sister. Although their relationship worsened, Jennings wrote in an undated poem that even in the face of disagreement, rows, hurtful words, and lack of loving-kindness, there was between them trust and responsiveness to need.[54] But elsewhere she wrote that she had found joy in places other than in her family.[55] That joy was in her relationship with Veronica Wedgwood.

Jennings claimed that there were few times in her life when she had not been in love with someone, and once her love was reciprocated, she was awakened and enchanted. "Love," she wrote, "is how I see the whole world and my own small life."[56] Her conundrum, which continued over years, was the relationship between love of God and love of a person and the role of passion and the desire to possess and be possessed. In the notebook poem "Solving a Problem" she asked: Is God only present when passion is subdued? Her answer was no, that the Incarnation meant that Christ as man can be everywhere evil is not present. While passion was dangerous, she believed that her love of another was part of her love of God and admitted that her life had been saved from grief by this understanding.[57] But in her relationship with Wedgwood she continued to struggle with these issues.[58]

Jennings considered Wedgwood her "rescuer," who at the death of Hildebrand James understood her grief and cared for her.[59] Their friendship blossomed. They were in daily "umbilical" telephone contact and had monthly reunions in London where they visited museums and attended cultural events. Jennings reveled in the fact that they traveled in grandeur and ate in elegant restaurants, but it was Wedgwood's presence that she cherished most.[60] She was moved by Wedgwood's keen intellect, unselfishness, humility, and warmth.[61] Their love was sometimes a game, a conversation, a touch on the hand. Jennings conceived of their relationship as almost sacramental.[62] In an unsent letter of 1982 she reveals her adulation of "Darling Veronica" and refers to herself as her "dependant."[63]

There is little evidence indicating what attracted Wedgwood to Jennings other than their mutual interests in poetry and art. But it may have been that Wedgwood needed to be needed by Jennings.[64] What is clear is that Wedgwood was aware of Jennings' jealousy of anyone who claimed her affection.[65]

Jennings had a certain anxiety about her relationship with Wedgwood, which is illustrated in one of her unpublished poems, "I Had a Love." In this Jennings speaks obliquely of her anxiety about the Wedgwood–Hope-Wallace relationship. Jennings writes that her love also had a love, and that this third love could overshadow her. She feared its "darkness" and never dared to move towards her love when this third one might be envious, resentful, or possessive.[66]

In her unpublished poems during the summer of 1982 Jennings records how she terribly missed Wedgwood and was "frantic" because they were out of touch for three weeks. Both grieving and full of rage, Jennings writes that she cursed Wedgwood in her mind, simultaneously acknowledging that she was behaving as a child in this regard.[67] When Wedgwood finally did return home, calls from Jennings were banned, ostensibly because they made Wedgwood "jumpy." Jennings was inconsolable, unsure how long she could endure this separation.[68] Cut off from Wedgwood, she writes that her love is being tested.[69] What was becoming clear, however, was that Wedgwood had substantial memory loss which would develop into Alzheimer's disease.

Jennings became increasingly desperate. She wrote of her anger, resentment, and contempt as well as her ongoing desire to serve Wedgwood.[70] Because they never fought, she was perplexed as to what had ended their relationship, but she refused to believe that this was a betrayal on Wedgwood's part.[71] In spring 1984 Jennings apparently received a "ghastly" letter from Wedgwood which indicated that she was cutting back on the money she would give Jennings for rent, then in another letter Wedgwood apologized and included a gift of £100. But the damage was done. Jennings was convinced that it was Hope-Wallace who had put Wedgwood up to this rejection.[72] Although she was beginning to realize that something was happening to Wedgwood's personality,[73] Jennings was haunted by loss of this relationship. Around Christmas 1985, after fifteen years of friendship, contact between Jennings and Wedgwood ceased.[74] In the last year and a half Jennings had only one telephone conversation with her, and she concluded that if Wedgwood could do without her so easily, she would accept that. Although hurt and angry, she did not want to be bitter.[75] Nonetheless Jennings, preoccupied with her own needs, was incapable of focusing on the tragedy afflicting her friend. Wedgwood was now gone from Jennings' life, but not from her memory.

17

Halcyon Days

Poetry is my mainspring,
Fulcrum, all
That matters most and
Even when I lost
A blithe and buoyant
Friendship and could
Feel
Nothing but rage and hurt I
Yet could trust
Poetry.[1]

"Drying Up"

A nd trust poetry she did. Although Wedgwood was lost to her, poetry was not. The years of the late 1980s proved to be ones of her acclaim and recognition as an important poet. On the eve of her sixtieth birthday she wrote of feeling healthy and vital and of dreaming of a whole lifetime ahead. As she looked back on the "rubble and debris" of her life, she saw her purpose. She was grateful for her childhood, which was still with her, for her rich memory, and even for those who hurt her as they strengthened her weak will.[2] She experienced a certain freedom and a diminishment of fear and shyness, and did not mind if she appeared a fool since now she did not care how others saw her. It was a birthday gift to say what she thought.[3] In pondering her life, she asked, what if she had made other choices? Had she missed opportunities? Had her shyness meant that she did not take risks? Might she have responded to one who loved her and therefore had a fuller life? She admitted to having gone down cul-de-sacs and made false beginnings, but sometimes these resulted in celebrations. She knew that writing came first, but she also knew that love and art were always intertwined.[4] She questioned: Was it too late at sixty to love another person? Might she have a new love before she died?[5] In a long litany of praise she wrote that love was "the thread of my life," "the magnet," "the true North / and the long beckoning / South," "the clarity out of confusion," and "the cure of any betrayal"[6] (Figure 17.1).

Jennings' sense of well-being combined with her public acclaim stood her in good stead as she confronted her principal loss, that of her friendship with Wedgwood. This preoccupation, which continued for years, was the one sadness in her life. While cognizant of Wedgwood's diminishing memory, she was baffled by why access to her was no longer possible. She was desperate to be in contact, and considered this break an abrupt and cruel ending to their years of friendship.

In a torrent of unpublished poems, she began to record her confusion and anger, convinced as she was that someone was controlling Wedgwood, ending their relationship, and casting her into exile. She conceived of Wedgwood's loss of memory as a kind of living death and hoped this death would be kind. She noted that she loved Wedgwood more deeply and dearly than any other person and that their love, which was intellectual and imaginative, was not spoiled by possessiveness. Although Wedgwood was locked in silence, Jennings thought of her obsessively every day even though she knew she must put her out of her mind.[7] She wrote that she did not want to be bitter, but she was. In "Bitter Fruit" she illustrates her confusion. "Can trust / Ever be retrieved? // Yes, there are many deaths but this today / Seems the worst I've ever known. You are / Distant in fact and distant in a way / You were not till you broke my trust, taught fear / Darker than I can say."[8] In "Growing Ahead" she asks: "Are you really lost / To me?"[9]

Jennings' distress over the end of this relationship was connected to her recognition that she could not go on without someone to love and look up to. Only in that way could she who was "half" become "whole." She confessed that she could only love God through people— men and women.[10]

The loss of Wedgwood's financial support imperiled Jennings' security. Her earnings came from writing, gifts, readings, awards, and a Civil List pension,[11] but this was not sufficient. To boost her income Michael Schmidt wrote to the Royal Literary Fund requesting it offer Jennings assistance, given her stature, her modest earnings, and the loss of her principal patron.[12]

Figure 17.1. Elizabeth Jennings, 1986, by Fay Godwin. © Courtesy of the British Library Board, image 083500

Jennings could be entrepreneurial when she needed to be. Since public readings brought in money and helped sell books, she augmented her efforts to secure these opportunities. She was invited to read at various venues, among others the Poetry Society and Newbury Literary Society in 1985, the latter arranged by John Wain. Since some of her poems had been translated into Italian, the Libreria Croce in Rome extended an invitation as well, but she declined to accept. In 1986 Roger Pringle again arranged for her to appear at the Stratford Poetry Festival, and she read her poetry at another venue where she was introduced by Anne Harvey. Harvey, a Catholic, became a friend who published Jennings' poems, arranged readings for her in schools and elsewhere, and consoled her in times of anxiety and depression. In 1987 Jennings read on B.B.C. Radio's *Woman's Hour,* and in 1988 she was at the Purcell Room at the South Bank Centre in London, and at Waterstone's in Stratford. Her presentations were clear and matter-of-fact, but her continual shuffling of papers made her less than a celebrity presence.

One of her assets was her first edition books and her own manuscripts, which she realized she could sell. Working principally with the London seller, Bertram Rota, she sold these materials to American universities which desired to augment their manuscript collections and had the money to purchase them. In subsequent years she became increasingly dependent on these sales,[13] although she continued to simultaneously petition her friends for monetary loans and gifts.

Happily Jennings' concerns about her finances and the end of her friendship with Wedgwood did not substantially diminish her sense of well-being experienced in the four-year period beginning in 1985. Early on in that year she kept a list of the good happenings which included publication of poems, receipt of funds from organizations, cherished fan mail, and opportunities to give readings and to have her poems reprinted.[14] By the end of this period she had reaped considerable success with the publication of *Extending the Territory,* her fourteenth book of poetry, and *Collected Poems: 1953–1985,* which garnered national acclaim, sold well, and ensured her success over the next five years. Her friend Peter Levi suggested that the publication of *Extending the Territory* marked a new, third phase of her writing, the earlier phases having been initiated by *Poems* (1953) and *Growing-Points* (1975).[15] She was entering halcyon days.

Extending the Territory lived up to its title. In its eighty-one poems Jennings increases her range of subject matter to include autobiographical themes, longer poems, and expanded use of free verse. Some poems are melancholic and focus on loss and death, but generally the poems about nature, God, and childhood are positive. Like bookends, memories of her earliest years begin and conclude the volume. The opening poem, "The Child's Story," is a paean of praise for her childhood, especially her love of the stars.[16] "Precursors," the book's final poem, is a remembrance of her youth and the role of poetry. "... I have come / To believe," she wrote, "that poetry is a restoration / Or else an accompaniment to what is lost / But half remembered."[17] In a life of many losses, poetry provided Jennings a way back to the Edenic bliss of childhood. She dedicated *Extending the Territory* to her friends Roger and Marion Pringle, who supported her both personally and professionally.

Reviews of *Extending the Territory* were numerous, but uneven in their evaluation. The detractors depressed her. John Lucas, writing in the *New Statesman*, criticized her "vapid" poems, with their unvaried language and uninteresting subject matter.[18] Robert Nye's review in *The Times* angered her; she called it a "nasty" review because he included comments about her mental illness. She wrote to Schmidt saying that Nye's claims were "rubbish," and insisted that there was nothing in *Extending the Territory* that gave any indication of her breakdown some twenty-five years before.[19] She was hurt, too, by David Gascoyne's critique, in which he opined that only one-third of the poems were excellent, and that some appeared to be confessional, subjective, and lacking in universality. But he concluded by calling the book a "triumphant anomaly."[20] Given that Jennings was an admirer of Gascoyne, and having claimed that he was the only living English poet other than Eliot who was in the mystical tradition, she might have expected more unequivocal praise from him.[21] She expressed her displeasure about his comments to Schmidt, who relayed her sentiments to Gascoyne directly. Gascoyne then responded with apologies to Jennings, explaining that the first paragraph of the review had been cut, and he added that since they were both poets who had spent time in psychiatric institutes, they might be more sympathetic toward each other.[22] A kindlier review in *The Observer* described her poems as "litanies of acceptance," and poems of "unfakeable naivety" which affect and involve the reader.[23] But the most munificent review was that of Peter Levi, who suggested that *Extending the Territory* was Jennings' best single collection thus far, "a brilliantly attractive book." He specifically praised her ability to recapture her early childhood and recover its sense of wonder. Calling her modest, authentic, and a poet with an inward fire, he went on to famously write that "she may be the last poet of what used to be called soul," "one of the few living poets one could not do without."[24] Levi's commendation and the Southern Arts Society Prize awarded to *Extending the Territory* gave her a great boost. The fact that the prize brought with it £1,000 must have softened the blow of any negative criticism the book generated.

The year 1985 was a productive one. Not only did *Extending the Territory* appear, but Pringle's Celandine Press printed 150 copies of her *In Shakespeare's Company*.[25] This handsome book contained twenty-three celebratory poems about Shakespeare's characters with accompanying illustrations. It was appropriately dedicated to John Gielgud, the Catholic Shakespearean actor and recipient of Oscar, Emmy, Grammy, and Tony awards, her correspondent over many years. In the book's preface Jennings wrote that these poems were a thank-you gift to Gielgud, to whom so many owed some of the greatest moments of their lives. Peter Levi was impressed with the little book, and called it "brilliant," "thrilling," a "virtuoso performance."[26]

Jennings' visibility was also enhanced by inclusion in two new anthologies. Her poems, along with those of Charles Causley, John Fuller, Vernon Scannell, and John Walsh, were incorporated into Anne Harvey's edition of the Penguin anthology of children's verse,[27] *Poets In Hand: A Puffin Quintet*. Jennings was thrilled by this publication. The following year Sebastian Barker published *Portraits of Poets*, which contained photographs and poems of some sixty poets born between 1898 and 1939. Only one-tenth of these were women, including Jennings, whose portrait and poem "I Feel" were included.[28]

For many years, reviewing books provided Jennings a way to bring in revenue and keep herself in the public spotlight. These reviews also documented her current interests. As an admirer of the poetry of Charlotte Mew, she praised Penelope Fitzgerald's biography of this haunted woman, asserting that even in the face of Mew's melancholy and suicide attempts, she remained one of England's most enduring poets.[29] In a review of the *Letters of John Clare*, the nineteenth- century poet, she wrote that these letters gave testimony to Clare's poetic genius, determination, and courage. She gave special note to his mental suffering, his childlike delight and sense of awe, characteristics she shared with him.[30] In appraising Amy Clampitt's *The Kingfisher*, Jennings observed that the author's lineage was with Marianne Moore, Elizabeth

Bishop, Frost, Stevens, and Lowell, and not with the confessional Plath or the feminist Adrienne Rich. Given this, she hoped that Clampitt might heal the breach between British and American poetry which had occurred beginning in the 1960s.[31]

A unique opportunity for visibility was also given Jennings when she was invited by Jeni Couzyn to be included in *The Bloodaxe Book of Contemporary Women Poets*. The book celebrated poets by gender, contended there was a conscious refusal in Britain to acknowledge women poets, documented the absence of women in poetry anthologies, and claimed that men disliked women's poetry because its content challenged them.[32] As such the *Bloodaxe Book* was obviously more than a compensatory anthology of women writers; it was a feminist tract, even though several of those included eschewed a feminist designation, as did Jennings. According to Peter Levi, Jennings claimed never to have felt discriminated against as a literary woman;[33] nonetheless, she was perplexed as to why there were not more women in the arts and called this "A Question with No Answer." As early as the 1960s Jennings expressed interest in this problem and wrote to the poet and editor Terence Tiller recommending he bring out a volume of poetry by women poets—Rossetti, Mew, Sitwell, Plath, Dickinson, Sexton, Bishop, Emily Brontë, and Marianne Moore. Her hope was such a book would point out the differences between men and women poets and address the "scarcity" of females in the tradition.[34] Jennings suspected this absence could not be explained merely by women's role as wife and child-tender, but that the loneliness of the woman artist was also a factor.[35] The book was not produced and without the analytical tools to critique women's place in the literary tradition Jennings had no way to think about the difficulty a woman had in speaking, as a poet must, in her own voice in a male-centered tradition.

The structure of Couzyn's book consists of brief autobiographical statements and several poems by each of eleven contemporary women poets, including Jennings, Plath, Stevie Smith, Raine, Denise Levertov, Anne Stevenson, and Jenny Joseph. Jennings' statement is an example of her gift of concealment or her discursive conversation.[36] She begins bizarrely by expressing her opposition to this kind of autobiographical self-examination because it exposes what she thinks of herself, makes her self-conscious about her work, and turns her inward toward her darkness. The remainder of her statement is given to a discussion of her Catholicism, which she reiterates came alive because of her visit to

Rome. Although she does not elaborate, she claims that her faith has influence on all that she does—her writing of poetry and her responsibility toward others and the suffering planet. She admonishes the reader, however, not to assume that she did not have problems with some religious tenets. Considering the focus of Couzyn's book, Jennings' statement is an odd one, but it does demonstrate her unwillingness to publicly expose her inner life. This refusal never diminished, and may explain in part her muted voice and diffident language, so often commented on by reviewers.

The public's positive response to Jennings' poetry increased her visibility. This is clearly illustrated in her most important publication of this period, *Collected Poems: 1953–1985*, which sold more than 35,000 copies, catapulted her to be included on the A-level syllabus, and resulted in her receiving the prestigious W. H. Smith Award, a prize which brought with it £4,000 and placed her on a par with other Smith Award recipients—including Raine, Heaney, and Larkin. To promote positive reviews and maximize sales of *Collected Poems*, an elaborate launch was planned. Blackwell's bookshops in both London and Oxford promoted the book and its release was arranged to coincide with Jennings' sixtieth birthday. Invitation lists for events were developed to include graduates of St. Anne's, representatives of all the major magazines and radio programs, friends, and admirers.[37] A book party was organized for the evening of Jennings' July birthday and held at the London home of her agent, Bruce Hunter of David Higham Associates. The effort proved successful; there were many positive reviews, and sales were such that a paperback edition was released the following year.

In her brief preface Jennings explained that the book's title, *Collected Poems*, was a misnomer; it did not contain all her previous poems, but her selection of the 301 of those she believed were worth preserving. Having eliminated many of her earlier hospital poems and others written between 1969 and 1982, this collection was offered as evidence that she was not a confessional poet. She reiterated that "Art is not self-expression" and that "'confessional poetry' is almost a contradiction in terms."[38] She went on to say, denying earlier statements, that she revised her poems extensively. This claim is inexplicable and paradoxical and might have been offered to counter the prevalent criticism that she wrote too much, and too much of it was unpolished. She dedicated the volume to Roy Fuller, a former professor of poetry at Oxford University.

Of the many reviews of *Collected Poems*, the *New Statesman's* was the most tepid, claiming both that the "dreary" Jennings had been eclipsed by her Movement colleagues, and that her poems about mental illness had the quality of "cool compassion" as compared to those of Plath and Lowell.[39] Other reviewers understood the importance of *Collected Poems*, even as they might criticize aspects of her work. One noted her emphasis on the tension between the self and the world, and the role of faith and art as mediators between them,[40] while another recognized her enduring talent to ask big questions even though her answers were often "bland."[41] Jennings' willingness to wrestle with difficult questions like love and death was highlighted by a third reviewer, who also sensed that her poems came from a life full of inner conflict and were written "with gloves on, and always from within doors or within a particular class."[42]

But other reviewers lauded the book. One compared her work to that of Czeslaw Milosz in that both rejected contemporary nihilism and offered a vision of goodness and order.[43] Fellow poet Anne Stevenson suggested that *Collected Poems* contained poems of wisdom and harmony and represented Jennings at her best. To her mind Jennings had a "rare . . . and extremely tough sensibility." Hers were some of "the finest lyric poems of the twentieth century."[44] Jennings was thrilled by this review.[45] *Acumen's* insightful reviewer hailed *Collected Poems* as serious poetry concerned with serious themes, the most important of which were the loss of the joy and hope of childhood and the desire for a substitute faith which would return one to that original condition.[46] *The Tablet's* commentator suggested that solitude was Jennings' principal theme, and while her tone was subdued, and there was some unevenness and repetition in her poems; they had emotional depth. He concluded that Jennings was technically accomplished and that she produced poems of originality and subtlety. His conclusion: her poetry was impressive.[47] Kingsley Amis, Jennings' friend since university days, wrote that she was a poet with a personal vision and the gift for making that vision immediate and shareable.[48] One American reviewer argued that Jennings was one of the finest poets since Thomas Hardy,[49] while another, admitting that Jennings' culture was foreign to Americans, submitted that her poetry nonetheless was important and had merit. But it was Peter Levi who best understood the intersection of Jennings' life and work. He advanced the notion that over a lifetime she wrote honestly and genuinely about important subjects, all the while enduring mental illness, financial insecurity, loneliness, and insults from critics for her manners, correct use of language, and for being a person of faith. In the face of this she remained steady as a rock, and her public continued to be faithful. Elizabeth Jennings was a "nourishing artist," a "triumph of integrity," who now at sixty was beginning to be recognized.[50]

The ceremony honoring Jennings with the W. H. Smith Award was held in 1987 with many of her old friends in attendance, including Alan Brownjohn and Grevel Lindop, among many others. Anne Harvey was enlisted by Michael Schmidt to ensure that Jennings not arrive inebriated—she was still drinking heavily, champagne being her favorite drink—and in an outfit smarter than her usual garb. Schmidt was concerned about her "sartorial presentation."[51] For the occasion she purchased new plimsolls and a sweater. Simon Hornby, president of W. H. Smith, and Kenneth Baker, Secretary of State for Education, were present and made remarks. Jennings gave a short speech that had a bit of sparkle, in which she allowed that she expected her *Collected Poems* to be in the window of every W. H. Smith bookshop in the country.

Since *Collected Poems* was reprinted in paperback, Jennings lobbied to have her favorite prose book, *Every Changing Shape*, reprinted as well. But that did not happen until almost a decade later. However, in 1988 Carcanet did bring out a new edition of her successful *The Sonnets of Michelangelo*.[52] Soon she would be listed on the A-level syllabus, which guaranteed that she would have minimum sales of 4,000 copies of *Collected Poems* each year.[53] Hoping to increase sales, she was spurred on to give readings in schools.[54] As Michael Schmidt wrote, to be on the A-level syllabus was to ensure one's immortality.[55] That might have been more important to Jennings than the money earned.

But she remained preoccupied about her finances. She persuaded Roger Pringle to purchase two manuscripts, "A Book of Spells," a collection of forty-four mostly previously published children's poems, and a 1986 iteration of her earlier autobiography.[56] She wrote him saying that she thought the autobiography was "quite valuable," and if he did not want it she would send it to the States,[57] meaning it would be sold to an American university. To help Jennings financially, Pringle purchased both manuscripts, but neither was ever published.[58] With the exception of a few paragraphs added to bring it up to the present, this truncated autobiography ended in 1960 with no mention of her breakdown or her relationship with "B." Although in hawking it she was probably driven principally by financial need, her effort was an indication that she wanted her life to be known, and that she thought it an important, a "valuable" life, which provided the context in which her poetry was nurtured.

Other small projects brought in money as well. William Meeuws of Thornton's bookshop suggested that she write a collection of poems on Oxford themes which he would publish and for which he would pay royalties in full when she turned in the manuscript.[59] Initially she wanted to dedicate the collection to Alec Guinness, but she changed her mind; the poems carried no dedication, although she later dedicated the poem "After a Painting Is Finished" to him.[60] Within two weeks Jennings composed sixteen poems on various aspects of Oxford—its landscape, rivers, churches, its university, students, and foreign inhabitants. One poignant poem is entitled "Loneliness," which alludes to the students who don't make friends and live alone. Their suffering becomes unbearable "until they reach / The gas-tap."[61] Another of these *Oxford Cycle* poems was an ode to the venerable Blackwell's bookshop, a Thornton competitor. When Meeuws realized this, he insisted it be deleted and that one praising Thornton's be substituted.

During this period Jennings was increasingly acclaimed, but she remained psychologically fragile. There were periods of four or five months when she was miserable because poems would not come to her. She was desperate to be seen as a valuable person and to receive the affection of others. This was illustrated by an incident which occurred at the death of the Dominican priest Osmund Lewry in April 1987. Lewry had been a great help to Jennings at the death of Hildebrand James in 1971, although she had not seen him in years. Right before Lewry died he sent Jennings a note saying he would "dearly love" to see her. Lamentably the letter arrived after his death. Jennings was devastated and wept profusely. She wrote five poems expressing her loss of someone who longed to see her and express his affection for her. She sent one of these poems on to Timothy Radcliffe, who the following year became provincial of the English Dominicans.[62]

Having turned sixty, Jennings felt well physically but was preoccupied and anxious; nonetheless she refused to take tranquilizers or pills to calm herself.[63] She pondered death and the loss of passion, desire, and power. She feared some disease would end her life, but she recognized that she yet had time to make amends for her sins of omission and commission.[64] Even with the preoccupations of aging, the late 1980s were halcyon days. She was victorious as never before. She had trusted poetry, and it had not betrayed her.

18

National Acclaim

> Even when grief is threatening, even when hope
> Seems as far as the furthest star.
> Poetry uses me, I am its willing scope
> And proud practitioner.[1]

"Against the Dark"

Poetry rescued Jennings again. She was its proud practitioner, particularly now. The publication of *Collected Poems* and reception of the W. H. Smith Award had worked their magic. Her cumulative success as a poet was increasingly evident. In 1989 Michael Schmidt wrote her: "Statistically speaking, you are now unrivalled as our best-seller. Indeed you must be one of the best-selling poets in England.... Few authors can claim the earned popularity that you now enjoy."[2] During the next five years Jennings would publish two more books of poetry, produce another autobiographical manuscript, be interviewed seven times in newspapers and on radio, and receive recognition for her poetic contribution to the nation.

Tributes, her twenty-first book of poetry, was published in 1989. Its poems were almost universally positive. Mining her own life as illustration, she wrote about childhood, friendship, poets, painters, and places. In other poems she reflected on the craft of poetry, a process which she admitted became more and more mysterious.[3]

As its title indicates, *Tributes* is offered as a celebration, in this case of a variety of artists. She honors poets—George Herbert, the Cornwall poet Charles Causley, and Philip Larkin, who had died a few years earlier. The Larkin poem opens with the lines: "The last thing you would have wanted— / A poem in praise of you."[4] She also honors painters—Turner, Caravaggio, Goya, and Chardin—and "shockers" like Warhol, Pollock, and Hockney—and mystics, namely Teresa of Avila and her favorite, Augustine. In other poems she reminisces about places which shaped her, especially those in Italy—Sant'Anselmo, Ostia Antica, Lake Albano, Florence, Assisi, and Siena.

Although she had previously written about friendship, in *Tributes* she includes poems commemorating her friends Tindal-Atkinson, Hildebrand James, and Veronica Wedgwood. In the poem "Friendship" she comments on the need to be lighthearted and not burdensome to new friends, and she restates that friendship in the last analysis must be about "Understanding and trust, / Loving-kindness, liberty."[5]

The book's poems about childhood recount her first six years in Boston, with all its pleasures and security;[6] her days of lying in the hay, picking flowers, and savoring apples and gooseberries.[7] In one autobiographical poem, "Legacies and Language," she traces her life from Boston to Oxford to Rome,[8] and in others she recalls her early rapture at mass and her creation of a childhood religion.[9] The bliss of childhood is eroded gradually as the child learns of time, which mocks and ensures loss. Only art and faith hint of immortality, when time ceases and one comes to "live in a power / whose medium is trust / and undemanding love."[10]

The most important poems of *Tributes* are those in which Jennings attempts to define the art of poetry. This is not a new theme for her, but it is greatly expanded here. Her most elegant description of poetry is of pigeons in flight. Gracefully, naturally, unexpectedly, they appear and then vanish. A poem begins in the same way, gathering force without the poet's intervention. A poem is sound which is not sought, but found.[11] In "House of Words" she writes of verbs, nouns, and adjectives sorting themselves out, as the poet waits to hear "the sound, the tune, the undertow of song."[12] Elsewhere she writes of the poem as imagination run wild, bringing back words or sometimes an entire poem. Without alteration, the poet lets "...language and music kiss / And marry and stay true."[13]

According to Jennings the central act of the poet, the "mainspring," is the act of waiting. Poems arrive in the quiet of night. First their music begins and the poet waits until the words come. Music and words are inextricably bound together, and when their union occurs, the poet experiences the stars shining their approval.[14] The function of poetry is to praise. Its images come from light and make song.[15] But poems also "…drive / Out the devils that darken love" and take on dreadful life disturbances and soften them.[16] Like all art, poetry is not escape, but rather a larger view, and because it tells the truth of both ecstasy and suffering, poems bring relief.[17] With its twisted language, meaning and metaphor, poetry is the most difficult of the arts,[18] but also its most accessible. In "The Feel of Things" she writes: "The poem is a way of making love / Which all can share. Poets guide the lips, the hand."[19]

Jennings' unsystematic poetics expressed in her poetry is further augmented in two articles published about this time in which she laments the lack of craftsmanship in contemporary poetry, rejects the idea that a person can be taught to be a poet, and weighs in on the use of rhyme, which makes readers feel safe because they learned it in school and can sing it.[20]

Writing poetry was central to Jennings' psychological health; it was also vocational. She attests in a later poem that poetry "keeps me enclosed, well-ordered and close-barred."[21] In a long unpublished poem on life's purpose she writes of seeing all things as thoughts in the mind of God. All pain and suffering are within God, who is always near and ready to lift all up to his grace. The poem ends with an affirmation of her own purpose as poet: "…and so I've learnt to believe / That art that's practised wholly selflessly / Is a tiny copy of God's transcendent dream / Where nothing's forgotten and 'is' takes over from 'seem.'"[22]

Within *Tributes* are poems which hint at the darkness she is never completely able to cast off. In "Two Together" she writes of the terrible temper she had as a child, which can still "burst out in fiery rages."[23] In another poem, she tells of family quarrels and angry accusations, and confesses that all have eaten of the shining apple which has ruined us.[24] But on balance, *Tributes* is one of Jennings' more optimistic volumes of poetry, reflecting her personal well-being at this time.

Reviewers confirmed this evaluation. Lawrence Sail, writing in *Stand Magazine*, commended the poems for their accessibility and vulnerability. He was especially taken with the poems of childhood and those which expressed joy and gratitude, but he acknowledged that the book includes dark poems as well.[25] An insightful reviewer suggested it was difficult to write about Elizabeth Jennings because the person and poet were intimately intertwined. Her poems reflect a person who was both tough and fragile, one who has suffered and been given the solace of love.[26] The *Times Literary Supplement* reviewer called Jennings a "craftswoman," praising her for the use of simile and her faith in a form suited for her poems.[27] *The Tablet* lauded her poetry as "nourishing," and releasing suffering and joy straight from the poet's heart to the reader.[28]

Any euphoria generated by Jennings' recent literary recognition was dampened the following year when on January 1, 1990 Madge Jennings died at age eighty-seven. Claiming to be ill, Jennings did not attend the funeral.[29] After her mother's death she continued to write poems about her, praising her mother's ability to comfort her and calm her rage, but regretting her own inability to express gratitude for her mother's thoughtfulness.[30] In a long poem, she described Madge Jennings as always kind, gentle, steadfast, innocent, and peaceful, a mother who supported her as a young poet. But now her mother's death meant that she was an orphaned child.[31]

During this time Jennings continued to live at 11 Winchester Road, where she felt increasingly oppressed by other residents, principally a young girl she called "schizophrenic," who sneered and jeered at her, knocked on her door at 2 a.m., and used obscenities, all of which tormented Jennings and brought her to tears.[32] At times, she could not bear it, and sought relief with friends like "Tommy" Tomlinson, Anne Scott,[33] or an unidentified woman named "Cotty," who offered her temporary housing. Apparently Cotty took Jennings into her "handsome" home and welcomed her into her family of young and old. In gratitude Jennings dedicated the opening poem of *Tributes* "For Cotty—A Letter of Thanks."[34] In this Jennings hailed Cotty as full of "sweet goodwill," as her "new found star" who opened her eyes again when she was blind. Unfortunately, nothing more is known of "Cotty," and she is not mentioned again.[35] At other times Jennings begged other friends, namely Prisca Tolkien or her newly-reacquainted friend Anne Harvey, to give her accommodation. Or she took refuge with Ruga Stanley, who provided companionship and a healing presence. When back in her own flat the highlight of Jennings' week was her Tuesday and Saturday visits with Ruga.[36] Later, in order to honor her, she wrote "Two Sonnets for a Czech Friend."[37] Jennings' unhappiness living at 11 Winchester was finally relieved when in September 1991 she secured new accommodation at 18A St. Margaret's Road, a place that was less expensive and had a sympathetic landlady.

The apex of Jennings' national recognition came on October 29, 1992 when Queen Elizabeth presented her with the medal of Commander of the British Empire (CBE) for highly distinguished and innovative contribution on a national level. When Jennings found out about the award she wrote Schmidt saying she could not believe the honor.[38] Aileen, a handsome woman and smart dresser, helped her sister ready for the occasion and accompanied her to the ceremony at Buckingham Palace. Jennings wore a flowered skirt, knitted sweater, red wool beret, black oversize duffel coat, tights, and lace-up shoes (Figures 18.1 and 18.2). A week or so after the ceremony there was a celebratory dinner at the venerable Rules restaurant in London. Michael Schmidt, who escorted her, had to explain to the restaurant staff that indeed Jennings, who arrived with her many carrier bags, was a famous poet.

After the ceremony Jennings received a letter advising her that the CBE brought with it a pension supplement of £250 per year.[39] This meant that she would now have an annual pension of £1,750. This would be supplemented by £2,100 from royalties paid out from David Higham Associates.[40] Additionally, she would earn money from speaking engagements, reviews, gifts, awards, and sales of her personal books and papers. But with less than £4,000 of secure annual income she continued to be worried about financial matters. When she had money she would hire a taxi to take her to Bath or Brighton, roundtrip forays

Figure 18.1. Elizabeth Jennings and Queen Elizabeth. Courtesy of British Ceremonial Arts Limited

162 ELIZABETH JENNINGS

Figure 18.2. Elizabeth Jennings and Aileen Albrow. Courtesy of Mark Albrow

of almost 200 miles in order to go on a spending spree. Often, when close to penury, Jennings undertook short assignments which brought in revenue: an essay on Emily Dickinson, reviews of the poems of R. S. Thomas and Alistair Elliot, a retrospective essay on becoming a poet, an introduction to *The Collected Poems of Ruth Pitter*, and, of course, poetry readings.[41]

As usual she was writing poems for another Carcanet volume. *Times and Seasons* appeared in 1992 and was dedicated to Simon Hornby, chairman of the W. H. Smith Company. One can imagine this dedication was offered to thank Hornby for the award she had received five years earlier. Slimmer than *Tributes*, *Times and Seasons* continued many of the same themes of nature, faith, art, and childhood, but its overall tenor was darker than her previous volume. What was new here was Jennings' return to the sonnet form for some of her verse and the inclusion of a few ecological poems. However, the bulk of the poems were autobiographical and focused on religion. In long sequences of poems on Christmas and Easter and poems about Mary, she recalls her own religious doubt, the suffering inflicted on her by religion, and her terrorizing first confession. Other poems are reminiscences of her discovery of poetry, her first love, the lost friendship with Wedgwood, and her mother's death. This last event prompted her to write other published and unpublished poems on this theme. In "Two Sonnets on Death" and "Death," she questions what happens after death. A remembered childhood experience of being drawn to the stars brought her to think that death might be like that, an "Undeserved blessedness."[42] There were fewer reviews of *Times and Seasons* than of *Tributes*, but she must have been pleased with *The Times Literary Supplement* lauding her for taking on the big questions and making them new, and for the accolade that she was "one of contemporary English poetry's major sublunary assets."[43] *The Tablet* praised Jennings for her mature and peaceful spirituality and her awareness of the world's suffering, and commended her for writing authentic religious poetry rather than devotional verse.[44]

Evidence of Jennings' popularity as a poet was increasing. Germaine Greer included two of her poems in *The Change—Women, Aging and the Menopause*,[45] and she was interviewed by Gerlinde Gramang for *Elizabeth Jennings: An Appraisal of Her Life*,[46] and by *The Times*, *Oxford Today*, *Oxford Poetry*, *The Independent*, the *Catholic Herald*,[47] and on the B.B.C. program *Desert Island Discs*.[48] During the open-ended questioning on this radio program, Jennings publicly revealed her likes and dislikes. If stranded on an island she would miss people and conversation. To sustain herself she would take with her music discs as diverse as "Surrey with the Fringe on Top" and her favorite Mozart horn concerto. She would also include a disc of Gielgud reading *Hamlet*. Her one allotted book would be *The New Oxford Book of American Verse*. During this B.B.C. program, she read several of her poems and gave details of her growing up and her journey to Rome. When asked why she wrote poems, she confessed that it was something she was able to do. When queried about what she would like to have, she answered, more money because she liked good food and wine and attending the cinema and theater.

True to form Jennings continued to take on large writing projects. In 1993 or 1994 she commenced writing yet another autobiography. In this long, handwritten essay entitled "Without Whom,"[49] she gives thanks for those persons without whom she might not have become a poet. She calls this a "sort of autobiography," believing as she does that autobiographies are egotistic and that the best of the genre are those which focus on others rather than the self. "Without Whom" is a curious document, which adds little to what had already been chronicled in her previous autobiographies, but it does reflect her mature thoughts on those who were important to her and the impact they had in shaping her life and poetry. It was a work of gratitude.

According to its synopsis, the eight chapters of "Without Whom" are ordered chronologically, but they are not presented as such in the one extant copy of this document.[50] Jennings begins with a chapter on Rome and her experience of religious renewal made possible by Tindal-Atkinson and others and the happiness and liberation which resulted. A second chapter is entitled "The Poets of the 1950s" and includes a discussion of her work in the library, her interaction with young poets, her earliest publications and their reception, and her collaboration with her Movement colleagues.

Another chapter veers off to include a discussion of literary influences, and a fourth is given over to C. V. Wedgwood. This section begins with a discussion about friendship, which in Jennings' mind is the greatest form of love that sinful creatures can hope for. She praises Wedgwood's virtues—her intelligence, graciousness, and modesty—and attests that their friendship was always lively and exciting, bonded as they were through poetry. Jennings recognizes that sometimes she herself was "difficult" and "introspective." She writes that their friendship was not "unsullied," although she offers no examples. Although she laments that she has not seen Wedgwood for ten years, she is nonetheless grateful to her for changing her and helping her to look outwards.

Jennings includes a chapter on Kingsley Amis, but in it focuses mostly on her years at the university, especially on her own romantic dalliances. The next three chapters describe her early life and are organized around her maternal grandparents, the Turners, her uncle Frank, and her teacher Miss Wilson. She reminisces about the loving care of her grandparents, the stimulation and encouragement of her uncle Frank, and Miss Wilson's influence in helping her discover poetry.

The strangest of the eight chapters is the one devoted to Nancy Waters, senior prefect and leader of Girl Guides. Jennings describes Nancy as intelligent, kind, and compassionate, and a person who had a deep moral effect on her. She admits that she worshipped Nancy from afar, that her "crush" on her was pure, and that she never wanted to narrow the distance between them because their relationship was not passionate, nor did it involve desire or egotism. Because of this, she did not fear its loss. Since Nancy Waters and Jennings almost never spoke to each other, it is difficult to understand how Waters might have influenced Jennings' literary life, but Jennings' inclusion of her in this "sort of autobiography" attests to the fact that this early relationship had a formative and memorable emotional influence on her.

At age sixty-seven Jennings had once again tried to make sense of her life by writing "Without Whom." She had experienced the death of her mother and accepted national acclaim for her work. Through it all, it was poetry which had kept her "enclosed, well-ordered and close-barred." She would need that stability in the next few years as she confronted dislocation and the death of Veronica Wedgwood.

19

Dislocation

...I have no one who
Cares for me totally,
No one to whom I come first
...there is no longer one
To whom I am the world, the centre, the heart,
The headstrong noonday sun,...[1]

"A Realisation"

In the mid-1990s Jennings experienced a dislocation which was both psychological and physical. She came to the realization that she was no longer the center of anyone's complete affection. Although she always counted on new loves to appear, now there were none. It was as if Veronica Wedgwood were already dead, given there had been no contact between them. Her loss was made worse by the death of her most loyal friend, Ruga Stanley, whom she had known from their time together at the Warneford Hospital. As a Jew and the only member of her family to survive the Holocaust, Stanley carried a lifelong sense of guilt. In May 1994 she unexpectedly committed suicide. Jennings believed that this desperate action was triggered by her viewing the film *Schindler's List*, which she had warned her not to see.[2] Ruga had been a faithful friend for thirty years, offering solace and healing as well as physical comfort. Now she was gone.

These personal losses were played out against a background of wrenching "homelessness." In 1993 Jennings was happy to leave her flat at Winchester Road and move to St. Margaret's Road, but then in May of the following year her empathic landlady, Mrs. Eleanor Wood, died suddenly. According to Jennings her possessions were packed up by Wood's son and sent off to storage in a garage in the countryside and she was evicted. During the next year and a half, she searched for permanent accommodations, all the while living at seven different addresses. She went as far as to post notices at newsstands, including one in the Oxford train station—"Elizabeth Jennings has nowhere to live. Can you help?"[3] She lived with Catholic friends, "Tommy," Anne Scott, in a series of B & Bs, which were very expensive and noisy, and in a one room council bedsit at 412 Banbury Road. Jennings moved her possessions from storage into the bedsit with the help of Wendy Hill, a typist who had been recommended to Jennings by Ruga a week prior to her suicide. When, in the process of the move, one of her many ornaments broke Jennings began banging her head on the wall.[4] She also lost her Commander of the British Empire medal, which was "heart-breaking." For a brief period, she was happy in the bedsit, but then she insisted she was burgled and robbed of £150, making her desperate to leave.[5] These many moves created great anxiety, and Jennings feared she might be recommitted to "the Bin."[6] Mostly she felt like a "waif" and "leper,"[7] a lost soul in need of a "haven," a place of solace and retreat, an "Eden," an "Acadia," a "Paradise."[8] It was only when she was surrounded by her many things, all ordered to her liking, that she felt secure. Now her unstable living environment began to take its toll. She had a "horror" of being alone without anyone to talk with. She complained of insomnia, and increasingly her conversation was more non-sequential and populated with tangential statements.[9]

Finally, Jennings was invited to live with the writer Christina Hardyment, whom she had met at a publisher's party a year or so before. Life with Hardyment and her four daughters was a happy time for Jennings, who felt included in family life. In gratitude, she later wrote "A Company of Friends," in which she described the Hardyment home as a "world of care," "abundant life," and a house "full of wisdom," and in another poem, "A Gift of Gratitude," she praised Christina for her "light-hearted, dazzling calm."[10]

At this point Jennings was sixty-eight years old and clearly very anxious about her financial future. Both Priscilla Tolkien and Anne Harvey gave her money and John Gielgud sent a contribution. She asked Michael Schmidt if he knew any well-off poets who might give her financial support, and then petitioned him for additional advances on book royalties, but that was not possible.[11] Since she had sold many of her first-edition books, she now auctioned off her dolls' house furniture and miniatures, only to be shocked at how little they were worth.[12] While her hope was that being on the A-level syllabus might make her "rich," in fact this venture did not bring in much money.[13] Given her financial insecurity, she must have been delighted when in May 1994 the Society of Authors selected her as the recipient of the Cholmondeley Award with its £2,000 prize. She was desperately in need of money and had not paid her income tax for either 1994 or 1995. She explained to the tax authorities that she had moved frequently, had increased expenses for housing, and that some of her property had been stolen.[14]

Jennings' housing nightmare ended when Prisca Tolkien found a sheltered accommodation for her at 64 Birch Court, Headington. Finally, by the end of 1995, she moved in and had a permanent address and phone number. Even after she took up residence at Birch Court, Christina Hardyment continued to invite her to Sunday dinner and take her on short trips and on holidays with her family.

For the next six years Jennings would live at Birch Court under the supervision of the warden, Catherine Jones, who not only cared about her but respected her as a poet. During most of her time there Jennings continued to follow her routine of spending her day in cafés and at the cinema in town, returning to her room at night, where she would write. Initially she occupied two rooms at Birch Court with enough space for her many possessions, but later she moved to a one-room accommodation. At this point Christina Hardyment helped her to shed some of her "unnecessary things" through a sale. Her dolls, toys, teddy bears, and big glossy books were spread out over ten tables and sold; this yielded a profit of £100. Since Jennings was a compulsive buyer it was difficult to limit her possessions. She loved to visit specialty shops, especially those which sold Christmas items. Sometimes Christina drove her into the countryside to the Christmas shop at Lechlade on the Thames where every inch of space was filled with the things Elizabeth loved: mechanical and musical toys, wind-up angels, snow globes, miniature knick-knacks, and Christmas decorations.[15]

Friends were relieved when Jennings finally was settled in Birch Court, but there was concerned she might be lonely. Therefore, Christina Hardyment put notices in both *Oxford Magazine* and *Oxford Today* announcing that Jennings needed visitors. While Jennings might feel she was not the center of any one person's life, she had a cadre of friends who made her life possible. However, she was sometimes unappreciative of those who helped her most. She once complained that she was disappointed in the cheap present Prisca had given her for Christmas, and then complained that Prisca would not lend her more money or let her live with her.[16] She wrote to Michael Schmidt saying she was not jealous of Christina and her world travels, but that she knew nothing of poverty.[17] And desperate for money, she berated Schmidt himself, saying he did not value her enough.[18] It was, however, these loyal friends who helped Jennings survive her last years.

In spite of her difficult living arrangements, Jennings proved to be extraordinarily productive during the three-year period 1994–6. *Familiar Spirits* was issued in 1994 and sold 1,100 copies in the first month. Although she initially wanted to dedicate the book to her landlady, Mrs. Wood, she changed her mind apparently because the woman was now deceased. Instead the Dominican priest Robert Ombres was the recipient of that honor. In a later volume, she inscribed the poem "Time's Element" for him.[19] Ombres and Jennings met first in the 1970s but then he left Oxford. On his return in the 1990s, their friendship was renewed. Jennings would attend his mass on Saturdays at 6 p.m. at Blackfriars, and they would sometimes meet to discuss his sermons, theology or other topics. They would frequently convene at the restaurant of the Randolph Hotel, before Jennings' exclusion from that establishment as an "undesirable customer."[20] Although Jennings does not elaborate on the reasons for barring her, one can imagine the fact that she looked disheveled and occupied a table for hours purchasing only one drink may in part explain her exclusion.

Familiar Spirits, her twenty-third book of verse, is appropriately titled. Its highly autobiographical poems reflect the loves of Jennings' early life—the people, places, and moments of unalloyed happiness of her youth. Her uncle, maids, grandfather, cousins, friends, family are all there as well as her exultations in nature. In an important poem, "Steps Towards Poems," she again explores the process of poem-making. She calls the poem "imagination's liberal side," "guess work of the intellect," and acknowledges that the poet does not understand how a poem is made, but always reveres it.[21] In two other poems the inward war which dominated so much of her life is again exposed. In "Two Sonnets on Love and Lust" and "The Modes of Love," she discusses different expressions of love, but what dominates is her concern for the peril of obsessive love. Lust is a "warden" which locks one inside. It is demanding, hurtful, and wounding, the madness of mind and heart, an "angry hunger, baleful thirst," a "fever," "a foul infection." It is "cruel" and "dark," a "deadly sin." There is no joy in it, only pain. It ends in death and loathing.[22] These ruminations still haunted a woman nearing age seventy.

Familiar Spirits, like many of her books, received mixed reviews with some critics dismissing her work as too autobiographical and out-of-fashion, and others responding positively to her efforts to focus on big questions and highlight the mystery of life. *The Tablet* recognized her as a poet "aging with vitality" and praised her best poems, which centered on the miracle of existence.[23] *Poetry Review* credited her with tackling the issues of love and death, and acknowledged that without self-pity or histrionics her poems offered both literary and spiritual nurture.[24] Jennings always valued applause from *The Times Literary Supplement*, but in this case the applause was muted. The reviewer lauded her best poems as technically elegant and moving, but noted that most of them were about simple and trite themes of personal relationships and family dynamics.[25] *London Quarterly* criticized her work as too autobiographical and "sweet" in a "lavender-scented way." Although she confronted profound questions like morality and art, the reviewer considered the outcome banal and was perplexed by Jennings' Puritanical views on sexual love and her seemingly contradictory obsession with it.[26]

Even though her books brought in some revenue, Jennings was always alive to how to augment her finances. In 1995 she signed a contract with Macmillan to publish *A Spell of Words: Selected Poems for Children*, to be edited by her friend Anne Harvey. The book was composed of many of Jennings' previously published children's poems and was the second book she dedicated to John Gielgud, her "pin-up" and patron.[27] She also continued to give radio readings. B.B.C. Radio 4 *Woman's Hour*, *Poetry Please*, *Words and Music*, and *Poetry Library* all gave her airtime.

Carcanet remained her principal publisher, with Schmidt editing, publishing, and marketing her books. In 1996 he managed to bring out three of her volumes even though in July of that year the Carcanet offices in Manchester were severely damaged in a truck bombing by the Provisional I.R.A. The release of *A Poet's Choice*, *In The Meantime*, and a paperback version of *Every Changing Shape* made it a banner year. At the same time, Enitharmon Press released *Collected Poems* by Ruth Pitter, which opened with a brief introduction by Jennings. Since this was the year of Jennings' seventieth birthday she was honored by her loyal friend Roger Pringle, who organized a tribute to her. Pringle introduced the program and Barbara Leigh-Hunt and Richard Pasco read some of her poems about childhood, nature, love, Italy, art, and religious experience, and the evening concluded with Jennings reading some of her own recent work.[28] This, the last of her readings at Stratford, was not her best. The dislocation and financial worries of the last two years were taking a toll on her physical and psychic life.

Her new books, however, kept her in the public eye. *A Poet's Choice* was a selection of poems which had influenced her over the years. It is no surprise that Shakespeare, Hopkins, and Herbert appeared prominently. In the introduction[29] Jennings discusses her own early discovery of poetry, which may have been meant to encourage young poets, and might explain the book's seemingly random dedication to "Blanche, Catherine, Julia and Katrina." These recipients of Jennings' affection may have been young women she chatted up in an Oxford café, and desiring to inspire them, she dedicated the volume to them. But not even Schmidt knew the identities of these four women.

In the Meantime came out two years after *Familiar Spirits* and gives evidence that Jennings continued to write prolifically. At this point Schmidt began to revise her work, but apparently she did not notice or contest this practice. Unlike in the past, when many of her poems focused on biblical or theological themes, those in *In the Meantime* were concerned with spiritual meaning and values. Appropriately the book was dedicated to her longtime Catholic friend Priscilla Tolkien. Its enigmatic title is explained in a poem of the same name, the last in the volume.[30] Although "in the meantime" is understood as a pause, one could also understand it as meaning "now," a signal that one does not know how much time is left. Jennings had a sense that death was not distant. In the poem "Lazarus," she speaks directly of death and what lies beyond life. She admits there are no words, no metaphor for the world beyond.[31]

Since most of the poems of *In the Meantime* are about the life of the spirit and its relationship to poetry-making, it was a fitting companion piece to the re-issued *Every Changing Shape*. It does contain, however, autobiographical poems about her grandparents, her mother, her childhood, her home and school, poems reminiscent of those in *Familiar Spirits*. These themes of life and spirit are joined together in the poem "Rome," the place where she encountered spirit and flesh as balanced, as working as one, and making her whole.[32] In "Mass," "Bread," "Consecration," and "Holy Communion" she writes of the uniting of the senses and spirit made possible by the Incarnation, the God made man, and captured now in the Eucharistic sacrament.[33] In other poems she links faith to poem-making. In "Seers and Makers" and "Hermits and Poets" she offers parallels between the artist and man of prayer.[34] In "Order" she explores life in the wilderness of the post-Edenic world in which to be human is to make order and find patterns.[35] In "Act of the Imagination" she lauds this faculty as essential for poem-making and for countering religious doubt.[36] *In the Meantime* is important as the most explicit poetic expression of Jennings' Catholic faith.

Perhaps because of its overtly religious content, the book was not as widely reviewed as Jennings' previous volumes of poetry. *The Expository Times* praised its ordered and lucid poems, and *The Times Literary Supplement*, while acknowledging Jennings' productivity, noted that her work was "strikingly uneven." The reviewer's insight that there was a disjunction between her poems of religious affirmation and those with an underlying current of discontent was salient.[37] Jennings' poetry continued to reflect both her exultation and faith and her melancholic experience of darkness.

The mid-1990s were difficult years for Jennings. Loveless and anxious about her future, she did what she always did—she wrote. Although convicted by reviewers of writing too much, she carried on not only to survive, but to fulfill her vocation. As she said, poem-making was something she could do. It was also what she had to do. Old age was not kind to her, yet in the coming years, even as her mental and physical health declined, she gained belated recognition.

20

Assurance beyond Midnight

> But I know well that now my spirit wakes
> And is assured....
> I feel in touch with everything that's peace
> And later on there will arrive with dawn
> A bold assurance and a synthesis
>
> Of what waits for me not much further on.
> But near enough to tell me faith is bold
> And proves itself in all that has been done
>
> To me and for me in a golden world.[1]
>
> "Assurance Beyond Midnight"

After decades of intermittent bouts of darkness, as she reached her mid-seventies Elizabeth Jennings was given a sense of peace. Hers had been "a golden world" and her spirit was now assured. But this gift, described in this final poem of her final book of poetry, was preceded by more illness and heartbreak. Her final peace would be hard-won.

Her living situation was ameliorated once she moved to Birch Court, but losses and ill health continued to plague her. Over the next five years her physical and psychic condition gradually deteriorated. She was frequently depressed and anxious, and manifested symptoms of paranoia. Although she admitted to feeling suicidal, she was sure she would not act on it. She was leery of any psychiatric help.[2] Her nutrition was poor, she did not sleep well, and her concentration was limited. She often refused to bathe and slept in her clothes. She was convinced that other residents were making noise twenty-four hours a day. Sometimes she would not answer her door, and at one point during a three-day period she pulled the alarm for help 149 times.[3]

She wanted nothing moved in her flat, although the bathroom and kitchen were filled with toys. In 1997 she nearly burned Birch Court down when the Christmas cards she had set between candles caught fire. She complained that she lost many books in the blaze.[4]

And there were also deaths. In 1997 her old beau Stuart died, but she said she felt nothing because their relationship was long ago.[5] A few days after Princess Diana died on August 31 she wrote an unpublished poem, "Public and Private Grief," in which she tells of the death of a young mother, the "queen of love," a person known for her goodness. Separated from her, the father is left to explain his wife's death to their children.[6] Jennings had some disagreement with Catherine Jones about Diana, and perhaps to assuage their differences she wrote "Apology to a Friend" and dedicated it to Jones.[7] Whatever their differences, Jennings appreciated not only Jones' care, but her respect for her poetry.

Desmond Albrow, her brother-in-law, was gravely ill as well and would die a few months later in January of the following year. Jennings did not attend his funeral, pleading illness, much as she had done for the funerals of each of her parents. After Albrow's death she tried to console her sister, but her attempts failed. Nonetheless she considered Aileen her "little mother" and she was her child, dependent on her sister's power.[8]

But it was Veronica Wedgwood's death from Alzheimer's disease in March 1997 which was the most devastating. Although Jennings had not seen Wedgwood for more than a decade, when she read her obituary she wept, remembering their long friendship and how Wedgwood had loved her and her poetry. Subsequent to Wedgwood's death Jennings wrote some twenty-eight additional poems about their relationship in which she lionized Wedgwood for her compassion, strength, nobility, imagination, trustworthiness, humor, and selflessness. She reminisced about their sharing of art and poetry, how Wedgwood stood by lovingly in times of her torment, how her touch healed her and set her free, and how her love taught her to love wholly in spirit. Jennings wrote that she prayed to Wedgwood and believed Wedgwood prayed for her.[9] The following year, in a poem about love in later life, Jennings admits that one no longer demands passionate reciprocity and is not swept up by the demands of heart and hands. The only fear is that love will end in death.[10] And now that had come to pass.

The highlight of what was otherwise a challenging year was her winning of one of the five Hamlyn Foundation Awards given to help artists overcome disadvantages and realize their potential. It brought with it a prize of the princely sum of £15,000, an amount Jennings attested she had never earned in any year. After receiving this windfall, she ordered a taxi and took off on a spending spree to Brighton.[11] Her purchases meant less room in her flat, making it even more hazard-ous.[12] Even with the Hamlyn bonanza she continued to hound Schmidt for money. Because a speaking engagement in Guildford had been bungled by Carcanet, she petitioned him to reimburse her for £200, and a week or so later she again wrote and asked for more money. He declined in both cases.[13]

As was her custom, Jennings continued to go into Oxford during the day and return to her room to write poems at night. She was insulted when people would ask "Are you writing still?" and responded to this "hated question" with the retort, "Are you breathing still?" Poetry was her "moon and sun" and it could not be turned off and on.[14] In her unpublished poems she continued to ponder the nature of her craft. In her youth, she almost worshipped poetry; it was food and drink, stronger than prayer.[15] Now she wrote of poetry's various powers. She claimed it was a sacrament, a gift and a way to pray.[16] It could heal the lonely and lost, haunt readers, and speak over continents. It was a gift of kindness and helped to grapple with fears. It brought contrition, fostered justice, and served as a harbinger of peace. "It was," she wrote, "an arc of good,"[17] but she also allowed that, like letters, poems were a place where secrets were told.[18]

As the years passed, her productivity waned, but she continued to write. *Praises*, which was dedicated to Catherine Jones, appeared in 1998.[19] It was a slim volume in the vein of *In the Meantime*, with a focus on the spiritual. The best of its poems linked the art of poem-making to timeless questions. In "The Largest Question" she queries what happens to the spirit when death removes the flesh. Her assur-ance is that God keeps spirits out of time.[20] And in another poem about Lazarus she describes his returning from the tomb and reenter-ing a strange world where spectators ask, "What was dying like?" Lazarus only weeps and whispers "dear God."[21] In other poems, she links poetry to faith. The poet's central capacity is imagination, which has the power to create alternative metaphors which can strengthen faith. She offers a full moon as metaphor for a "Host held up / For everybody's eyes / To see and understand the high and deep / Salvation in the skies…"[22]

Reviews of *Praises* were not numerous. *The Tablet* linked Jennings' popularity to the innocence of her poems, and suggested that while her subject matter was quotidian, the heavenly was always near at hand.[23] *The Reader* noted that the poems were joyful and confident, even though they emerged from a complex reality.[24] A more expansive review was carried by *The Times Literary Supplement*, in which her writing was compared with that of Henry Vaughan. For this reviewer both Jennings and Vaughan understood the joys of the Edenic world, emphasized childhood, and wrote in elegiac form. While Jennings' poetry might be repetitive and her language somewhat "shop-worn," he commended *Praises* for its treatment of interconnected subjects— religion, the ordinary, suffering, and art.[25]

One can imagine that Jennings would have been cheered if she read a letter in *The Times Literary Supplement* from the Australian Catholic poet Les Murray, who had been nominated as England's poet laureate. Murray demurred, saying that as he was not a British citizen he could not be laureate to "ER II," but that he proposed instead Elizabeth Jennings. In defending his choice he wrote: "The variety, depth and continuing vivacity of her work are astonishing, and she has humanity, a balance that might strike just the right note for her country in times when it needs a guru." He suggested that the selectors choose a "real poet," one who upheld poetry, rather than a sloganeer.[26] Murray's suggestion went nowhere, and Andrew Motion was appointed instead. It was not until eleven years later that Carol Ann Duffy became England's first female poet laureate.

Recognition of Jennings' artistic achievement by St. Anne's College, her alma mater, finally came in January 1998 when Gina Pollinger, Gillian Reynolds, the radio broadcaster, and other alumnae organized an evening of "Words and Music," including selections from Debussy and Chopin and readings from Jennings' poetry and the novels of fellow alumna, Penelope Lively. Jennings attended the event in her distinctive dress: a black skirt, white blouse, and green plimsolls.[27] Since she had great anxiety about the evening, the actress Janet Henfrey, another St. Anne's graduate, was enlisted to read her poetry. As it turned out, prior to her arrival Jennings had several glasses of wine, which must have relaxed her, and in the end she read some of her own work from *Collected Poems*. It was a festive evening with many of Jennings' friends in attendance: Anne Harvey, Aileen Albrow, Anthony and Ann Thwaite, and Christina Hardyment, among others. Even Germaine Greer, broken leg and all, arrived from Cambridge.[28] Jennings was grateful for the acclaim and friendship.[29]

By 1999 Jennings' health began to fail. She contracted flu and then developed severe back pain which sent her to the Radcliffe Hospital for almost two months. She spent Christmas of that year as a patient, but at least some monotony would have been relieved when her two Dominican friends, Robert Ombres and Tim Calvert, visited her.[30]

Given her failing health and the deaths of Wedgwood and Ruga Stanley, Jennings began to ponder her own death, asking how she might face life without flesh.[31] Some twenty years earlier she speculated what she would do on her last day of life. She would forget the past, not ask for a priest, eat a meal with her Roman friends, and indulge herself by counting who would feel at a loss because of her death.[32] But now she had other aspirations. She wanted Verdi's *Requiem* played and Herbert's poems read.[33] She wished to die in July, the month she was born,[34] and preferred a death which gave her time to repent all her sins. Her desire was to be buried under a star-studded sky and a full moon on the shores of Lake Albano, not far from Castel Gandolfo, the Pope's summer residence,[35] a place she long ago walked with Tindal-Atkinson and where she found solace in her faith.

Feeling vulnerable, Jennings nonetheless continued to write poems and to work on a long essay on the person who had given her both inspiration and understanding of her own life—Gerard Manley Hopkins.[36] Written during her hospital stay and recuperation, the essay is recorded in part on hospital stationery. It is extant as a jumble and confusion of papers with extensive corrections. Although the comparisons are not made directly, Jennings saw her own life and that of Hopkins in much the same light. He validated her vocation and linked suffering and creativity. Like her, he lived in a time of great anti-religious sentiment, yet his greatest gift was an ability to capture the innocence of an Edenic world in his joyful and fresh language. His admiration for Duns Scotus brought him to experience the presence of God in all things and express his exultation in poetry. Although Jennings considered Hopkins' dual vocation as priest and poet as advantageous, his sensual personality, attraction to others, and desire to grasp the beauty of the physical world caused him great conflict. It was his propensity to fall in love, rather than conflict over belief, which haunted him. When alone with God in prayer he faced this impasse head on. Yet in Jennings' mind, it was conflict which made Hopkins' poetic achievement possible.

She admitted that while Hopkins' poetry was unique and daring, it was difficult for contemporary readers to comprehend, given that Christianity was not fashionable and society was both uninterested in and greatly uncomfortable with moral and religious passion. Although fragmented and unfinished, Jennings' essay on Hopkins gives some insight into her late-life preoccupations, her longstanding interest in the life and work of this spiritual companion, and their commonly shared "inward war."[37]

Accidents and illnesses continued to plague her. In March 2000 she fell and fractured her foot, and then in the first part of 2001 she was admitted again to the hospital on account of ulcers and an intestinal obstruction. Since there was concern she would die, Prisca arranged for a priest to give her the sacrament of last rites.[38] Jennings spent four months in recovery. As usual, she kept on writing.

The poems of this period were gathered into her last volume of poetry, *Timely Issues*, which she dedicated to her physician, the gerontologist Hywel W. Jones. Because she was weak and less able to concentrate, Michael Schmidt edited this work as well as a new volume of *New Collected Poems*. Jennings would not live to see either in print. The poems of *Timely Issues* stand as Jennings' final joyful testimony to the abating of her inward war. This was expressed most poignantly in "Night Song," in which she speaks of God's work being completed and all being gathered in response to his call. "We come to him at last, / Some slow, some fast."[39] Although the work was not widely reviewed, *The Times Literary Supplement* commended *Timely Issues* as a celebration both of life and of the creative impulse that overcomes illness and death.[40] At the core of the book is Jennings' experience of the suspension of time while under anesthesia. She attests that it was the tender attention of a nurse named Alyson that calmed her and by her touch and care helped her to come to new revelations.[41] Jennings emerged from surgery with a "hard-learned awe" and an ability to see "skies of sifted gold." She now knew how to deal with the enemies of darkness and fear, as well as how to praise.[42] She had been to a mysterious place where the sun was a beacon lighting up the earth, where no clocks ticked, and colors were more brilliant than the rainbow. There she could "hear" radiance and "touch" "sights."[43] Elsewhere she wrote of a door opening in the East, a feeling of being enriched and having her imagination restored.[44] Returning to consciousness, she wrote: "And yet what wonders hit me when I crossed / The threshold back to consciousness to find / All things aglow with grace."[45] In the process of being close to death, she experienced new powers[46] and desired to find love and happiness.[47] After receiving communion, she wrote a homage to Gerard Manley Hopkins in which she confirmed that the tiny piece of Eucharistic bread saved her. She gave thanks and confessed: "I know my flesh behaves // Oddly, but I know also I am / Within Heaven's confines."[48]

Once she felt healthy again she returned with gratitude to making poems. She praised imagination, and wrote homages to Herbert, Traherne, and Graves. The final poems of *Timely Issues* reflect Jennings' interest in religious subjects. In them she tells of monks and prophets, of a Eucharist which unites Bethlehem and Jerusalem, and of the diversity of saints. She includes poems on Christmas, New Year, Epiphany, and Whitsun, that feast when the Holy Ghost teaches "men the way to die / And never to feel lost."[49] In one of her last poems, "Perfection," Jennings acknowledges that every person dreams of a "perfected, holy thing," but ultimately finds it does not last or satisfy. Rather it is "personal truth" which brings one to one's knees and allows one to endure suffering.[50] *Timely Issues* closes with her "bold assurance" of peace and meaning in all that is.[51]

Discharged from the hospital, Jennings returned to Birch Court in early August of 2001. But her life there was increasingly difficult. She was weak, losing weight, and unstable on her feet. After she fell and broke her hip she needed additional care. Christina Hardyment wrote a letter to Elizabeth's friends urging them to visit and asking if anyone knew of an appropriate care facility for her.[52] The Rosebank Care Home in the village of Bampton, a fourteen-bed residence with a garden, became her ultimate haven. By the end of August 2001 Jennings was moved there. Her health deteriorated rapidly, even though her care was excellent, and friends came to visit, including Prisca, who came once a week. At some point Jennings was informed she had been awarded the honorary degree of Doctor of Divinity by the University of Durham. As she was unable to travel to Durham to receive the award, representatives from the theology and English faculties planned to present the degree to her in person in Bampton, but circumstances overtook that plan.

On Friday, October 26, 2001 Prisca, who had power of attorney, visited in the afternoon and found Elizabeth peacefully sitting in a

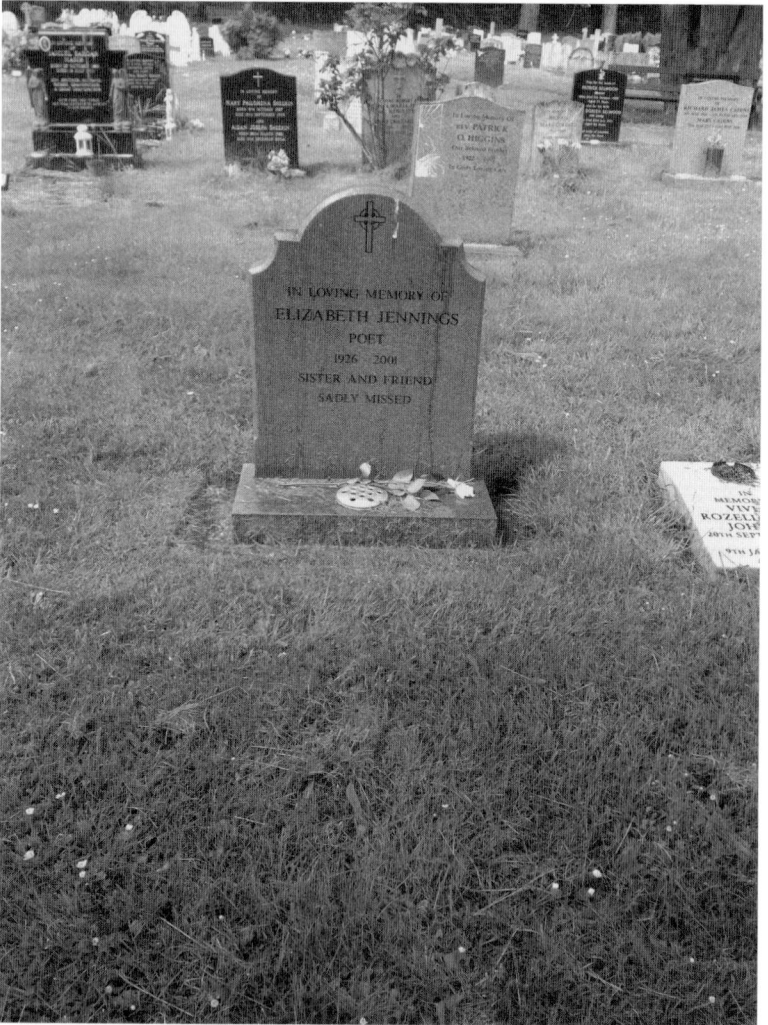

Figure 20.1. Elizabeth Jennings' grave, Wolvercote Cemetery, Oxford. Dana Greene

chair. Elizabeth inquired about her parents and those of Prisca, all of whom she assumed were still living. About two hours later Elizabeth rang the bell for assistance and then died in her room of a massive hemorrhage and heart attack. It was 6 p.m. and the inward war had finally ceased.

Jennings' body was cremated, and her ashes were placed in an urn which Prisca kept in her study, a sign of their lifelong friendship. The funeral mass, held on November 6, 2001 at St. Gregory's and St. Augustine's, was organized by Prisca and Christina and was presided over by the chaplain of the Radcliffe Hospital, David Hartley. Several rows of mourners—friends, family, and parishioners—filed into the small church. No Verdi was played, no Herbert poems were read. Prisca read "The Dance," a poem which celebrated that where Christ was, there was the dance. All creation—sunrise, stars, and sunset, prayer and death—were a part of the dance, this "constant movement."[53] Christina read "A Company of Friends," which Jennings had written years before to honor her family's warmth and generosity, and "Night Song," which speaks of God's work having now been done,[54] was read by Mark Albrow, Jennings' nephew who represented the family. When the mass ended, those gathered were invited to repair to the nearby Cotswold Lodge Hotel, a grand Victorian mansion on Banbury Road, to celebrate Jennings' life.

Since her wealth was insignificant, when her estate was probated there was no tax applied to what remained.[55] Her possessions were packed up, and later hundreds of her toys and knick-knacks, many still in their wrapping, were put on sale, the proceeds going to the Save the Children Fund.[56]

In early 2002 a private burial was held in the Wolvercote Cemetery, a short walk from Jennings' family home on Banbury Road. She would be interred not on the shores of Lake Albano, but in the place where she had lived her life. Mourners gathered, prayers were offered, ashes were buried, and a stone was placed. The marker read simply— Elizabeth Jennings, Poet, 1926–2001, Sister and Friend, Sadly Missed (Figure 20.1). The main attraction of this Catholic section of the cemetery is the grave of J. R. R. Tolkien, which is visited by multitudes of adoring fans. Jennings' grave draws few visitors. Marked only by a single tree, the stone is set apart, much as Jennings was in life. What remains is her poetry. It is in this, her "beautiful art," that Elizabeth Jennings lives on. It is as she would have wanted.

Epilogue—Life as Poetry, Poetry as Life

[Poetry is]
... this
 Demanding, impatient, moody,
Aching, recalcitrant,
Kind, perceptive
Honest, yes
Beautiful
Art. It is my life my,
Raison d'être.[1]

"Writing Poems: Primary Source"

For Elizabeth Jennings poetry was "quite literally a way of life,"[2] a "temporary home."[3] Both "torturous" and "rapturous," poem-making was her way of loving, of communing. It gave meaning, solace, and order to her life. She confirmed that she existed for poetry: " ... my poetry is me, [it] justifies my existence."[4] Poetry was her "mainspring," her "fulcrum."[5] It "saved" her, and was necessary for life itself.

For sixty years Jennings gave herself to her craft, offering pleasure and consolation to her many readers. Poetry was her gift to them. As previously noted, she was the author or editor of some forty-eight books of poetry, prose, and anthology which sold between 200,000 and 225,000 copies.[6] At her death, all major newspapers in the United Kingdom ran long obituaries documenting her achievement. Praise was lavished on her as never before. Writing in the *Financial Times*, Ruth Padel declared that Jennings was "one of the best-loved British poets in the last fifty years."[7] In an earlier review, she wrote that "[h]er work is a mix of directness and grace, informed by the mystical and religious traditions of English poetry."[8] *The Guardian's* obituary, written by Jennings' friend Grevel Lindop, confirmed her popularity and her capacity to write poems of "startling power." He added that over the years she developed a simple style and an original personal voice. She took on difficult subjects and mentored generations of student poets.[9] The anonymous obituary in the *Daily Telegraph*, a paper which for years published Jennings' reviews, hailed her development from a "thinking poet to a poet of feeling and suffering." She was described as prolific and unclassifiable.[10] *The Times'* obituary led with comments about her graceful and formal poems which were not negatively influenced by her personal crises. It commended her straightforward gifts and her critical faculties while also noting she was a shy, sensitive, nervous person and an irritable reviewer.[11]

It is not happenstance that the obituary by Michael Schmidt in *The Independent* was the most comprehensive and insightful, given that he had known Jennings for years, was her editor since 1975, and had a deep grasp and appreciation of both her strengths and limitations. With authority, he asserted that Jennings was "the most unconditionally loved writer of the generation of poets of the Movement," attributing her popularity to her feel for ordinary people and her honest, straightforward, non-ironic, and non-satiric verse, which was generally written in strict form.[12] While he lamented that her transcendent concerns were anachronistic in the contemporary world,[13] "[h]er best poems were something more than literature."[14] In his preface to her posthumously published *New Collected Poems*, Schmidt wrote that what set her off from "her wry, sour-puss contemporaries" was her combination of "passion, purity and the prosaic."[15] The last of these descriptors was contested by Anthony Thwaite, who claimed that irrespective of her limitations Jennings survives as a "classic."[16] *The Tablet*, for which she wrote for many decades, cited her focus on the personal and local as prisms through which love and grace were revealed.[17]

Summative reflections on her entire corpus were included in reviews of her *New Collected Poems*, published in 2002. For example, the *London Review of Books* suggested that to read her work in its entirety was to enter a "blur," and although she was shy and could not "market" herself, what she did offer "was an appreciation of the value of spirituality and a quietly dauntless focus on vocation—a religiously structured commitment that made her life very hard, very unremunerated, and her best poetry very releasingly true."[18] When the *Tablet* reviewer considered her *New Collected Poems*, he pointed out her "craftsman like versification," her "psychological perceptiveness," and her "painterly eye." Her long-term orientation was toward greater openness, and her "catholicity" was in her ability to use a seemingly narrow poem as a way through to consideration of a larger question.[19] A common criticism of Jennings' corpus was that her early work was best and the later inferior.[20] Nonetheless scholarship evaluating the sweep of her work continued. Another edition, *The Collected Poems*, appeared in 2012,[21] a French edition of her poems was undertaken,[22] the Elizabeth Jennings Project was created,[23] and *Elizabeth Jennings and the Sacramental Nature of Poetry* was published.[24]

And friends found ways to honor her. The National Portrait Gallery, which houses Rollie McKenna's photograph of Jennings, sponsored "Timely Issues: A Celebration of the Life and Work of Elizabeth Jennings,"[25] St. Anne's College, her alma mater, hosted "An Evening of Readings and Reminiscences of Elizabeth Jennings"[26] in 2004, and in 2016 the college sponsored an Elizabeth Jennings Symposium.[27]

Others memorialized her in various ways. As part of the 2002 Traherne Festival the Hereford Cathedral Choir performed a concert in her honor; Janet Henfrey gave readings of her poems in various churches; the staff at the Rosebank Care Center planted a tree on the grounds in her memory; poets wrote elegies for her;[28] and in 2003 the city of Oxford named a lovely new street off the Woodstock Road in her honor. Elizabeth Jennings Way is park-like and winds by the canal leading to the Thames (Figure p. 188). It stands as a permanent and bucolic reminder of Jennings' love of nature and of the city of spires she called home.

It may be that it is only when biography clears away the detritus of Jennings' life that a fuller appreciation of her achievement will be possible. She was a woman who, facing formidable psychological, financial, and cultural obstacles, won for herself a large following of readers, and in so doing expanded the poetry-reading audience substantially. She had numerous admirers, many of whom appreciated that she spoke to and for them. What yet remains unexplored are her ideas about the art of poetry and its relationship to religious experience—in other words, her insights into poetics and theopoetics.[29]

Jennings' contribution to these fields is discursive, unsystematic, descriptive, and buried in both her prose and poetry. Early on she writes that her comments about poetry are inadequate and she hopes

Elizabeth Jennings Way, Oxford. Courtesy of University of Oxford/Richard Lofthouse

she will be judged on her practice and not her theory. But she then goes on to write about the nature of poetry, the making of poems, the role of poetry in society, and its relationship to prayer and the mystic life. For Jennings, the function of poetry is to discover order in a post-Edenic world marked by chaos, time, decay, and darkness. Poetry restores what is lost and only half-remembered. It halts time and, like love, religious ritual, and the experience of nature, it holds back darkness and gives brief access to the transcendent, offering hope in the midst of despair. She suggests that the best poems are those which show order emerging from conflict. For her, the poem moves not from the general to the particular, or from one abstraction to another. Neither is it concerned with theoretical ideas, but with ideas expressed in images, metaphors, and similes. Although poetry must be personal, the poet's experience is shaped and ordered by means of imagination, emotion, technical skill, and intellect. As a consequence the poet's individual experience is transcended. The poem which emerges is an autonomous phenomenon, one independent of its creator.

Jennings, analogizing poem-making to love-making, calls it a mysterious creation of rhythm and unity. The poet conceives and swells as the poem grows in its dark home. Poets are "saints of verse," those who have allowed some power or "invisible presence" to work within them. It is not that they are more sensitive, wiser, or more prophetic than others, but they are more willing to face fear. They order disorder, push through the dark, reach beyond individual isolation, and discover relationships, while communicating the deepest human experiences. They show humanity the heights it can reach, but they are, as Plato suggested, dangerous in that they challenge accepted laws and customs. Jennings differs with Auden, who claims that poetry makes nothing happen. Although for her poetry is an end in itself, and rarely prompts one to act, it seeks truth, not by advancing a code of ethics, but rather by describing a world where there is peace, kindness, and justice.[30] Through words poetry reinstates what once was known and now is lost or almost lost.

Poetry is a restoration, but it is also "a way of looking," of seeing the world. As such it is a gateway to the numinous, like the Eucharist, and analogous to prayer and mystical experience. Given these insights about the nature of poetry, Jennings can be understood as an early contributor to the field of theopoetics, the study of poetry as an embodied dimension of human experience, an offering of legitimate evidence of the intersection of divine and human interaction.

Jennings' thoughts on the making of a poem and its relationship to mysticism were first expressed in *Every Changing Shape*. In that book she reconnects with the sacramental tradition of poetry which links back through Hopkins to earlier writers. For her, poetry and mysticism share many of the same functions in the human mind and imagination. They emerge from the same creative source and require their practitioners to engage with darkness and shadows. Neither is abstract or impersonal. Both the creative imagination of the poet and the experience of the mystic are "gifts."

While Jennings distinguishes between the poet and the mystic, she sees strong similarities between the poet and the priest. Both serve as mediators, uttering words that transform. Both demand self-mastery and a willingness to wait in darkness. The priest's prayer and offering of Eucharist are gestures of hope that help one enter a larger reality and satiate one's hunger. Likewise the poet creates the poem, offering it as a "secular sacrament."

Jennings is aware of the difficulty Christian poets have in the contemporary world, given the hostility or indifference to religion and the absence of a robust religious culture. She urges these poets to either rebel against their culture or reinterpret Christian symbols in a new way for their times.[31] It is this second option that she embraced.

Poetry was Jennings' lodestar and beacon; she clung to it in her search for personal meaning and wholeness. In the process she created a "demanding, impatient, moody, aching, recalcitrant, kind, perceptive, honest, yes—beautiful art." It is among the shards of that "beautiful art" that one "finds" Elizabeth Jennings and evidences of her inward life. Although she might have concurred with Virginia Woolf that "... one can't write directly about the soul. Looked at, it vanishes ...,"[32] the fact is that in Jennings' case glints of her "soul" are accessible in her poetry. What emerges from this search is a complex person who belies the caricatures of either "Botticelli's angel" or "Bag Lady of the Sonnets."

The legacy of Elizabeth Jennings is not restricted to her poems, poetics or theopoetics, but must include her lived vocation, her relentless attempt to enact the poetic vision she encountered in ordinary life and to offer it to her contemporaries. In the face of formidable odds— loneliness, rejection by critics, financial insecurity, and physical and mental fragility—she persisted. Her life stands as witness to the poetic imagination, a means of experiencing life and enhancing its vitality. Poetry was for her a way of being, it was life itself.

Notes

PROLOGUE

1. Michael Holroyd, *Works on Paper: The Craft of Biography and Autobiography* (Washington, D.C.: Counterpoint, 2002), 19.
2. Michael Schmidt, "Preface," *New Collected Poems* (Manchester: Carcanet, 2002), xix.
3. "An Impertinent Interviewer," *The Collected Poems*, ed. by Emma Mason (Manchester: Carcanet, 2012), 909–10. Published posthumously. Unless indicated otherwise, all poems are referenced to this volume.
4. Michael Schmidt, "Obituary: Elizabeth Jennings," *The Independent* (October 31, 2006), 6.
5. "No Consolation," Georgetown University (GT), Elizabeth Jennings Papers (EJP) 2, Box 18, Folder 3.
6. "Poetry Is," GT, EJP 2, Box 17, Folder 6.
7. "A Metaphysical Point about Poetry," 775.
8. "Times There Are," GT, EJP 2, Box 24, Folder 4.
9. "Darling Veronica," GT, EJP 2, Box 22, Folder 4.
10. Eavan Boland, *Object Lessons* (New York: W. W. Norton, 1995), ix.
11. "A Fear," 73.
12. "A Metaphysical Point about Poetry," 775.
13. *Poetry Today* (London: Longmans, Green, 1961), 56.
14. "I Count the Moments," 435.
15. "The Powers of Poetry," University of Delaware (UD) Elizabeth Jennings uncatalogued Pooh Bear Notebook, 98-36, September 2, 1997.
16. "The Gift," UD, uncatalogued poems, 01-10 1996–2000, January 3, 2000.
17. "A Way to a Creed," 467.
18. "Sufism," 392.
19. Wallace Stevens, Aphorisms from Adagia. http://giveitaname-giveitaname. blogspot.com/2009/04/from-adagia-wallace-stevens.html.
20. "What Poetry Aspires To," GT, EJP 2, Box 15, Folder 4.

CHAPTER I

1. "Light to Dark," 461.
2. See "Autobiography," MS, 1986 (hereafter "Autobiography 1986"), in possession of Roger Pringle, affirming her belief in her early memories. Other

unpublished autobiographical works provide detail. These include: "The Inward War," Washington University (WU), MS, n.d. *circa* 1967, Box IV, Notebooks I and J, hereafter "The Inward War"; "An Autobiography by Elizabeth Jennings," UD, MS, 186 (unless otherwise noted all citations refer to this collection), Series III.2, Box 6," hereafter "An Autobiography"; "As I Am," GT, TS, *circa* 1969, EJP 2, Box 32, Folder 1, hereafter "As I Am"; "Without Whom," Boston College (BC), MS *circa* 1993, Series IV, Box 16, Folder 6, hereafter "Without Whom." Poems are filled with autobiographical detail, even though Jennings claims her poems are not autobiographical. Every effort has been made to link the poems to descriptions from interviews or her several autobiographies.

3. "Boston, Lincolnshire Childhood," 900. Published posthumously.

4. "A Moment of Childhood," 460.

5. "The First Six Years," 605.

6. Ibid.

7. "A Child by the Sea," GT, EJP 2, Box 19, Folder 3.

8. "Untitled Autobiographical Statement," GT, EJP, 2, Box 25, Folder 8.

9. Baptismal Register of St. Mary's Boston provided by Canon A. P. Dolan, Diocesan Archivist.

10. "Essay," WU, Box 9, Notebook D.

11. "Autobiography 1986," 2.

12. "Her Wisdom," 629–30.

13. "The Inward War," Notebook I, Chapter 1.

14. "Our Maids," 688. Although many were sacked, Jennings did not consider the family's maids bad people. She had a more congenial view of her nannies.

15. "In Memory of a Gardener in Childhood," GT, EJP 2, Box 15, Folder 8.

16. "The Inward War," Notebook I, Chapter 1; "First Six Years," 605–6.

17. "Hide and Seek," GT, EJP 2, Box 25, Folder 1.

18. "The Inward War," Notebook I, Chapter 1; "My Grandmother," 89.

19. "Untitled Autobiographical Statement."

20. "The Wrong Sex," UD, Box 3, Folder 63; "Unwanted Child," BC, Notebook, Box 6, Folder 7; "Traumatic Birth," UD, Series II, Box 4, Folder 64.

21. "The Secret Brother," 221–2; "Invisible Brother," GT, EJP 2, Box 25, Folder 5.

22. "Autobiography 1986," 1–7.

23. Ibid.

24. "A Bird in the House," 500.

25. "The Inward War," Notebook I, Chapter 1.

26. "Without Whom," "The Turners," 1–9.

27. "Sea Music," UD, uncatalogued, 01-10 1996–2000.

28. "A Cliff Walk in North Devon When I Was Twelve," 689.

29. "Boston," 767–8.

30. "The Child's Story," 499.
31. "Among the Stars," 697.
32. "A Child in the Night," 380.
33. "Sea Love," 294.
34. "Sea Music," UD, uncatalogued, 01-10 1996–2000.
35. "The Sea," 285.
36. "Precursors," 546.
37. "In a Garden," 310.

CHAPTER 2

1. "Spirit of Place," GT, EJP 2, Box 23, Folder 10.
2. "Longings," UD, Series II, Box 4, Folder 70.
3. "Country Sounds," 785–6.
4. Information about life at Banbury Road was gleaned from the several autobiographies, "Gardens: A Childhood One," GT, EJP 2, Box 28, Folder 2; "North Oxford Once," UD, Daisy Notebook, uncatalogued, Poems April 29, 1997; "Bicycles in Summer," 696; "Country Sounds," 795.
5. "The Inward War." Notebook J. Chapter has no number.
6. "Standing Outside," WU, Box 5, Poems O–S, 1964–5.
7. "Fairground," 564–5.
8. "My Father," GT, EJP 2, Box 20, Folder 2.
9. "Essay on My Father," WU, Box 9, Notebook D.
10. Priscilla Tolkien, "Beginnings and Endings," *PN Review* 31, Issue 1 (Sept.-Oct., 2004): 9–10.
11. "Ugly Duckling," BC, Notebook, Box 2, Folder 6.
12. "Disappointment," GT, EJP 2, Box 25, Folder 2.
13. "Fear," GT, EJP 2, Box 8, Folder 4.
14. "One Kind of Catholic," GT, EJP 2, Box 25, Folder 1.
15. "An Autobiography," Chapter I, "The Toys and the Honeysuckle."
16. "Her Wisdom," 629–30. "Facts of Life," UD, uncatalogued Notebook with red and blue horse, 98-36, December 24, 1997; "Facts of Life," GT, EJP 2, Box 27, Folder 5.
17. "Without Whom," "Miss Wilson," 1–8.
18. "Six-Year-old's Punishment." GT, EJP 2, Box 27, Folder 7. "The Inward War," Notebook I, Chapter 2.
19. "Legacies and Language," 586–7.
20. Jean Ward, "Elizabeth Jennings: An Exile in Her Own Country." *Literature and Theology* 21, No. 2 (June 2007): 198–213.
21. "Confession," GT, EJP 2, Box 24, Folder 8; "The Dark of Religion," GT, EJP 2, Box 8, Folder 9.
22. "First Confession," 660.
23. "Early Rituals," 917; "Nursery," 675, "Saying Mass," UD, uncatalogued blue, orange, green Notebook October 25, no year.

24. "A Serious Game," 504.
25. "A Sky in Childhood," 505; "An Education," 441; "Among the Stars," 697.
26. Jennings wrote many poems about Oxford, both published and unpublished. See "Spell of Oxford," "Up for the First Time," "Oxford: A Prologue," "Rivers and Churches," in *An Oxford Cycle: Poems* (Oxford: Thornton's Book Store, 1987); "A Tribute Oxford," 73; "Oxford," GT, EJP 2, Box 25, Folder 10; "Legacies and Language," 586; "Roots: From Lincolnshire to Oxfordshire," GT, EJP 2, Box 20, Folder 6.

CHAPTER 3

1. "Debt to a Teacher," GT, EJP 2, Box 23, Folder 2.
2. "Without Whom," "Miss Wilson," 1–8.
3. "The Liberation," 723.
4. "Without Whom," "Miss Wilson."
5. "To My Sister," GT, EJP 2, Box 6, Folder 12.
6. "Blood Bonds, Family Feelings," 693.
7. Elizabeth Jennings, "Saved by Poetry," *The Tablet* (May 15, 1993): 13.
8. School Notebook, GT, EJP 3, Box 4, Folder 9.
9. "The Sea as Metaphor," 592–3.
10. "Classroom," 507–8.
11. Elizabeth Jennings, "Introduction," in *A Poet's Choice* (Manchester: Carcanet, 1996), xii–xiv.
12. "Lepanto," GT, EJP 2, Box 23, Folder 5.
13. "As I Am," "First Writing," 19–20; Candida Crewe, "Bag Lady of the Sonnets," *The Times* (November 23, 1991): 10–11.
14. "Lepanto," GT, EJP 2, Box 23, Folder 5; "Debt to a Teacher," GT, EJP2, Box 23, Folder 2.
15. "English Lesson," 907–8.
16. "Autobiography 1986," 22.
17. "Saved by Poetry," 13.
18. Crewe, 10–11.
19. "Two Sonnets," 739–40.
20. "The Call of the Sea," 829. Published posthumously.
21. "Moonlight on the Oxus," 830. Published posthumously.
22. "On the Death of My Godfather," UD, Series II, Box 4, Folder 67; Elizabeth Jennings, *Let's Have Some Poetry* (London: Museum Press, 1960), 13–19; "An Uncle and Godfather," 687.
23. "Without Whom," "Uncle Frank," 1–13.
24. *Let's Have Some Poetry*, 19.
25. "The Dead Bird," 232. Jennings included this early poem in *The Secret Brother and Other Poems*, a subsequent volume of poetry for children.
26. Elizabeth Jennings, "Elizabeth Jennings," in *Contemporary Authors Autobiography Series* 5, ed. Adele Sarkissian (Detroit, MI: Gale Research Co., 1987): 107.

27. "Without Whom," "Nancy Waters," 1–4; "A Gift Preserved," GT, EJP 2, Box 25, Folder 2; "Every Changing Shape," WU, Box 9, Notebook C; "First Love," 656–7; "An Explanation," BC, Notebook Box 4, Folder 11; "An Autobiography," Chapter VI, "Confusion." In another poem entitled "First Love," 691, she writes of a pure love which does not ask for reciprocity, but worships from afar. In this poem, she uses the name "Emma" which may have been a substitute for Nancy.
28. "Without Whom," "Nancy Waters."
29. "An Autobiography," Chapter VI, "Confusion."
30. "Hero-Worshipper," GT, EJP 2, Box 22, Folder 5.
31. "A State of Love," GT, EJP 2, Box 15, Folder 3.
32. Jennings wrote an unfinished play during this same time. "Untitled Play." BL, Notebook B 52598B, 1941–2.
33. This name derives from the red dye food coloring used for decoration. The dye is obtained from insects and used in pre-Hispanic Mexican rituals.
34. "A Childhood Religion," 607; "The World We Made," 685–6; "An Autobiography," Chapter V, "Shadows."
35. "After Doubt," GT, EJP 2, Box 6, Folder 13.
36. Nottingham Diocesan Archives, Register for St. Mary's Boston, Lincolnshire. Her confirmation was held at Church of Saint Gregory and St. Augustine, June 17, 1939.
37. "The First Words," GT, EJP 2, Box 25, Folder 1.
38. "Age of Doubt," 753; "First Doubt," GT, EJP 2, Box 25, Folder 2.
39. "Passage from Childhood," 89.
40. "Teenagers," 753.
41. "A Child's Religion," GT, EJP 2, Box 8, Folder 8.
42. "An Autobiography," Chapter VI, "Confusion."
43. "The Dark of Religion," GT, EJP 2, Box 8, Folder 9.
44. "As I Am," "Confusion," 24.
45. This is undated and was a gift to Roger Pringle.
46. "Whitsun Sacrament," 320. The sacrament of confirmation brings with it a new name and is administered at Pentecost.
47. "Late Childhood," GT, EJP 2, Box 15, Folder 2.
48. "Adolescence," 833–4.
49. Crewe, 10–11.
50. "An Autobiography," Chapter VIII, "The Last of Childhood."
51. "As I Am," "The Toys and the Honeysuckle," 5; "Intimations," 9; "First Writing," 20; "My Parents," 29; "An Autobiography," Chapter VI, "Confusion."
52. "An Autobiography," Chapter VI, "Confusion."
53. Ibid.
54. "An Autobiography," Chapter VII, "My Parents"; "As I Am," "Confusion," 27.
55. "Abuse of a Sacrament," 907.
56. "A Childhood Horror," 651–2.

57. "The Second World War," http://www.wilmots.me.uk/phpBB3/view-topic.php?f=2&t=17.
58. "Wings of the War," 827. Published posthumously.
59. "Adolescence," 833–4.
60. "Autobiography 1986," 25–6.
61. "My Father," GT, EJP 2, Box 20, Folder 2.
62. "My Father's Father," 692.
63. "My Grandmother," 89.
64. "My Sister's First Child," GT, EJP 2, Box 18, Folder 7; "A Shock," BL, ADD MS 52599 Modern Literary MSS, Vol. IX up to 1964; "An Illegitimate Baby- For A," GT, EJP 2, Box 16, Folder 5.
65. Elizabeth Jennings, "Author's Introduction to *Collected Poems*, 1967." Reprinted in *Poetry Book Society: The First Twenty-Five Years*, ed. Eric W. White (London: Poetry Book Society, 1979), 40.
66. "The Inward War," Notebook J, no chapter title given.

CHAPTER 4

1. "First Term," *An Oxford Cycle*, 11.
2. Jennings details her years at the university in *Contemporary Authors Autobiography*, 103–15; "An Autobiography," Chapter VIII, "The Last of Childhood;" Chapter X, "Falling in Love;" Chapter XI "When Exams were Over"; "Untitled Entry," GT, EJP 2, Box 25, Folder 3; "First Love," 656, "First Love," 691, and "C. S. Lewis Lecturing in Magdalen Hall in 1946: A Tribute," 891; "Autobiography 1986," 30–41; "As I Am," "The University," "Falling in Love," "New Life Ahead," 36–61.
3. For information on St. Anne's Society and the College see "St. Anne's College, Oxford: A Brief History" by David Smith, http://www.st-annes.ox.ac.uk.
4. In this case she means she was almost asked to leave the university for academic reasons. She was ill prepared in a few subjects.
5. "C. S. Lewis Lecturing in Magdalen Hall in 1946."
6. "Grace," GT, EJP 2, Box 25, Folder 4.
7. Jennings often offers multiple explanations for the same event. At one point she writes that Stuart was in Japan, in another place that he was in Thailand. It is unknown whether he was in both countries. She also cites that her father ended her relationship with Stuart and alternatively that both she and Stuart decided to end it. In other places she says she left Oxford to follow Stuart to London and alternatively that she left Oxford because she was not a scholar and she wanted to earn money. I have tried to follow the most plausible explanations.
8. College Register, St. Anne's College.
9. Matthew Arnold, "The Study of Poetry," http://www.poetryfoundation.org.

10. Email from David Smith, Librarian, to Dana Greene, October 7, 2014 and Clare White, Librarian, to Dana Greene, April 7, 2017. The M.A. is awarded separately from the B. Litt. Any student who completes the B.A. is entitled for a fee to be awarded the M.A. seven years after matriculation.

11. Crewe, 10–11.

12. "The Poetry of Kingsley Amis," GT, EJP 2 Box 28, Folder 5; "Without Whom," "Kingsley Amis," 1–7.

13. "The Elements," 3.

14. "The Clock," 5.

15. "Modern Poet," 4.

16. Kingsley Amis, *Memoirs* (New York: Summit Books, 1991), 109.

17. William Bissett, "Elizabeth Jennings," in *The Dictionary of Literary Biography*, 27, *Poets of Great Britain and Ireland, 1945–60*, ed. Vincent B. Sherry (Detroit: Gale Research, 1984), 163–70.

18. "Elizabeth Jennings" in *A Poet Speaks: Interviews with Contemporary Poets*, ed. Peter Orr (New York: Barnes & Noble, 1966), 93.

19. Information on these various influences is found in Elizabeth Jennings, *Let's Have Some Poetry*, 41–53; Gerlinde Gramang, *Elizabeth Jennings: An Appraisal of Her Life as a Poet, Her Approach to Her Work and a Section of the Major Themes of Her Poetry* (Lewiston, New York: Edwin Mellen Press, 1995), 17–25.

20. "An Autobiography," Chapter XII, "New Life Ahead;" Chapter XIII, "Future Plans."

21. "An Autobiography," Chapter XII, "New Life Ahead."

CHAPTER 5

1. Elizabeth Jennings to Paul West, February 9, 1953. Paul West Papers, Special Collections Library, Pennsylvania State University (PSU), RBM 2594, Series 2, Sub-series 1, Box 33, and Folder 6. All subsequent references to the Jennings/West correspondence refer to this citation.

2. Elizabeth Jennings to Michael Hamburger, October 21, 1952, Michael Hamburger Papers. Brotherton Library (hereafter Brotherton), University of Leeds. Location: B. C. Hamburger.

3. "An Autobiography," Chapter XIV, "The Deep Dismay"; "A Life in the Day of Elizabeth Jennings," interview with Chris Oram, *Sunday Times* (July 27, 1980), 62.

4. "A Life in the Day of Elizabeth Jennings," interview with Rosalyn Chissick, *Sunday Times* (March 17, 1996), 53–4.

5. "My Father," GT, EJP 2, Box 20, Folder 2.

6. "As I Am," "Deep Dismay," 65–72.

7. "An Autobiography," Chapter XIV, "New Ways of Knowing." Long after Day-Lewis' death Jennings wrote the unpublished, "For Cecil Day Lewis," lauding his integrity. GT EJP 2, Box 26, Folder 11, December 1986.

8. *Six Women Poets* (Oxford: Merton College, 1952).

9. "An Autobiography, Chapter XIX, "Abroad and at Home"; "As I Am," "Abroad and At Home," 92–6.

10. Elizabeth Jennings to Paul West, PSU, February 9, 1953.

11. Alan Brownjohn, "A Preference for Poetry: Oxford Undergraduate Writing in the Early 1950s," *The Yearbook of English Studies*, 17; *British Poetry since 1945*, Special Number (1987), 62–74 (London: Modern Humanities Research Association).

12. Paul West, "Tutors: My Many Mentors at Oxford, from Lincoln College to All Souls, Linger like Spirits in the Mind," *The American Scholar* 83, No. 1 (winter, 2014). www.theamericanscholar.org.

13. "Without Whom," "Poets of the 1950s," 1–40.

14. Ibid.

15. Elizabeth Jennings to Paul West, PSU, July 19, 1952 and June 7, 1953.

16. Adrienne Rich to Jack and Marie Sweeney, January 25, 1956. Jack and Marie Sweeney Papers, University College Dublin Archives. AL 52/287, August 24, 1955–Oct. 17, 1966. http://www.ucd.ie/archives. I am grateful to Hilary Holladay for bringing this information to my attention.

17. Elizabeth Jennings to Paul West, PSU, February 1, 1952.

18. "The Substitute," 12–13.

19. Elizabeth Jennings to Paul West, PSU, July 19, 1952.

20. "An Autobiography," Chapter XVII, "Oxford and London;" Chapter XVIII, "Oxford and London Again."

21. "An Autobiography," Chapter XVIII, "Oxford and London Again."

22. Donald Hall to Dana Greene, letter, October 26, 2015.

23. "An Autobiography," Chapter XXI, "Of Illness and Other Things." This is confirmed by a letter from Jennings to Martin Seymour-Smith, April 26, 1953. University of Texas (UT), Robert Graves Collection, MS, 1707, container 4.12, MS-RG-MSC-08 and 08-01.

24. "Elizabeth Jennings," No. 1 (Oxford: Fantasy Press Poetry Series, Oxford University Poetry Society, 1952). Apparently, there was another pamphlet series, the Roebuck pamphlets, founded by Martin Seymour-Smith, in which Jennings' poems were to also appear but most of its poems were already included in her 1953 *Poems*. It is unclear whether the Roebuck pamphlet ever appeared. Elizabeth Jennings to Martin Seymour-Smith, May 29, 1953. UT, Robert Graves Collection, Letters MS, 1707, container 4.12 MS-RG-MSC-08 and 08-01.

25. "An Autobiography, Chapter XVIII, "Oxford and London Again."

26. "Without Whom," "Poets of the 1950s," 1–40.

27. Ibid., 27.

28. Elizabeth Jennings, *Poems* (Swinford/Oxford, England: Fantasy Press Poets Series, 1953).

29. "Delay," 11.

30. *An Anthology of Modern Verse, 1940–1960.* Chosen and with an introduction by Elizabeth Jennings (London: Methuen & Co., 1961).

31. "The Arrival," 22.

32. "The Island," 28.

33. Anne Ridler, "Introduction," *Poems* (Oxford: Fantasy Press, 1953), vii–viii.

34. Peter Redgrove, "Representative Poets," review of David Stacton's *An Unfamiliar Country* and Elizabeth Jennings' *Poems, The Times Literary Supplement* (December 4, 1953): 778.

35. This comment is repeated in an anonymous review of Jennings' 1967 *Collected Poems,* "Cool Comfort," *The Times Literary Supplement* (September 21, 1967): 840.

36. Elizabeth Jennings to Michael Hamburger, August 3, 1953. Michael Hamburger Papers, Brotherton, Location: B. C. Hamburger.

37. "Autobiography," Chapter XXII, "The Art of Verse."

38. "An Autobiography," Chapter XX, "Festivals and Anthologies"; *New Poems 1956: A PEN Anthology,* eds. Dannie Abse and Stephen Spender (London: M. Joseph), 1956.

39. "In the Night," 51.

40. Elizabeth Jennings to Paul West, PSU, February 9, 1953.

41. "For A Child Born Dead," 47–8.

42. "Answers," 53. Larkin included five of Jennings' poems in his anthology.

43. Thomas Kinsella, review of *A Way of Looking* in *Prose Occasions, 1951–2006,* ed. Andrew Fitzsimons (Manchester: Carcanet, 2009), 159–61.

44. Elizabeth Jennings to Anthony Thwaite, March 25, 1956. Anthony Thwaite Papers, Bodleian Library (Bodleian), MS. Eng. C 7982.

45. Philip Larkin to Elizabeth Jennings, February 4, 1956. BL, ADD 52599. Modern Literary MSS, IX up to 1964, 119–20.

46. W. S. Merwin to Elizabeth Jennings, January 1, 1956. BL, ADD 52599, Modern Literary MSS, IX up to 1964, 113.

47. J. R. R. Tolkien to Elizabeth Jennings, December 3, 1955. BL, ADD 52599, Modern Literary MSS, IX up to 1964, 111.

48. Kathleen Raine to Elizabeth Jennings, January 17, 1956. BL, ADD 52599, Modern Literary MSS, IX up to 1964, 115–17.

49. Elizabeth Jennings to Robert Graves, n.d., Canellun Collection. Archives of St. John's College, Oxford. This is a letter in which Jennings thanks Graves for his letter of congratulations.

50. Elizabeth Jennings, "Unfinished Manuscript about Italy," GT, EJP 2, Box 31, Folder 26.

51. Vita Sackville-West to Elizabeth Jennings, February 22, 1956. BL, ADD 52599, Modern Literary MSS, IX up to 1964, 122.

52. Doris Lessing won the Somerset Maugham Award in 1954. The next woman recipient was Angela Carter, who received the award in 1969.

CHAPTER 6

1. Elizabeth Jennings, Poetry To-Day (London: Longmans, Green & Co., 1961), 56.
2. "As I Am," "Oxford and London Again," 90.
3. Press, "Interview," 91.
4. Martin Dodsworth, "The Movement: Never and Always" in *The Oxford Handbook of Contemporary British and Irish Poetry*, ed. Peter Robinson (Oxford: Oxford University Press, 2013), www.oxfordhandbooks.com.
5. David Perkins, A *History of Modern Poetry: Modernism and After* (Cambridge, MA: Harvard University Press, 1987), 418–43.
6. Robert Conquest, ed., *New Lines* (London: Macmillan, 1956), xi–xviii.
7. Stephen Regan, "Larkin and the Movement," in *The Cambridge History of English Poetry*, ed. Michael O'Neill (Cambridge: Cambridge University Press, 2010), 879–96; Blake Morrison, *The Movement: English Poetry and Fiction of the 1950s* (Oxford: Oxford University Press, 1980); Ian Hamilton, "The Making of the Movement," in *British Poetry since 1960: A Critical Survey*, eds. Michael Schmidt and Grevel Lindop (Manchester: Carcanet Press, 1972), 70–3; Jerry Bradley, *The Movement: British Poets of the 1950s* (New York: Macmillan, 1993), 1–10; John Press, *Rule and Energy: Trends in British Poetry since the Second World War* (London: Oxford University Press, 1963); Anthony Thwaite, *Contemporary English Poetry: An Introduction* (London: Heinemann, 1964); Martin Dodsworth, "The Movement: Never and Always," in *The Oxford Handbook of Contemporary British and Irish Poetry*, ed. Peter Robinson (Oxford: Oxford University Press, 2013), www.oxfordhandbooks.com.
8. Edward Short, "A Faithful Poet," *The Weekly Standard* 18, No. 22 (February 18, 2013), http://www.weeklystandard.com/a-faithful-poet/article/700492.
9. Press, "Interview," 91–6.
10. Gramang, 25–30.
11. Richard Bradford, *The Odd Couple: The Curious Friendship between Kingsley Amis and Philip Larkin* (London: Robson Press, 2012), 197.
12. *Let's Have Some Poetry*, 93–105; *Poetry To-Day*, 9–21; "Ten Years After: The Making of a Movement," *The Spectator* (October 1, 1964): 30.
13. "Introduction," *An Anthology of Modern Verse*, 7–12.
14. Ibid.
15. *Let's Have Some Poetry*, 24–5.
16. Elizabeth Jennings, "Reflections on Reviews," UD, Series III.4, Miscellaneous Prose.
17. Press, "Interview," 93.
18. There is no definitive evidence as to the dedication, but since *Let's Have Some Poetry* was a book to entice young people to read poetry, the dedication may have been to Jonathan Butterfield, son of Isabel and Dr. John

Butterfield, whom Jennings had met recently and who loved poetry. Alternatively, it may have been dedicated to Jonathan Price, fellow poet associated with Fantasy Press.

19. Ibid. 24–40, 55–67, 136–7.
20. "Order," 735.
21. *Let's Have Some Poetry*, 113.
22. Ibid. 23–7, 113.
23. "An Autobiography," Chapter XXII, "The Art of Verse."
24. "Without Whom," "Poets of the 1950's;" Press, "Interview," 91–6.
25. "Writers Prospect," WU, Box 7, no notebook.
26. Elizabeth Jennings, "A Difficult Balance," *The London Magazine 6*, No. 11 (November 1959): 27–30.
27. Elizabeth Jennings, "Hall's American Poetry," WU, Box 11, Notebook M.
28. "Fountain," 77–8.
29. "Annunciation," 80.
30. "A Fear," 73.
31. "As I Am," "The Return," 150–2.
32. Anthony Thwaite, "Forms of Assurance," review of *A Sense of the World*, *The Spectator* (September 4, 1958): 24.
33. Alan Ross, "In the Shadows," review of *A Sense of the World*, *The Times Literary Supplement* (October 31, 1958), 628; John Heath-Stubbs, "Poets and Poetry," review of *A Sense of the World*, *Encounter* (February 1959), 72–3; Philip Larkin, "Reports on Experience," in *Further Requirements: Interviews, Broadcasts, Statement and Book Reviews, 1958–85*, ed. Anthony Thwaite (Ann Arbor: University of Michigan Press, 2004), 178–80.
34. "An Autobiography," Chapter XXII, "The Art of Verse."
35. "Autobiography 1986," 46.

CHAPTER 7

1. "Three Months in Rome: In Memory of Somerset Maugham," GT, EJP 2, Box 31, Folder 20.
2. "Autobiography 1986," 46.
3. "Toward Contemplation," 833.
4. "A Confession," 95.
5. "Unfinished Manuscript about Italy," GT, EJP 2, Box 31, Folder 26.
6. "A Conversation in the Gardens of the Villa Celimontana, Rome," 75.
7. "Unfinished Manuscript about Italy."
8. "Lake Albano Outside Rome," 559.
9. "A Debt to a City," GT, EJP 2, Box 19, Folder 10.
10. "Without Whom," "Rome," 11.
11. "The Power of Rome," GT, EJP 2, Box 23, Folder 11.
12. "Without Whom," "Rome," 16.

13. Ibid., 28.
14. "Harvest and Consecration," 91–2.
15. "David Jones the Poet," WU, Box 7, no notebook, no date.
16. "Visit to an Artist," 101.
17. "Cradle Catholic," UD, Series II.2, Folder 56. This poem is different from a much later poem of the same title.
18. Elizabeth Jennings, "A Poet Argues that There is No Such Thing as a 'Catholic Writer' Just a Plain and Simple Writer," *Catholic Herald* (August 18, 1967): 4.
19. "*Pensées,*" April–June 1957. WU, Box 8, Notebooks A and B.
20. Ibid., No. 34.
21. Ibid., No. 93.
22. Ibid., No. 127.
23. Ibid., No. 99.
24. "Reflections," WU, Box 8, Notebook C, April 17, 1958.
25. "Letter from Assisi," 79–80.
26. "Men Fishing in the Arno," 109–10.
27. "Which City?" GT, EJP 2, Box 5, Folder 6.
28. "An Autobiography," Chapter XXVI, "The Return." Angelyn Hays, "Elizabeth Jennings," in *British Writers* V, eds. George Stade and Sarah Hannah Goldstein (New York: Charles Scribner's & Sons, 1999), 205–21.
29. Elizabeth Jennings, ed., *The Batsford Book of Children's Verse* (London: B. T. Batsford, 1958).
30. "Reflections," WU, Box 8, Notebook C, April 17, 1958.

CHAPTER 8

1. Elizabeth Jennings, *Every Changing Shape* (Manchester: Carcanet, 1996). First published in London by André Deutsch and in PA by Dufour 1961, 30.
2. The best bibliography of Jennings' reviews and articles for this early period is Maria Antonietta Marghella's dissertation, "Love, Knowledge, Art, Religion: An Analysis of Elizabeth Jennings' Poetry," Università di Roma "La Sapienza," 1988. In this she lists more than one hundred reviews and articles for the period 1954–68.
3. *Penguin Modern Poets 1: Lawrence Durrell, Elizabeth Jennings, R. S. Thomas.* (Harmondsworth, UK: Penguin, 1962). Roy Fuller in reviewing this volume commended Jennings' thoughtfulness and sensitivity to horror and pain. "In Search of An Audience," *Times Literary Supplement* (April 20, 1962), 266.
4. "Introduction." *An Anthology of Modern Verse*, 7–12.
5. Jennings thought Yeats was the greatest of the modern poets. She admired Graves and her poetry shared much with Muir. She liked Empson, but not his followers, whom she thought only wanted to be clever. She was particularly critical of A. Alvarez. Elizabeth Jennings to Martin Seymour-Smith,

April 26, 1953. UT, Robert Graves Collection, Letters MS, 1707, container
4.12. MS-RG-MSC-08 and 08-01.

6. *The Sonnets of Michelangelo*, translated by Elizabeth Jennings with an introduction by Michael Ayrton (London: The Folio Society, 1961).

7. Ibid., Translator's Note, 6–7.

8. "Essay on Poetry and Mysticism," MS. Notebooks. n.d., Elizabeth Jennings Collection of Papers. Berg Collection of English and American Literature, New York Public Library (hereafter NYPL). In this essay, written *circa* 1961, Jennings examines the major differences and similarities between the poet and the mystic. Both share passivity and openness of ideas and emotions, although the poet is more self-conscious. Both want to lose themselves, encounter darkness and conflict, share a sense of being possessed, and require concentration and surrender. However, the poet desires to make, while the mystic wants to love. For the poet to come to some aspect of truth, he uses imagination, while the mystic achieves this through denial, prayer and love. The poet is concerned with form, clarity or communication, but the mystic is not.

9. "Literary Tradition," BC, Poetry Notebook, Box 1 Folder 7a, 1973.

10. Elizabeth Jennings to Peter Levi, October 9, 1961. Peter Levi Papers, BC, 1986–98, Box 11, Folder 15.

11. Elizabeth Jennings to Anthony Thwaite, September 8, 1961, Bodleian MS. Eng.c.7982, Fools. 1–63.

12. Christine Brooke-Rose, "A Poet Among the Mystics," review of *Every Changing Shape and Song for a Birth or a Death*, *The Times Literary Supplement* (October 6, 1961): 660.

13. "Interview with Elizabeth Jennings" conducted by E. A. Sturzl, February 1982, *Acumen Magazine* (April 1985): 8–16.

14. "Introduction from *Song for a Birth or a Death*," in *Don't Ask Me What I Mean: Poets in Their Own Words*, eds. Clair Brown and Don Patterson (London: Picador, 2003), 135.

15. Peter Levi, "The Sinews of Poetry," review of *Song for a Birth or a Death* and *Every Changing Shape, Time and Tide* 42, No. 30 (July 27, 1961): 1241.

16. "Song for a Birth or a Death," 87.

17. "Interview of Elizabeth Jennings with Gerlinde Gramang," in *Elizabeth Jennings: An Appraisal*, 101.

18. "Song for a Birth or a Death," 87.

19. "Family Affairs," 87–8.

20. "Passage from Childhood," 89–90.

21. "At Mass," 96.

22. "Notes for a Book of Hours," 93–5.

23. "To A Friend with a Religious Vocation," 105–6.

24. "The Clown," 101–4.

25. "World I Have Not Made," 91.

26. "No Child," 114.

27. "The Instrument," 115.
28. "Unfulfilled," 113.
29. "Remembering Fireworks," 115
30. "Preface," *Collected Poems, 1953–85* (Manchester: Carcanet, 1986), 13.
31. "What Poetry Aspires To," GT, EJP 2, Box 15, Folder 4.

CHAPTER 9

1. "To a Friend with a Religious Vocation," 105–6.
2. "As I Am," "An Autobiography," Chapter XXIX, "A Wider Scope," 169–76.
3. "Autobiography 1986," 60.
4. William John Hughes Butterfield was professor of experimental medicine at Guy's Hospital, London, and later Lord Butterfield.
5. "An Autobiography," Chapter, XXX, "Love Returning."
6. Ibid., 156.
7. "The Instrument," 115.
8. Jennings, *Contemporary Authors Autobiography Series*, 115.
9. "Making Love," WU, Box 4, Poems J–N, 1964–6.
10. "Demands of Love," GT, EJP 2, Box 17, Folder 3. This poem was written in 1980 as she recalls her tryst with "B."
11. "My Three Needs," GT, EJP 2, Box 22, Folder 4, 1982.
12. "An Autobiography," Chapter XXVIII, "New Friends."
13. "The Dominican Friars—England & Scotland," http://godzdogz.op.org/godzdogz/fr-sebastian-bullough-o-p-1910-1967. R. C. Fuller, "Sebastian Bullough O.P. 1910–1967," *Scripture: The Quarterly of the Catholic Biblical Association* (January 1968): 1–4.
14. Photographs. GT, EJP 2, Box 31, Folder 25. There are two photographs of this priest in tennis garb and one in clerical dress.
15. Jennings, *Contemporary Authors Autobiography Series*, 115.
16. Interview with Gina Pollinger conducted by Rachel Buxton and Emma Mason, October 4, 2008, London. The English publisher was André Deutsch and the American publisher may have been Dufour.
17. *Recoveries: Poems* (London: Deutsch and New York: Dufour, 1964).
18. "Sequence in Hospital," 159–63.
19. Thomas Kinsella, review of *Recoveries*, *New York Times Book Review* (December 20, 1964). Reprinted in *Prose Occasions, 1951–2006*, ed. Andrew Fitzsimons (Manchester: Carcanet, 2009), 219–21.
20. Anthony Thwaite, "How to Confess," review of *Recoveries*, *Times Literary Supplement* (June 11, 1964): 512.
21. Donald Hall and Robert Pack, eds. *New Poets of England and America*. (New York: Meridan Books, 1957), 136–44. Thirteen of Jennings' poems were included.

22. Derwent J. May, "New Lines—or Sidelines?" review of *New Lines 2* by Robert Conquest, *The Times Literary Supplement* (September 6, 1963): 673.

23. "Gambling," MS Poems, No. 4. Berg Collection, NYPL.

24. Crewe, 10–11.

25. "An Autobiography," Chapter XXX, "Love Returning." Here she insists that the frustration of this affair was a part of the cause of her impending mental breakdown.

26. "The Question," 855. Published posthumously. "Spinsters," WU, Box 5 Poems O–S, 1964–5.

CHAPTER 10

1. "Attempted Suicides," 197–8.

2. "A Suicide," BL, ADD MS 52599, Modern Literary MSS, IX up to 1964.

3. "The Dead Selves," *c.*1963, 837. Published posthumously.

4. Elizabeth Jennings to Anthony Thwaite. Anthony Thwaite Papers Special Collections, Brotherton Library, University of Leeds. *The Listener*, February 19, 1963.

5. Recent research indicates that children who experience sustained traumatic brain injuries may develop anxiety, phobias, and depression later in life. This is especially true for women. "Childhood Brain Injury May be Tied to Anxiety and Depression Later in Life" by Madeline Kennedy, *Washington Post,* June 20, 2017, E-8.

6. "An Autobiography," Chapter XXXII, "Breakdown."

7. "As I Am," "Breakdown," 195.

8. Ibid., 197–8.

9. "Duty Doctor," 838–9. Published posthumously.

10. "Taking Life," WU, Box 6, Poems T–Z, 1964–6.

11. Jennings records these events in "As I Am," "Breakdown," "Mental Hospital," "Movements Outwards," "Christmas and Afterward," "Spain," "Out of the Hospital" and "Back Again," 189–238; "An Autobiography," Chapter XXXII, "Breakdown," and Chapter XXXVII, "Out of the Hospital and Back Again."

12. "Dream of Sickness" and "Time Out of Mind," two prose pieces, describe her time in the Warneford. MS., Berg Collection, NYPL, *circa* 1965.

13. Gramang, "Interview," 96.

14. "A Year Later," WU, Box 6, Poems T–Z, 1964–6.

15. She recorded this in a poem "A Birthday in Hospital—Written on the Day," 212.

16. "On Being Told by a Psychiatrist that One is Emotionally Immature," UD, Box 3, Folder 71.

17. "Diagnosis and Protest," 193–4.

18. "Interrogator," 195–6.

19. "Poem about the Breakdown of a Breakdown," 218.
20. "Psychotherapeutic Treatment," UD, Series II.1, Folder 41, Poems 1963–6; "An Autobiography," Chapters XXXII, "Breakdown;" Chapter XXXIII, "Mental Hospital;" Chapter XXXIV, "Movements Outward." These chapters describe her admission to and stay in the Warneford.
21. "The Volcano," WU, Box 6, Poems T–Z, February 20, 1966. Another poem "Volcano and Iceberg," 238, uses many of the same images.
22. "The Conversant," "Decision," "Depression," "Dethronement," WU, Box 2, Poems. All loose.
23. "Surely?," UD, Series II.1, Folder 46, Poems. Dated November 10, probably 1964.
24. "No Consolation," GT, EJP 2, Box 18, Folder 3.
25. "You Won't Tell Anyone Will You?," WU, Box 7, no notebook. Acquired in 1967.
26. "The Treatment," 848. Originally written *circa* 1963–6. Published posthumously.
27. "Two Ways," 849. Originally written *circa* 1963–6. Published posthumously.
28. "After the Catastrophe," 852–3. Published posthumously.
29. "Grove House, Iffley," 207.
30. "Dependence," 858–9. Published posthumously.
31. "An Autobiography," Chapter XXXVI, "Spain."
32. "As I Am," "Movements Outward," 211. According to Jennings, Hildebrand reported to her that Spencer believed 70 percent of her problems were due to her father. This information was given to her in letters from Hildebrand. These letters do not appear to be extant.
33. "My Room," 214.
34. WU, Box 8, Notebook D.
35. "Prayer for a Sick Poet," WU, Box 8 Notebook D, June 28, 1965.
36. "Script for BBC 'Woman's Hour,'" WU, Box 7, no notebook, 1965.
37. "Voices," WU, Box 6, Poems T–Z, 1965–6, August 28, 1965.
38. "The Mind Has Wounds," 843. Published posthumously.
39. "Prayer for A Poet Who Attempted Suicide," UD, Series III.4, Box 6, Folder 86, Misc. Prose.
40. "Prayer," 856–7. Published posthumously.
41. Elizabeth Jennings to Seymour Spencer, 1965. Oxfordshire Health NHS Foundation Trust. Privately held by Mark Albrow.
42. "Matador," 253, was published later in 1969.

CHAPTER 11

1. *Let's Have Some Poetry*, 41–53.
2. *The Mind Has Mountains* (London: Macmillan, 1966); *The Secret Brother and Other Poems for Children*, illustrated by Meg Stevens (London: Macmillan, 1966).

3. "Diagnosis and Protest," 193–4.
4. "In a Mental Hospital Sitting-room," 193.
5. Seamus Heaney, "Words and Rhymes," review of *The Mind Has Mountains*, *The Times Literary Supplement* (July 14, 1966), 616.
6. Alasdair Claire, review of *The Mind Has Mountains*, *Encounter* (November 1967), 76.
7. "Van Gogh" and "Van Gogh Again," 196, 211–13.
8. "Caravaggio's Narcissus in Rome," 208.
9. "Samuel Palmer and Chagall," 202–3.
10. "Love Poem," "Thinking of Love," 210, 211.
11. "One Flesh," 210–11.
12. "Friends," 228.
13. Press, "Interview," 93–6.
14. Gramang, "Interview," 96.
15. *Frost* (London: Oliver & Boyd, 1964), 1–18.
16. *Christianity and Poetry* (London: Burns & Oates, 1965). This was published in the United States as *Christian Poetry* (New York: Hawthorn, 1965).
17. G. S. Fraser, "Christianity and Poetry," review of *Christianity and Poetry*, *The Times Literary Supplement* (July 1, 1965), 559.
18. Jennings, "A Poet Argues," 4.
19. Anthony Thwaite, "Elizabeth Jennings," in *Contemporary Poets*, 2nd ed., ed. James Vinson (London: St. James Press, 1975), 778.
20. Maureen Moran, "The Heart's Censer: Liturgy, Poetry and the Catholic Devotional Revolution," in *Ecstasy and Understanding: Religious Awareness in English Poetry*, ed. Adrian Grafe (New York: Continuum, 2008), 40–1.
21. "For Emily Dickinson," 284.
22. "Emily Dickinson and the Poetry of the Inner Life," in *Review of English Literature* 3, No. 2 (April 1962), 78–87.
23. "Without Whom," "Poets of the 1950s," 35.
24. Press, "Interview," 91–6. See also, *Poetry To-day*, 51. This might be substantiated by the fact that Donald Hall in his *New Poets of England and America* (1957) included several American women poets, but Jennings was the sole English woman poet.
25. "Without Whom," "The Poets of the 1950s," 36.
26. Jennings wrote this unpublished article discussing the social limitations of spinsters. "Spinsters," WU, Box 5, Poems O–S, 1964–5.
27. For consideration of the role of women poets in England see Maura Dooley, ed., *Making for Planet Alice* (Newcastle on Tyne: Bloodaxe Books, 1997); Vicki Bertram, ed., *Kicking Daffodils: Twentieth Century Women Poets* (Edinburgh: Edinburgh University Press, 1997); Jan Montefiore, *Feminism and Poetry, Language, Experience, Identity in Women's Writing* (London: Pandora, 1987).
28. "A Simple Sickness," WU, Box 5, Poems O–S, November 11, 1965.

CHAPTER 12

1. "An Impertinent Interviewer," 909–10. Published posthumously.
2. "Thinking of My Father's Future Death," 862; "To My Father," 864. Both poems were published posthumously.
3. "To My Father," WU, Box 6, Poems T–Z, December 10, 1965.
4. "Visit to a Nursing Home," UD, Series II.2, Folder 52. See also, "For My Dead Father," 261.
5. "A Disagreement with Freud," GT, EJP 2, Box 22, Folder 6, July 1982.
6. "A Dreadful Truth," GT, EJP 2, Box 17, Folder 3, August 1980.
7. "The Known Thing," UD, Series II.2, Folder 52.
8. "Nobody's Fault," GT, EJP 2, Box 5, Folder 10, December 1977.
9. "Ten Years After My Father's Death," 877. Published posthumously.
10. "Apology to My Dead Father," GT, EJP 2, Box 11, Folder 2, October 1979.
11. "Essay," WU, Box 9, Notebook D.
12. "An Explanation for My Mother," GT, EJP 2, Box 11, Folder 4, October 1979.
13. Elizabeth Jennings to Barbara Cooper, UD, uncatalogued MS 305, Box 1, Folder 3, 1965–8. This letter is dated July 18. Jennings apologizes for not having written in a long time. Presumably, this was written in 1968.
14. "Different Loves," GT, EJP 2, Box 5, Folder 9, December 1977; "Stages of Love," GT, EJP 2, Box 13, Folder 7, March 1980; "Full Circle," GT, EJP 2, Box 13, Folder 9, March 1980; "Passion" and "Spoilt Love," GT, EJP 2, Box 24, Folder 8, April 1983.
15. *Collected Poems, 1967.* London: Macmillan, 1967.
16. Michael Schmidt conceives of the volume in this way given that it was followed by volumes with few memorable poems. Schmidt, "Preface," *New Collected Poems*, xxi.
17. Elizabeth Jennings, "Introduction," *Collected Poems* reprinted in *Poetry Book Society: The First Twenty-Five Years*, ed. Eric W. White (London: London Poetry Book Society), 1979, 40.
18. Anthony Thwaite, *Twentieth-Century English Poetry: An Introduction* (London: Heinemann, 1978), 116.
19. "Cool Comfort," review of *Collected Poems* by Elizabeth Jennings, *Times Literary Supplement* (September 21, 1967): 840.
20. Julian Symons, "Clean and Clear," review of *Collected Poems*, *New Statesman* (October 13, 1967): 476.
21. Blunden is quoted by Margaret Byers in "Cautious Vision: Recent British Poetry by Women" in *British Poetry since 1960: A Critical Survey*, eds. Michael Schmidt and Grevel Lindop (Manchester: Carcanet, 1972), 82.
22. Edward Lucie-Smith, ed., *British Poetry Since 1945* (Baltimore, MD: Penguin, 1970), 136.
23. Elizabeth Jennings to Barbara Cooper, 1965–8. UD, uncatalogued MS 305, Box 1, March 6 *circa* 1967.
24. "Women's Autobiographies," WU, Box 10, Notebook C. This handwritten manuscript is a brief review of autobiographies by Zoe Procter, Mary

Reed Bobbitt, and Dorothy Alben. There is no indication as to where this review appeared.

25. "Without Whom," "Synopsis," 3.

26. "The Inward War," WU, Box 12, Notebooks I and J.

27. "An Autobiography," UD, MS, Series III.2, Box 6.

28. "We Poets," UD, Notebook Lucidities, 1964–7, Series II.2, Folder 54, 1969.

29. "As I Am," GT, EJP 2, Box 32, Folder 1.

30. "Nobody Knows," WU, Box 4, Poems J–N, 1964–6, October 3, 1966.

31. C. and J. Literary Agents to Elizabeth Jennings, GT, EJP 1, Box 2, Folder 28.

32. Cicely Veronica Wedgwood to Elizabeth Jennings, GT, EJP 1, Box 2, Folder 6, March 22, 1969.

33. "To One Who Read My Rejected Autobiography," 272.

34. This untitled autobiography was given to Roger Pringle, founder of the Celandine Press, in 1986 to be considered for publication, but it was never published.

35. "Without Whom," BC, *circa* 1990, Series IV, Box 16, Folder 6. It is unclear whether this manuscript was ever offered for publication. The sale of this to Boston College meant that her four autobiographical statements were sold to four different university archives.

36. *The Animals' Arrival* (London: Macmillan, 1969).

37. Michael Mott, "Recent Developments in British Poetry," review of *The Animals' Arrival, Poetry* CXVIII, No. 2 (May 1971): 110–11.

38. The Peter Levi Papers, BC, MS 1986–98, Box 11, Folder 15 contains information on the Levi/Jennings relationship. See also Brigid Allen, *Peter Levi, Oxford Romantic* (Oxford: Signal Books, 2014).

39. "Peter Levi," WU, Box 11, Notebook N.

40. "A Letter to Peter Levi," 257–8.

41. "A Brief Study of Eliot and His Life," BC, Series IV, Box 16, Folder 5.

42. Veronica Wedgwood to Elizabeth Jennings, GT, EJP 1, Box 2, Folder 12, August 1, 1970.

43. Seymour Spencer to Elizabeth Jennings, GT, EJP 1, Box 2, Folder 24, June 3, 1970.

44. Veronica Wedgwood to Elizabeth Jennings, GT, EJP 1, Box 2, Folder 7, June 19, 1969 and Box 2, Folder 7, July 4, 1969.

45. Veronica Wedgwood to Elizabeth Jennings, GT, EJP 1, Box 2, Folder 7, August 4, 1969.

46. John Wain to Elizabeth Jennings, GT, EJP 1, Box 2, Folder 3, July 19, 1969.

47. John Wain, "Green Fingers: For Elizabeth Jennings in Oxford," *Critical Quarterly* 9, No. 3 (1967), 197–9, https://Johnwain.wordpress.com/green-fingers-two excerpts.

48. *A Choice of Christina Rossetti's Verse*, selected and with an introduction by Elizabeth Jennings (London: Faber & Faber, 1970), 9–12.

49. Christopher Busby to Elizabeth Jennings, GT, EJP 1, Box 2, Folder 28, A-6 Correspondence with publishers, April 19, 1972.

50. "Untitled Essay on Christina Rossetti," UD, Uncatalogued Manuscripts, black notebook, poems, March 12, 1997.
51. *The Story of My Heart: An Autobiography* by Richard Jefferies with an introduction by Elizabeth Jennings (London: Macmillan, 1968), UD, Series III.3, Box 6, Folder 83.
52. *Wuthering Heights and Selected Poems* by Emily Brontë with an introduction by Elizabeth Jennings (London: Pan Books, 1967), 1–15.

CHAPTER 13

1. "Drying Up," GT, EJP 2, Box 30, Folder 3.
2. "Interview with E. A. Sturzl, 8–16.
3. "Not Owning," BC, Poetry Notebook, Box 1, Folder 7a, 1973; "Moving In," 263–4.
4. "Cleaning-Up," GT, EJP 2, Box 14, Folder 7; "Laid Open," GT, EJP 2 Folder 6; "Moving Again," GT, EJP 2, Box 16, Folder 4; "Collectors," GT, EJP 2, Box 5, Folder 3.
5. Veronica Wedgwood to Elizabeth Jennings, GT, EJP 1, Box 2, Folder 8, April 1970.
6. "The Longing," GT, EJP 2, Box 1, Folder 5; "Concerning a Vice," GT, EJP 2, Box 1, Folder 6.
7. "Longings," 279.
8. Veronica Wedgwood to Elizabeth Jennings, GT, EJP 1, Box 2, Folder 13, December 28, 1970.
9. *Lucidities* (London: Macmillan, 1970; New York: Dufour).
10. Wedgwood to Elizabeth Jennings, GT, EJP 1, Box 2, Folder 13, December 2, 1970.
11. Terry Eagleton, "Adjusting the Art to the Self," review of *Lucidities*, *The Times Literary Supplement* (December 11, 1970): 1436.
12. Roy Fuller, "Mysterious Clarities," review of *Growing-Points*, *The Times Literary Supplement* (July 4, 1975): 718.
13. Byers, 83–4.
14. "Vocations," 273.
15. "A Decision," 266.
16. "A New Elegy for a Friend Dead Seven Years," GT, EJP 2, Box 15, Folder 4, May 1980.
17. "All Through Life," GT, EJP 2, Box 5, Folder 7, November 13, 1977.
18. Jennings wrote many unpublished poems about James' death including: "My In Memoriam," BC, Poetry Notebooks, Box 1, Folder 1; "The End of the Year, 1971," BC, Poetry Notebooks, Box 1, Folder 1; "After a Friend's Death," GT, EJP 2, Box 17, Folder 11; "Three Elegiac Sonnets," GT, EJP 2, Box 26, Folder 11; "Ten Years After a Death," GT, EJP 2, Box 21, Folder 4; "Fifteen Years after a Death," GT, EJP 2, Box 30, Folder 4;

"An Elegy after Twenty Years at Guernsey," GT, EJP 2, Box 27, Folder 1; "A Pitiful State," GT, EJP 2, Box 1, Folder 6; "All Through Life," GT, EJP 2, Box 5, Folder 2.

19. "After a Time," 317.

20. She gives this description in her chapter on Wedgewood in "Without Whom," "Cecily Veronica Wedgwood," 1–5.

21. "In Confidence," GT, EJP 2, Box 26, Folder 3 and "Worshipper," GT, EJP 2, Box 31, Folder 22.

22. "O Goodness," GT, EJP 2, Box 1, Folder 6.

23. "Historian at Work," BC, Notebook, Box 1, Folder 8, September 1973.

24. In 1972 Wedgwood sent a request for support for Jennings from the Arts Council. Since Wedgwood was a member of the Arts Council, one might assume a grant was awarded. Veronica Wedgwood to Michael Schmidt, Rylands, CPA 2/2/153/26, March 3, 1972.

25. C. V. Wedgwood to Michael Schmidt, Rylands, CPA 2/2/153/25, October 26, 1971.

26. C. V. Wedgwood to Vivien Greene, November 2, 1971. Letter owned by Roger Pringle.

27. C. V. Wedgwood to Michael Schmidt, June 17, 1973, Rylands CPA 2/2/153/47, May 1, 1973; 48; August 14, 1974/55.

28. C. V. Wedgwood to Michael Schmidt, October 26 and November 2, 1971, Rylands, CPA 2/2/153/25.

29. Elizabeth Jennings, "The State of Poetry—A Symposium," *Poetry Magazine*, Nos. 29–30 (Spring/Summer, 1972): 25–7.

30. *Relationships* (London: Macmillan, 1972).

31. Alasdair Maclean, "Marble Fun," review of *Relationships*, *The Listener* 89, No. 2295 (March 22, 1973): 389–90.

32. "Elegy for W. H. Auden," 327.

33. Elizabeth Jennings to Peter Levi, August 1, 1972, Peter Levi Papers, BC, MS 1986–98, Box 11, Folder 15.

34. "The Inward War: A Critical Biography of Gerard Manley Hopkins," UD, Series III.1, Prose, Pose 1964–73, Box 5. *Circa* 1973.

35. Ibid., Box 5, Folder 74, 1–80.

36. *Every Changing Shape*, 107.

37. "Hopkins in Wales," 328.

38. *Every Changing Shape*, 109.

39. See Barry Sloan, "Poetry and Faith: The Example of Elizabeth Jennings," *Christianity and Literature*, 55, No. 3 (Spring, 2006): 393–414 for an illuminating discussion of Jennings' poetry and faith, and Michael Wheeler, "Elizabeth Jennings and Gerard Manley Hopkins," in *Hopkins Among the Poets: Studies in Modern Responses to Gerard Manley Hopkins*, ed. Richard Giles (Hamilton, ON, Canada: The International Hopkins Association Monograph Series, 3, 1985), 104–6.

40. "The Inward War: A Critical Biography of Gerard Manley Hopkins," 1–5.
41. "An Attempt to Define Poetry," BC, Notebook, Box 4, Folder 2, October 29–November 4, 1978.

CHAPTER 14

1. "Revival," 264.
2. Elizabeth Jennings to Barbara Cooper, June 22, 1974, UD, uncatalogued MS 305, Box 1, Folder 4.
3. "Accepted," 343.
4. "New York," GT, EJP 2, Box 6, Folder 8; "New York," GT, EJP 2, Box 5, Folder 6; "Patriotism," GT, EJP 2, Box 7, Folder 3.
5. *Seven Men of Vision: An Appreciation* (London: Vision Press), 151–72.
6. "David Jones: The Poet," WU, Box 7.
7. "Elegy for David Jones," BC, Notebook, Box 1, Folder 10.
8. "Cradle Catholic," UD, Box 2, Folder 57, April 1972.
9. "Cradle Catholic," 380. This is a published poem of the same previously cited title but with different content, published a few years later.
10. Veronica Wedgwood to Michael Schmidt, October 22, 1973, Rylands, CPA 2/2/2/153, 49.
11. "Rembrandt's Late Self-Portraits," 324; "Mozart's Horn Concertos," 324; 355.
12. Sturzl, "Interview," 8–16 and "Three Score and Ten: Elizabeth Jennings," interview with Elizabeth Jennings by Ian McMillan. *The Living Poet* Series 1, Episode 27 (May 1983), http://www.bbc.co.uk/programmes/b080xzf4. Rebroadcast November 4, 2016. On air only through 2017.
13. Crewe, 10–11.
14. Gramang, "Interview," 96.
15. Veronica Wedgwood, "The Poet of Changing Moods," review of *Growing-Points*, *Daily Telegraph* (April 17, 1975): 13.
16. Fuller, "Mysterious Clarities," 718.
17. Alan Brownjohn, "Hymenoptera," review of *Growing-Points*, *New Statesman* (May 30, 1975): 732–3.
18. Edward Levy, "The Poetry of Elizabeth Jennings," review of *Growing-Points*, *Poetry Nation* 5 (Spring 1975): 62–74.
19. John Matthias, "Pointless and Poignant," review of *Growing-Points*, *Poetry* (March 1977): 347–50.
20. Almost all these poems are in the Georgetown collection with some others at Boston College.
21. "A Reflection from Pascal," 381.
22. "Night Love Song," GT, EJP 2, Box 4, Folder 1.
23. "Faith," GT, EJP 2, Box 3, Folder 12.
24. "The Clown," 101–4.
25. "The Awkward One," GT, EJP 2, Box 3, Folder 14.

26. "The Clown," GT, EJP 2, Box 8, Folder 2.
27. "The Truth About the Clown," GT, EJP 2, Box 17, Folder 7; "Jester Today," UD, Series II, 1, Folder 62; "My Birthday," BC, Notebook, Box 4, Folder 1.
28. She mentioned "imagined experience" as it relates to Hopkins. *The Inward War: A Critical Biography of Gerard Manley Hopkins*, 48.
29. "Autobiography," 1986, 65.
30. "The Poetry Reading," WU, Box 8, Notebook C.
31. There is almost no market research on poetry readers during this period, but these conclusions derived from a survey of 400 readers of *New Poetry*. See "The State of Poetry," survey by *New Poetry* (London, Workshop Press, 1978).
32. Elizabeth Jennings to Michael Schmidt, February 1, 1976, Rylands, CPA 2/1/41/22.
33. In 1976 she traveled to both Greece and Spain.
34. "Living in the Country," "Various Landscapes," GT, EJP 2, Box 4, Folder 3; "Living in the Country, A Village Called Freeland," GT, EJP 2, Box 4, Folder 7; "Country Wisdom," GT, EJP 2, Box 4, Folder 5.
35. Elizabeth Jennings to Michael Schmidt, August 12, 1977, Rylands, CPA 2/2/59.
36. Elizabeth Jennings to Michael Schmidt, Rylands, November 1978, CPA 2/1/41/50, June 22, 1976 and CPA 2/2/59.
37. "Old People's Nursing Home," 372–3; "Ways of Dying," 370; "Death of an Old Lady," 374–5.
38. "Near the End of Life," BC, Notebook, Box 6, Folder 7.
39. "Like a Dutch Toy In a Way," GT, EJP 2, Box 5, Folder 10.
40. "Ugly Duckling," BC, Notebook, 1976, Box 2, Folder 6.
41. "Fear," GT, EJP 2, Box 8, Folder 4.
42. "Classic Fear," GT, EJP 2, Box 3, Folder 6.
43. Elizabeth Jennings to Peter Levi, September 4, 1977, Peter Levi Papers, MS 1986–98, BC, Box 11, Folder 15, and Elizabeth Jennings to Michael Schmidt, November 1978, Rylands, CPA 2/2/2/59.
44. "Attempt to Stop Over-Working," GT, EJP 2, Box 1, Folder 4.
45. E. Jane Dickson, "The Café Society of a B & B Poet," *Daily Telegraph* (October 29, 1994): 16.
46. Press, "Interview," 91–6.
47. Short, and BC, Notebook, December 23, 1976–January 3, 1977, Box 2, Folder 10. In this latter the award is misnamed.

CHAPTER 15

1. "Into the Hour," 421.
2. "Reflections on Spain," GT, EJP 2, Box 3, Folder 10 and "Spain," GT, EJP2, Box 3, Folder 11.

3. "To My Mother at Seventy Three," 373; "An Explanation for My Mother," GT, EJP 2, Box 11, Folder 4; "My Mother," UD, Box 3, Folder 67.
4. "Reflection After a Visit to My Mother," GT, EJP 2, Box 17, Folder 2.
5. "To My Sister," GT, EJP 2, Box 4, Folder 2; "To My Sister," BC, Notebook Box 4, Folder 6.
6. Elizabeth Jennings to Peter Levi, September 4, 1977, Peter Levi Papers, BC, MS1986.098, Box 11, Folder 15; "Peter Levi," WU, Box 11, Notebook N.
7. "A Priest Abandons His Office," GT, EJP 2, Box 6, Folder 10. This was written the year after Levi left the priesthood.
8. "In Memory of Robert Lowell," GT, EJP 2, Box 4, Folder 2.
9. *Six Oxford Poets* (Oxford: Bodleian Library, 1977).
10. Carol Cisman, Joan Keefe, Kathleen Weaver, eds., *The Penguin Book of Women Poets* (Harmondsworth: Penguin, 1978) and John Wain, ed. *An Anthology of Contemporary Poetry: Post-War to the Present* (London: Hutchinson, 1979); Michael Schmidt, ed., *An Introduction to Fifty Modern British Poets* (London: Heinemann, 1979); Michael Schmidt, ed., *Eleven British Poets* (London: Methuen, 1980).
11. Elizabeth Jennings to Michael Schmidt, November 2, 1979, Rylands, CPA 2/3/81/60.
12. Secretary for Appointments to Elizabeth Jennings, February 11, 1980, Rylands (Elizabeth Jennings Papers, EJP), Acc 2011-002, Box 1/1.
13. This is the estimate of Michael Schmidt. Interview with the author, May 14, 2015, Manchester.
14. "Birthplace," GT, EJP 2, Box 3, Folder 10. Jennings has six unpublished poems titled "Birthplace."
15. "A Difficult Return," BC, Notebook, Box 4, Folder 8.
16. "In Praise of Italy" and "I Have Walked," GT, EJP 2, Box 9, Folder 2; "Salute to Bibbiena, Tuscany," GT, EJP 2, Box 9, Folder 3; "The Meaning of Cities" and "A Litany of Myself," GT, EJP 2, Box 10, Folder 2; "A Vow," GT, EJP 2, Box 11, Folder 7; "The Influence of the South," GT, EJP 2, Box 12, Folder 8.
17. "A Litany of Myself," GT, EJP 2, Box 10, Folder 2.
18. John P. White, "At Some Imagined Limit," review of *Consequently I Rejoice*, *The Tablet* (May 27, 1978): 10.
19. Anne Stevenson, "Snaffling and Curbing," review of *Consequently I Rejoice*, *The Listener* 98 No. 2530 (October 13, 1977): 486–7.
20. Julian Symons, "A Distilled Despair," review of *Moments of Grace* and *Selected Poems*, *The Times Literary Supplement* (February 1, 1980): 112.
21. Jennings dedicated "After a Painting is Finished," 554–5 to Alec Guinness, a fellow Catholic.
22. Elizabeth Jennings to Anne Harvey, July 11, no date. Uncatalogued. Rylands.
23. "A Candid Statement," GT, EJP 2, Box 16, Folder 11 and "A Just Tribute," GT, EJP 2, Box 22, Folder 5.
24. "An Education," 441.

25. "Beseeching," 430.

26. "The Whole Bestiary," 426.

27. "Euthanasia," 442–3.

28. "Christmas Suite in Five Movements," 450–2.

29. "I Count the Moments," 435.

30. Sloan, 393–414.

31. *Winter Wind* (Sidcot: Gruffyground Press, 1979).

32. *After the Ark* (Oxford: Oxford University Press, 1978).

33. Veronica Wedgwood to Michael Schmidt, December 6, 1978, Rylands, CPA/2/2/153/78.

34. Elizabeth Jennings to Howard Sergeant. MS. Hull Historical Society, September 24, 1978.

35. "The Paranoid," GT, EPJ 2, Box 1, Folder 5.

36. Veronica Wedgwood to Michael Schmidt, December 4, *circa* 1978, Rylands, CPA 2/2/153/4.

37. "Nobody's Fault," GT, EJP 2, Box 5, Folder 10.

38. "Loyalty," GT, EJP 2, Box 5, Folder 10.

39. "Loyalty," GT, EJP 2, Box 4, Folder 5.

40. "Confession," GT, EJP 2, Box 24, Folder 8.

41. "The Explanation" and "Hierarchies," BC, Notebook, Box 4, Folder 11.

42. "Hero-worshipping," GT, EJP 2, Box 15, Folder 6.

43. "Loyalty," BC, Notebooks, Box 3, Folder 11.

44. "Need," GT, EJP 2, Box 6, Folder 8.

45. "Without Whom," "Cecily Veronica Wedgwood," 11.

46. "All This To Do," GT, EJP 2, Box 8, Folder 7 and "Paradox," GT, EJP 2, Box 7, Folder 10.

47. "One Regret," GT, EJP 2, Box 9, Folder 6.

48. "Different Loves," GT, EJP 2, Box 5, Folder 9.

49. "Happy Memory," GT, EJP 2, Box 9, Folder 2.

50. "All This To Do," GT, EJP 2, Box 8, Folder 7.

51. "The Joining," GT, EJP 2, Box 11, Folder 3.

52. "Rivals," GT, EJP 2, Box 12, Folder 2.

53. "When I Spoke Least of Love," GT, EJP 2, Box 13, Folder 1.

54. "Song for One Abroad," GT, EJP 2, Box 17, Folder 7.

55. "In Love," GT, EJP 2, Box 11, Folder 2.

56. "Love of a Rare Kind," GT, EJP 2, Box 1, Folder 3.

57. "A Litany for Friendship," GT, EJP 2 Box 1, Folder 5 and "Asking Too Much," GT, EJP 2, Box 1, Folder 6.

58. "A Late-Night Letter in Tuscany," GT, EJP 2, Box 9, Folder 3; "A Letter After a Holiday in Tuscany," GT, EJP 2, Box 9, Folder 3; "Friendship," GT, EJP 2, Box 17, Folder 4; "In Absences," GT, EJP 2, Box 8, Folder 9.

59. "A Vexed Question," GT, EJP 2, Box 5, Folder 10.

60. "Late Night Letter in Tuscany."

61. "A Litany of Myself," GT, EJP 2, Box 10, Folder 2.

CHAPTER 16

1. "Rescued," 474.
2. "Unity," GT, EJP 2, Box 16, Folder 3.
3. "On Not Opting Out," GT, EJP 2, Box 15, Folder 3.
4. "On the Move Again," GT, EJP 2, Box 18, Folder 2.
5. "Snooker," 604.
6. Crewe, 10–11, and de Muth, "Wondering about the Individual Sheep."
7. Elizabeth Jennings to Michael Schmidt, Rylands, CPA, Acc 3, Box 195/3/29, n.d.
8. Elizabeth Jennings to Michael Schmidt, June 26, 1984, Rylands, CPA, Acc 3, Box 267/3/127, 100–59.
9. John Mole, "Crepuscular and Plain," review of *Celebrations and Elegies*, *The Times Literary Supplement* (July 16, 1982): 770.
10. Michael Schmidt to Elizabeth Jennings, January 11, 1980, Rylands, CPA 2/3/81/62.
11. Michael Schmidt to Elizabeth Jennings, November 16, 1982, Rylands, CPA Acc 3, Box 267/3/154, MS 100–59.
12. Roger Pringle, ed., *A Garland for the Laureate: Poems presented to Sir John Betjeman on His 75th Birthday* (Stratford-upon-Avon: Celandine Press, 1981).
13. John Wain to Elizabeth Jennings, October 5, 1984, GT, EJP 1, Box 2, Folder 4.
14. Elizabeth Jennings to Philip Larkin, February 14, 1984, Hull Historical Society, Hull History Centre.
15. "A Wish to Help," GT, EJP 2, Box 20, Folder 4.
16. Sturzl, "Interview," 8–16.
17. Crewe, 10–11.
18. "Off Top," unpublished limerick in possession of Roger Pringle.
19. "A Terrible Lesson," GT, EJP 2, Box 19, Folder 9; "A Terrible Lesson," GT, EJP 2, Box 19, Folder 8; (two poems with the same title); "Shock and Understanding," GT, EJP 2, Box 20, Folder 2.
20. "Poland, December 1981," GT, EJP 2, Box 20, Folder 4; "A Polish Vigil," GT, EJP 2, Box 20, Folder 4.
21. "The Unprivileged," GT, EJP 2, Box 23, Folder 12; "Northern Ireland, February 1982," GT, EJP 2, Box 23, Folder 12; "Late News," GT, EJP 2, Box 23, Folder 3; "Talk of War," GT, EJP 2, Box 23, Folder 11; "War," GT, EJP 2, Box 23, Folder 11.
22. "Aborted," GT, EJP 2, Box 4, Folder 5; "Abortion," GT, EJP 2, Box 12, Folder 9; "Abortion," GT, EJP 2, Box 12, Folder 8; "Abortion," GT, EJP 2, Box 13, Folder 2; "Abortion," GT, EJP 2, Box 24, Folder 6. She wrote these poems over the course of many years.
23. "After the Falklands War," GT, EJP 2, Box 23, Folder 11; "The Falklands Island Invasion, April 1982," GT, EJP 2, Box 21, Folder 3.

24. Cecil Woolf and Jean Moorcroft Wilson, eds., *Authors Take Sides on the Falklands* (London: C. Woolf Publishers, 1982): 114–15.
25. "Poet at the Pictures," interview with Hermione Lakers, *Oxford Today*, Trinity issue, 1989: 34.
26. "The Nature of Prayer," GT, EJP 2, Box 21, Folder 1; "Psalm and Poem," GT, EJP 2, Box 19, Folder 7; "The Nature of Prayer," GT, EJP 2, Box 19, Folder 10; "A Question of Love," GT, EJP 2, Box 18, Folder 11; "Every Mass," GT, EJP 2, Box 19, Folder 8; "And to You," GT, EJP 2, Box 20, Folder 7; "Searching for Truth," GT, EJP 2, Box 23, Folder 11; "Times There Art," GT, EJP 2, Box 24, Folder 4; "An Attempted Explanation," GT, EJP 2, Box 14, Folder 4; "Reasons for Belief," GT, EJP 2, Box 16, Folder 8.
27. Donald Davie, *The New Oxford Book of Christian Verse* (Oxford: Oxford University Press, 1981).
28. Elizabeth Jennings, *The Batsford Book of Religious Verse* (London: Batsford, 1981): 9–10.
29. C. H. Sisson, "Divine Rhyme," review of *The Batsford Book of Religious Verse*, *The Spectator* (June 26, 1981): 23.
30. Elizabeth Jennings, *In Praise of Our Lady* (London: Batsford, 1982): 11–12.
31. Elizabeth Jennings, *A Dream of Spring*, illustrated by Antony Rossiter (Stratford-upon-Avon: Celandine Press, 1980).
32. "From Light to Dark," 461.
33. "A Way to a Creed," 467.
34. Elizabeth Jennings, *Italian Light and Other Poems*, illustrated by Gerald Woods (Eastbourne: Snake River Press, 1981).
35. "Sources of Light," 497.
36. "I Beg for Light," 496–7.
37. "The Voices of Plain Chant," 496.
38. "Over and Over," 473.
39. Mole.
40. Veronica Wedgwood, "Tuscan Idylls," review of *Celebrations and Elegies*, *Daily Telegraph* (June 3, 1982): 14.
41. Douglas Dunn, "Unremittingly Prolific Poet," review of *Celebrations and Elegies*, *Glasgow Herald* (May 5, 1982): 8.
42. "Art in a Violent World," GT, EJP 2, Box 15, Folder 5; "What Poetry Is," GT, EJP 2, Box 14, Folder 2; "The Responsibility of Poetry," GT, EJP 2, Box 14, Folder 3; "Poetry Is," GT, EJP 2, Box 17, Folder 6; "What Poetry Aspires To," GT, EJP 2, Box 15, Folder 4; "What Poetry is Not," GT, EJP 2, Box 20, Folder 9; "The Purpose of Art," GT, EJP 2, Box 19, Folder 8; "The Use of Imagination," GT, EJP 2, Box 21, Folder 3; "Imagination," GT, EJP 2, Box 24, Folder 9; "Poetry," GT, EJP 2, Box 14, Folder 10; Elizabeth Jennings to Michael Schmidt, January 24, 1984, Rylands, CPA Acc 3, Box 267/3/7 100–59.
43. "Youth," GT, EJP 2, Box 16, Folder 3; "Rejection," GT, EJP 2, Box 14, Folder 4.

44. "One Kind of Catholic," GT, EJP 2, Box 25, Folder 1.
45. "Passion" and "Spoilt Love," GT, EJP 2, Box 27, Folder 8.
46. "Romantic Dalliances," GT, EJP 2, Box 20, Folder 3.
47. "Full Circle," GT, EJP 2, Box 13, Folder 9. Jennings' early loves are con-
    firmed in two published poems of this period, "Heyday," 476, and "First
    Admirers," 479.
48. "The Death of a Great Nurse," GT, EJP 2, Box 22, Folder 6, and
    Gramang, 96.
49. "After a Death," GT, EJP 2, Box 20, Folder 9.
50. "Who Forgives Who?" GT, EJP 2, Box 20, Folder 10. This poem was
    written in 1982; James died in 1971.
51. "Questions About Marriage," GT, EJP 2, Box 20, Folder 10.
52. "Friendship," GT, EJP 2, Box 20, Folder 10; "Friendship," GT, EJP 2,
    Box 18, Folder 3.
53. "For My Sister Aged 38 Years," MS, Poems, Group of 92, No. 2, Berg
    Collection, NYPL.
54. "For My Sister and Brother-in-Law," poem in possession of Mark
    Albrow.
55. "A Love Poem Written While with My Family," GT, EJP 2, Box 19, Folder 2.
56. "In Or Out of Love," GT, EJP 2, Box 18, Folder 5.
57. "Solving a Problem," GT, EJP 2, Box 19, Folder 8.
58. There is not sufficient extant evidence to determine the physical rela-
    tionship between Jennings and Wedgwood. Georgetown University and
    the Rylands Library have limited Wedgwood materials, and the Bodleian
    Library's collection of Wedgwood's material contains nothing about
    Jennings. Jennings had the gift of concealment. On the one hand, she
    discriminated between homosexual tendencies and homosexual acts as
    evidenced in her evaluation of Hopkins. It is unknown whether her public
    claim that she was chaste applied to both male and female relationships.
    One piece of evidence from this period which cannot be explained is an
    unpublished poem entitled "Infidelity," GT, EJP 2, Box 21, Folder 4, April
    1982 in which Jennings writes of female infidelity and the speaker's fear of
    having been duped. However, there is no way to determine whether this
    is in fact descriptive of an event, the paranoid concern of a fearful Elizabeth
    Jennings, or a monologue written from imagined experience.
59. "Rescuer," GT, EJP 2, Box 22, Folder 1.
60. "For a Friend Not Seen for a Year," GT, EJP 2, Box 25, Folder 5.
61. "Dependence," GT, EJP 2, Box 16, Folder 11, and "Friend Who Is an
    Historian," GT, EJP 2, Box 17, Folder 1.
62. "Never Quite the Same," GT, EJP 2, Box 22, Folder 1.
63. "Darling Veronica," July 22, 1982, GT, EJP 2, Box 22, Folder 4.
64. "Meeting a Great Writer," GT, EJP 2, Box 22, Folder 6.
65. "Veronica Wedgwood to Michael Schmidt, December 4, 1978, Rylands,
    CPA/2/2/153/4.

66. "I Had a Love," WU, Box 11 Notebook Q, Poems 1981. See also letter from Elizabeth Jennings to Anne Harvey, January 23, 5–8, in which Jennings complains of her relationship with an unnamed friend. Uncatalogued Rylands.
67. "From Rage to Grief," GT, EJP 2, Box 22, Folder 1; "A Jinx," GT, EJP 2, Box 22, Folder 1.
68. "Love and Sickness," GT, EJP 2, Box 22, Folder 3.
69. "Life-Line Suspended," GT, EJP 2, Box 22, Folder 2.
70. "For a Friend Not Seen for a Year," GT, EJP 2, Box 25, Folder 5.
71. "Left in the Air," GT, EJP 2, Box 23, Folder 1.
72. Elizabeth Jennings to Michael Schmidt, Rylands, November 13 and 26, 1984, CPA Acc 3, Box 267/3/112 100–59.
73. Elizabeth Jennings to Ruga Stanley, July 3, 1985. UD, Uncatalogued MS 306, Folder 2. In this letter Jennings refers to the 1984 letter. Elizabeth Jennings to Michael Schmidt, Rylands, April 7, 1984, CPA Acc 3 267/3/133 100–59.
74. Elizabeth Jennings to Michael Schmidt, January 11, 1986, Rylands, CPA Acc 3, box 267/3 Correspondence 1982-881-99.
75. "Loss and Time," GT, EJP 2, Box 25, Folder 7.

CHAPTER 17

1. "Drying Up," GT, EJP 2, Box 30, Folder 3.
2. "On My Sixtieth Birthday," 887, published posthumously; "Grace" and "Let Me Be Grateful," GT, EJP 2, Box 25, Folder 4; "Unusual Gratitude," GT, EJP 2, Box 25, Folder 6.
3. "Holding Your Tongue," GT, EJP 2, Box 26, Folder 12.
4. "Otherwise," GT, EJP 2, Box 27, Folder 6.
5. "Reflections at Sixty," GT, EJP 2, Box 27, Folder 11; "Elegy for Myself," 890, published posthumously.
6. "Once Again," GT, EJP 2, Box 26, Folder 6.
7. "Elegy for the Living," GT, EJP 2, Box 25, Folder 10; "Early Ageing," GT, EJP 2, Box 25, Folder 11; "Against Pity," GT, EJP 2, Box 26, Folder 4; "Tribute to an Absent Friend," GT, EJP 2, Box 27, Folder 2; "Death Before Death," GT, EJP 2, Box 26, Folder 2; "A Friendship in Silence," GT, EJP 2, Box 27, Folder 7; "Lost Love," GT, EJP 2, Box 26, Folder 3.
8. "Bitter Fruit," 530.
9. "Growing Ahead," 532.
10. "Trust" and "Two Losses," GT, EJP 2, Box 26, Folder 5.
11. Letter to Elizabeth Jennings regarding her retirement, May 27, 1981, BC, MS 17, Folder 30, and Peter Levi, "Otherwise Engaged," *The Independent* (March 12, 1987): 12.
12. Michael Schmidt to the Royal Literary Fund, September 10, 1985, Rylands, CPA Acc 3, Box 267/3. Correspondence 1982-881-99.

13. American institutions which purchased Jennings' manuscripts included, among others: Washington University, University of Delaware, Georgetown University, Boston College, and the New York Public Library.

14. "List—January–May 1985," UD, Letters and Poetry Manuscripts, MS 282, Folder 6.

15. Peter Levi, "A Sense of Inward Fire," review of *Extending the Territory*, *The Spectator* (October 19, 1985): 33.

16. "The Child's Story," 499.

17. "Precursors," 546.

18. John Lucas, "Review of *Extending the Territory*," *New Statesman* 110, No. 2851 (November 15, 1985): 28.

19. Elizabeth Jennings to Michael Schmidt, January 21, 1985. See Critics on Jennings in Jane Dowson, *The Elizabeth Jennings Project*, http://www.elizabethjennings.dmu.ac.uk/home.html.

20. David Gascoyne, "A Poet's Experience," review of *Extending the Territory*, *The Tablet* (September 14, 1985): 16.

21. *Every Changing Shape*, 190.

22. David Gascoyne to Michael Schmidt, November 18, 1985, GT, EJP 1, Box 1, Folder 16.

23. Peter Porter, "Cassettes of Atrocity," review of *Extending the Territory*, *The Observer*, (September 1, 1985): 19.

24. Levi, "A Sense of Inward Fire," 33.

25. *In Shakespeare's Company* (Shipston-on-Stour, Warwickshire: Celandine Press, 1985).

26. Peter Levi, "Poetry," review of *Collected Poems*, *PN Review* 53, No. 3, 1986, 89–90. In this review Levi comments on *In Shakespeare's Company* as well.

27. Anne Harvey and Charles Causley, eds., *Poets in Hand: A Puffin Quintet* (Harmondsworth: Penguin, 1985).

28. Sebastian Barker, *Portraits of Poets* with photographs by Christopher Barker (Manchester: Carcanet, 1986).

29. Elizabeth Jennings, review of *Charlotte Mew and Her Friends*, *Daily Telegraph*, GT, EJP 2, Box 31, Folder 29.

30. Elizabeth Jennings, review of *Letters of John Clare*, ed. Mark Storey, GT, EJP 2, Box 31, Folder 28. No date.

31. Elizabeth Jennings, "Water Music," review of *The Kingfisher* by Amy Clampitt, *The Spectator* (August 3, 1984): 25.

32. Jeni Couzyn, *The Bloodaxe Book of Contemporary Women Poets* (Newcastle upon Tyne: Bloodaxe Books, 1985): 13–29.

33. Levi, "Otherwise Engaged," 12. Levi asserts this without evidence.

34. Elizabeth Jennings to Terence Tiller, December 22, *circa* 1963 from the Warneford Hospital. Correspondence, Berg Collection, NYPL.

35. "A Question With No Answer," WU, Box 11, Notebook P, 1981.

36. Elizabeth Jennings in Couzyn, 98–100.

37. Elizabeth Jennings publicity lists, Rylands, CPA Acc 5/1/Box 1.

38. "Preface," *Collected Poems 1953–1985*, 13.
39. Robert Sheppard, "Review of *Collected Poems*," *New Statesman* (August 21, 1987): 22.
40. Lawrence Sail, "Recapturing Hope," review of *Collected Poems*, *Poetry Review* (December 1986): 42–3.
41. Simon Rae, "Overwhelming Questions," review of *Extending the Territory*, *The Times Literary Supplement* (May 30, 1986): 586.
42. Anna Adams, "Review of *Collected Poems*," *The Green Book* 2, No. 7, 1987.
43. M. D. Aeschliman, "Moments of Grace," review of *Collected Poems*, *Reflections* (Winter, 1990): 13.
44. Anne Stevenson, "A Rage for Order," review of *Collected Poems*, *Sunday Times* (September 14, 1986): 55.
45. Elizabeth Jennings to Anne Harvey, September 27. No year. Uncatalogued Ryands.
46. William Oxley, "Review of *Collected Poems*," *Acumen* (April 5, 1987): 81–3.
47. Bernard Bergonzi, "Religious Poet," review of *Collected Poems*, *The Tablet* (September 13, 1986): 13–14.
48. Kingsley Amis, "Books Now for Christmas," review of *Collected Poems*, *The Spectator* (December 6, 1986): 34.
49. Thomas D'Evelyn, "Two Contemporary Poets: Graham and Jennings: Plot Apart in Form and Subject," *Christian Science Monitor* (August 12, 1987): 213.
50. Peter Levi, review of *Collected Poems*, *PN Review* 53, No. 133 (1986): 89–90.
51. Crewe, 10–11.
52. *The Sonnets of Michelangelo* sold well from the time of its first publication in 1961. There were editions published by Allison & Busby in 1969, Doubleday in 1970, and Carcanet in 2002.
53. Dowson, The Elizabeth Jennings Project, www.elizabethjennings.dmu.ac.uk/home.html, literary career, 1980s.
54. In order to commemorate these readings, Jennings wrote an unpublished poem, "Reading Poetry at a School, July 9, 1992," 894.
55. Michael Schmidt to Elizabeth Jennings, June 1, 1987, Rylands, CPA, Acc 3, Box 267/3 Correspondence 1982-88-99.
56. Manuscript copies of both "A Book of Spells" and "Autobiography, 1986" are in possession of Roger Pringle.
57. Elizabeth Jennings to Roger Pringle, March 28, 1987. Letter owned by Pringle.
58. Roger Pringle to Dana Greene, email, July 11, 2016.
59. Statement by Wim Meeuws, July 1, 2013, GT, EJP 3, 151109, Box 4, Folder 1. *An Oxford Cycle: Poems* (Oxford: Thornton's Ltd, 1987).
60. "After a Painting Is Finished," 554.
61. "Loneliness," 12.
62. "O Happy Death," 618–20; "A Letter from the Dead," 620–1; "A Song for Death," 621–2; "Death of a Dominican Priest at Easter," 622–3, and "An

Elegy for O. L. OP," GT, EJP 2, Box 27, Folder 5. See also Elizabeth Jennings to Timothy Radcliffe and Simon Robson, October 28, 1987, and Timothy Radcliffe to Elizabeth Jennings, February 10, 1988. BC, MS 17, Folder 9.

63. "Worry," GT, EJP 2, Box 30, Folder 16.
64. "Two Sonnets on Death," GT, EJP 2, Box 2, Box 26.

CHAPTER 18

1. "Against the Dark," 592.
2. Michael Schmidt to Elizabeth Jennings, July 7, 1989, Rylands, CPA Acc 5-2, Box 6/6.
3. "Poetry Sometimes...," 673.
4. "For Philip Larkin," 550.
5. "Friendship," 575–6.
6. "First Six Years," 605–6.
7. "Psalm of Childhood," 565.
8. "Legacies and Language," 586–7.
9. "Easter Vigil and Mass," 600, and "A Childhood Religion," 607.
10. "The Force of Time," 610–11.
11. "Pigeons Suddenly," 590.
12. "House of Words," 587–8.
13. "The Luck of It," 591.
14. "Waiting," 596.
15. "Against the Dark," 592.
16. "Some Words of My Mother's in Childhood," 563–4.
17. "I Heard a Voice," 593–4.
18. "The Arts," 557.
19. "The Feel of Things," 584.
20. Elizabeth Jennings, "The State of Poetry," *Agenda* 27, No. 3 (1989), 40–1, and "Questionnaire on Rhyme," *Agenda* 28, No. 4 (1991), 24.
21. "Living by Love," 679–80.
22. "A Realisation," 897. Published posthumously.
23. "Two Together," 572.
24. "All That Departing," 579–80.
25. Lawrence Sail, review of *Tributes*, *Stand Magazine* 31, No. 4 (Autumn 1990), 48–50.
26. C. H. Sisson, "How Spirit Speaks to Spirit," review of *Tributes*, *The Spectator* (September 2, 1989): 30.
27. Glyn Maxwell, "Faith in Form," review of *Tributes*, *The Times Literary Supplement* (May 5, 1989), 495.
28. Herbert Lomas, "Straight from the Heart," review of *Tributes*, *The Tablet* (March 25, 1989): 25.
29. "Cousins, Aunts, Uncles," 693–4.
30. "The Happy Regrets: Last Words for My Mother," 683–4.

31. "Sudden Remembrance," 629.
32. "Schizophrenic," GT, EJP 2, Box 26, Folder 1, and "Schizophrenia," undated and published posthumously, 938.
33. "Left in Charge," 677. Dedicated to Anne. This may refer to Anne Scott.
34. "For Cotty—A Letter of Thanks," 547.
35. There is no reference to Cotty in the voluminous Jennings materials, nor do people who lived in Oxford at that time and knew Jennings recognize the name.
36. Elizabeth Jennings to Ruga Stanley, BC, 1993–47, Box 16, Folder 16–18.
37. "Two Sonnets for a Czech Friend," 673.
38. Elizabeth Jennings to Michael Schmidt, June 20, 1992, Rylands, CPA Acc 6-1, Box 22/10.
39. Sir Robin Catford to Elizabeth Jennings, January 26, 1993, BC, Box 17, Folder 30.
40. Report from David Higham Associates, February 1993, BC, MS, Box 17, Folder 21. This estimate pertains to 1993 only.
41. Jennings, "Emily Dickinson and the Poetry of the Inner Life," 394–401; "Priest Poet," review of Counterpoint, *The Tablet* (January 19, 1991): 17–18; "A Wanderer's Voice," review of *My Country: Collected Poems of Alistair Elliot*, *The Tablet* (May 26, 1990): 24; "Saved by Poetry," 13; "Introduction," *Collected Poems of Ruth Pitter* (Petersfield: Enitharmon Press, 1990): 15.
42. "Two Sonnets on Death," 898, published posthumously, and "Death," 667.
43. Will Eaves, "Ceremonial Forms," review of *Times and Seasons*, *The Times Literary Supplement* (January 15, 1993): 23.
44. Bernard Bergonzi, "Faith of a Poet," review of *Times and Seasons*, *The Tablet* (February 6, 1993): 14–15.
45. Germaine Greer, *The Change—Women, Aging and the Menopause* (London: Hamish Hamilton, 1991): 372–5. See also Rosemary Dinnage, "Happy Cronehood!," review of *The Change* by Germaine Greer, *The Times Literary Supplement* (October 25, 1991): 6.
46. Gramang, "Interview," 93–101.
47. Crewe, 10–11; Lakers, 34; Sinead Garrigan, "An Interview with Elizabeth Jennings," *Oxford Poetry* 6 (1992): 103–7; de Muth, "Wondering About the Individual Sheep," *The Independent* (October 20, 1994); "Not Averse to Conviction," interview with Paul Goodman, *Catholic Herald* (March 1, 1991): 7.
48. Sue Lawley, "Interview with Elizabeth Jennings," *Desert Island Discs*, B.B.C. Radio 4 (January 3 and 8, 1993), http://www.bbc.co.uk/programmes/p0093x99.
49. "Without Whom," BC, Series IV, Box 16, Folder 6.
50. There is a discrepancy between the ordering of the manuscript as described in Jennings' opening synopsis and its actual ordering. The latter ordering is followed in this discussion. Also, Jennings indicates that there is a chapter on London included in the manuscript, but this is not extant.

CHAPTER 19

1. "A Realisation," 695. This published poem shares the same title with a poem mentioned earlier, but it is in fact a different poem.
2. De Muth, "Wondering about the Individual Sheep."
3. "Obituary of Elizabeth Jennings," *The Tablet* (November 3, 2001): 31.
4. Wendy Hill to Dana Greene, email October 10, 2015.
5. Elizabeth Jennings to Anne Harvey, January 16, 1995. Uncatalogued, Rylands.
6. Elizabeth Jennings to Michael Schmidt, July 1995. Cited under Michael Schmidt correspondence. www.elizabethjennings.dmu.ac.uk/home.html.
7. "At Home," "A New Flat," UD, 01–10, 1996–2000, uncatalogued.
8. "Home," BC, Series V, Box 16, Folder 8.
9. Dickson, 16; de Muth, "Wondering about the Individual Sheep."
10. "A Company of Friends," 792–3, and "A Gift of Gratitude," 783–4.
11. Elizabeth Jennings to Michael Schmidt, August 30, 1994, Rylands, CPA Acc 6-3, Box 34, Folder 7; November 17, 1994, Folder 9.
12. Elizabeth Jennings to Michael Schmidt, Rylands, December 25, 1995, CPA Acc 8, Box 10, Folder 7.
13. "A Life in the Day Of," interview with Elizabeth Jennings by Rosalyn Chissick, *Sunday Times* (March 17, 1996): 53–4. Jennings remained on the A-level syllabus until the late 1990s.
14. Draft of a letter to "Dear Sirs," August 7, 1995, BC, Series IV, Box 17, Folder 31.
15. Interview with Christiana Hardyment, May 18, 2015, Oxford.
16. Elizabeth Jennings to Rebecca Stanley, December 26, no year, BC 1993–47, Box 16, Folders 16–18; Elizabeth Jennings to Anne Harvey. Written from Birch Court, no date. Uncatalogued, Rylands.
17. Elizabeth Jennings to Michael Schmidt, June 7, 1996, Rylands, CPA Acc 8, Box 19, Correspondence, 1995–96.
18. Elizabeth Jennings to Michael Schmidt, September 27, 1994, Rylands, CPA Acc 6-3, Box 34 Folder 4.
19. "Time's Element," 749.
20. Short, "A Faithful Poet."
21. "Steps Towards Poems," 705.
22. "Two Sonnets on Love and Lust," 708, and "The Modes of Love," 714–19.
23. Chris Moore, "Two Women, Two Voices," *The Tablet* (October 15, 1994): 21.
24. Gwyneth Lewis, "Annunciations," Poetry *Review* 84, No. 4 (Winter 1994): 60.
25. JLeS [*sic*], review of *Familiar Spirits*, *The Times Literary Supplement* (May 5, 1995): 29.
26. Kirsten Luckins, "Differing Poetic Responses to the Big Questions," *London Quarterly*, No. 5 (February 14–May 15, 1995): 30.
27. Anne Harvey, ed., *A Spell of Words: Selected Poems for Children* (London: Macmillan, 1997).

28. Roger Pringle to Dana Greene, email, August 13, 2016.
29. *A Poet's Choice* (Manchester: Carcanet, 1996): xiii–xiv.
30. "In the Meantime," 754.
31. "Lazarus," 752.
32. "Rome," 748–9.
33. "Mass, I," 741–2; "Mass II," 743–4; "Bread," 744–5; "Consecration I," 745; "Consecration II," 745–6; "Holy Communion," 747.
34. "Seers and Makers," 732, and "Hermits and Poets," 732–3.
35. "Order," 735.
36. "Act of Imagination," 734.
37. Gordon Wakefield, "God and Some English Poets: Elizabeth Jennings," *The Expository Times* 109, No. 10 (1997); Clive Wilmer, "Poetry and Prayer," *The Times Literary Supplement* (July 25, 1997): 25.

CHAPTER 20

1. "Assurance Beyond Midnight," 822–3.
2. Jennings' condition is documented in Clinical Notes from the archives of the Oxfordshire Health NHS Foundation Trust. Statements were written by Jackie Stayt, Community Mental Health Nurse, March 26, 1997; June 24, 1997; and May 25, 1999. These documents are in the possession of Mark Albrow.
3. Catherine Jones, "Elizabeth Jennings: Her Last Six Years," Rylands, CPA Acc 15, Box 6 2/6.
4. Elizabeth Jennings, UD, Box 97-38, uncatalogued Notebooks, March–April 1997.
5. Gemma Simms, "Secret Poets Revealed," *Oxford Mail* (June 18, 1998): 14.
6. "Public and Private Grief," UD, Box 98-36, uncatalogued Pooh Bear Notebook, September 2, 1997.
7. "Apology to a Friend," 763, and "Reconciliation," UD, Box 98-83, uncatalogued Wallace and Gromit Silly Bear Notebooks, May 6, 1998.
8. "At Odds" (For My Sister), UD, Box 98-82-83, uncatalogued Black and Red Notebook, June 9, 1998.
9. Almost all these poems are in uncatalogued materials at the University of Delaware.
10. "Late Love," UD, 01-10 1996–2000, Notebook, August 21, 1998.
11. Max Davidson, "Her Prize Money Is in the Bag," *Daily Telegraph* (December 13, 1997): 7.
12. Jennings' love of knick-knacks is described in the poem "My Shops," UD, Box 98-36, uncatalogued flower-covered notebook, December 4, 1997.
13. Elizabeth Jennings to Michael Schmidt, October 17, 1998; Michael Schmidt to Elizabeth Jennings, October 22, 1998; Elizabeth Jennings to Michael Schmidt, October 25, 1998; Rylands, CPA Acc 10, Correspondence 1998, Box 4, 9 and 10.

14. "The Hated Question," UD, Box 98-36, uncatalogued Wallace and Gromit reindeer notebook, December 13, 1997.
15. "The Value of Poems," UD, Box 98-36, uncatalogued, blue, orange, green, yellow notebook, October 25, *circa* 1997.
16. "The Gift," UD, uncatalogued, 01-10 1996–2000, January 3, 2000.
17. "The Powers of Poetry," UD, Box 98-36, uncatalogued Pooh Bear notebook, September 2, 1997.
18. "Like Letters," UD, Box 98-36, uncatalogued blue, orange, green yellow notebook, October 25, *circa* 1997.
19. *Praises* (Manchester: Carcanet, 1998).
20. "The Largest Question," 785–6.
21. "A View of Lazarus," 756.
22. "A Full Moon," 760–1.
23. Chris Moore, "A Clutch of Poems," review of *Praises*, *The Tablet* (March 20, 1999): 19.
24. Jane Davis, "Praises," *The Reader* 5 (Autumn/Winter, 1998): 41–4.
25. Michael O'Neill, review of *Praises*, *The Times Literary Supplement* (December 25, 1998): 28–9.
26. Les Murray, "Letter—Selecting the Poet Laureate," *The Times Literary Supplement* (December 11, 1998): 17.
27. Jones, "Elizabeth Jennings."
28. Gillian Reynolds to Dana Greene, emails, July 2016.
29. Apparently, there were hard feelings between St. Anne's and Jennings since at some point Gina Bollinger had asked the then principal, Ruth Deech, if the college would provide a permanent accommodation for Jennings. The request was declined.
30. Elizabeth Jennings to Michael Schmidt, September 1999, Rylands, CPA Acc. 11 Box 4/1 and Box 4/5, November 1, 1999.
31. "Death," UD, uncatalogued teddy bear notebook, 01-10 1996–2000, October 1998–April 1999 and January 6, 1999.
32. "I Ask Myself," GT, EJP 2, Box 3, Folder 11, February 1977.
33. Elizabeth Jennings to Michael Schmidt, September 13, 1993, Rylands, CPA Acc. 6-3 Box 34, Folder 16.
34. "A Wish," GT, EJP 2, Box 3, Folder 6.
35. "Of Dying," UD, Box 97-38, uncatalogued heart notebook, May 11–July 17, 1997.
36. "The Vision and Popularity of Gerard Manley Hopkins," *circa* 1999. Uncatalogued, Rylands.
37. In his preface to Jennings' *New Collected Poems* (Manchester: Carcanet, 2002), xix, Michael Schmidt states that Jennings wrote a long, unfinished essay and a sequence of poems about Hopkins and that she was fascinated by his chastity and by differences between male and female chastity and their implications for the imagination. In the material now in the Rylands

Library I was unable to find confirmation of Jennings' interest in Hopkins' preoccupation with chastity.

38. Elizabeth Jennings to Anne Harvey, August 8, *circa* 2001. Uncatalogued. Rylands. Letter, Priscilla Tolkien to Dana Greene, August 28, 2016. Privately held.
39. "Night Song," 819–20.
40. Sian Hughes, "Except for Sudden Darks," review of *Timely Issues*, *The Times Literary Supplement* (November 23, 2001): 2.
41. "Tenderness," 807–8.
42. "Regions of Memory," 792.
43. "One More Place of Memory," 810.
44. "Some Months After an Anaesthetics," 807.
45. "Lost Time," 808.
46. "An Awareness," 806.
47. "After Four Months of Illness," 809.
48. "Homage to Gerard Manley Hopkins: After Receiving Communion in Hospital," 801–2.
49. "Whitsun," 820.
50. "Perfection," 822.
51. "Assurance Beyond Midnight," 822–3.
52. Christiana Hardyment to Friends of Elizabeth Jennings, August 9, 2001, Rylands, CPA Acc 15, Box 6/2/18/Correspondence 2001–3.
53. "Dance," 793.
54. "Night Song."
55. Statement. High Court of Justice, District Probate Registry, Oxford. December 7, 2001. The estate devolved to Aileen Albrow and did not exceed £210,000; therefore it was not taxed.
56. "Poet's Toy Passion Will Help Children," *Oxford Mail* (May 27, 2002), http://www.oxfordmail.co.uk/news/6593609.

EPILOGUE

1. "Writing Poems: Primary Source," GT, EJP 2, Box 27, Folder 9.
2. Jennings, in *Bloodaxe Book*, 100.
3. "Advice to Myself and Other Poets," GT, EJP 2, Box 30, Folder 2.
4. Ibid.
5. "Drying Up."
6. This approximation is based on Michael Schmidt's estimate that Carcanet sold some 170,000 copies of her books. Additionally, Jennings published another nineteen books with other publishers prior to moving to Carcanet in 1975. Five of these were published by Macmillan, which did runs of at least 1,000 copies. Eleven more books were published by other houses after Jennings signed on with Carcanet. According to World Catalog, fifteen

of Jennings' books had ten or more editions, with *The Sonnets of Michelangelo, Every Changing Shape, Growing-Points, Poetry to-day, Frost,* and *An Anthology of Modern Verse* having the most.

7. Ruth Padel, "Fortunes of War, Love and Peace," review of *New and Collected Poems, Financial Times* (April 20, 2002): 4.

8. Ruth Padel, "The Sunday Poem," *The Independent* (October 17, 1999): 13.

9. Grevel Lindop, "Elizabeth Jennings," *The Guardian* (October 31, 2001), http://www.theguardian.com/news/2001/oct/31/guardianobituaries. books.

10. "Poet Whose Verse Drew on Her Christian Faith but Offered Experience Rather than Sermons," "Obituary of Elizabeth Jennings Poet," *Daily Telegraph* (October 30, 2001): 25.

11. Obituary, "Elizabeth Jennings," *The Times* (October 31, 2001): 19.

12. Michael Schmidt, "Obituary, Elizabeth Jennings," *The Independent* (October 31, 2001): 6.

13. Michael Schmidt, ed., *Lives of the Poets* (New York: Knopf, 1999): 836–40.

14. Schmidt, "Obituary," 6.

15. Michael Schmidt, "Preface," *New Collected Poems*, xix–xiv.

16. Anthony Thwaite, "'Angel' into 'Bag-lady,'" *Sunday Telegraph* (April 21, 2002), http://www.telegraph.co.uk/culture/4727712/Angel-into-bag-lady.html.

17. Anthony Haynes, "Most Catholic Poet," review of *New Collected Poems, The Tablet* (April 13, 2002): 19–20.

18. Robert Crawford, "Locked and Barred," review of *New Collected Poems, London Review of Books* (July 24, 2003): 31–2.

19. Anthony Haynes, "Most Catholic Poet," review of *New Collected Poems, The Tablet* (April 13, 2002): 19–20.

20. Thwaite, "'Angel' into 'Bag-lady',", and Gerry Fenge, "Journeys of the Self," *The English Review* (September 1, 2000): 26.

21. Emma Mason, ed., *The Collected Poems*. This contains all Jennings poems which appeared in book form except those in *An Oxford Cycle* and *In Shakespeare's Company*. Some previous unpublished poems are also included in Mason's edition.

22. This is forthcoming from Editions L' Harmattan.

23. See The Elizabeth Jennings Project, www.elizabethjennings.dmu.ac.uk/home.html.

24. Anna Walczuk, *Elizabeth Jennings and the Sacramental Nature of Poetry* (NY: Columbia University Press, 2018).

25. This was held on September 8, 2002 with Janet Henfrey, Anne Harvey, and Michael Schmidt reading.

26. This event was held on March 27, 2004 with many of Jennings' friends in attendance and Anne Harvey, Janet Henfrey, Michael Schmidt, Gina Pollinger, Christina Hardyment, and Priscilla Tolkien reading Jennings' poetry.

27. Principal presenters at this October 29, 2016 symposium were: Jane
    Dowson, Dana Greene, Emma Mason, and Michael Schmidt.
28. See Jeremy Reed's "Late Roses," written in memory of Elizabeth Jennings,
    This is How You Disappear (London: Enitharmon, 2007), 27–8, and Jane
    Davis, "Elizabeth Jennings," *PN Review* (January–February 2002), 11.
29. For examples of attempts to understand Jennings' contribution to poetics
    and theopoetics see Barry Sloan, 393–414; Joseph R. Teller, "'The misrule
    of our dust': Psychoanalysis, Sacrament, and the Subject in Elizabeth
    Jennings' Poetry of Incarnation," *Christianity and Literature* 57, No. 4 (2006):
    531–57; and Stephen McInerney, "'Art with its Largesse and its Own
    Restraint': The Sacramental Poetics of Elizabeth Jennings and Les Murray,"
    in *Between Human and Divine*, ed. Mary R. Reichardt (Washington, D.C.:
    Catholic University of America Press, 2010): 207–25.
30. Material included in the two previous paragraphs was drawn from the
    following poems included in GT, EJP 2: "At Poetry Readings," Box 26,
    Folder 9; "An Error," Box 26, Folder 11; "The Saints of Verse," Box 27,
    Folder 9; "A Large Analogy," Box 27, Folder 8; "Poetry and Truth," Box 28,
    Folder 2; "Disagreement with Auden," Box 30, Folder 3; "The Ethics of
    Verse," Box 30, Folder 4; "Plato Was Right," Box 30, Folder 8; "The Place
    of Self," Box 30, Folder 8; "Making the Poem," Box 30, Folder 20; "The
    Feel of Things," 584; and "Precursors," 546. Elizabeth Jennings to Michael
    Schmidt, January 24, 1984, Rylands, CPA Acc 3, Box 277/2/7; "Uncle
    Frank" in "Without Whom," 10; "The Poet and His Public Today," WU,
    Box K, Notebook B; "The Value of Poetry," WU, Box 7; *Don't Ask Me
    What I Mean: Poets in Their Own Words*, 132–5; *Every Changing Shape*, 108.
31. Materials included in the three previous paragraphs were drawn from
    diverse sources including: *Every Changing Shape*, 9, 10, 17–18, 30, 44, 56, 68,
    95, 189, 215–22, 224, 232; *Poetry To-day*, 55; "Saved by Poetry," 613; "Poems
    of Consecration," GT, EJP 2, Box 30, Folder 9; *Christian Poetry*, 92–101,
    102–15.
32. Virginia Woolf, "Letter to Leonard Woolf," February 27, 1926, in
    A Writer's Diary (New York: Harcourt, Brace, 1954), 84–5.

Bibliography

ARCHIVAL RESOURCES CONSULTED

Bodleian Library, Oxford, Department of Manuscripts, Western Mss. Eng.c. 7982, Anthony and Ann Thwaite Papers (Bodleian).

British Library, London, Modern Literary Manuscripts, MSS. Vols. VIII, IX, MS 52598-89, (BL).

Brotherton Library, Special Collections, University of Leeds. Letters Database. Letters Database to and from Elizabeth Jennings (Brotherton).

Catholic Nottingham Diocesan Archives, "Elizabeth Joan Jennings."

District Probate Registry at Oxford, Elizabeth Joan Jennings, December 7, 2001.

Georgetown University, Booth Family Center for Special Collections, Elizabeth Jennings Papers Mss. Series 1, 2, 3 (GT).

Hull History Centre, Letters of Elizabeth Jennings (Hull).

John J. Burns Library, Boston College. Elizabeth Jennings Papers, MS 2007.018 and Peter Levi Papers, MS 1986–98 (BC).

John Rylands University Library, University of Manchester Library, Carcanet Press Archive, *Critical Quarterly* Archive (Rylands).

New York Public Library, Berg Collection, Elizabeth Jennings Collection of Papers, Mss. brg/19298#c222641 and Correspondence, brg/19298#222653 (NYPL).

Pennsylvania State University, Eberly Family Special Collections, Paul West Papers (PSU).

St. Anne's College Archive, Oxford.

St. John's College Library, Canellum Collection, Letters from Elizabeth Jennings to Robert Graves, Oxford.

University of Delaware Library, Special Collections, Elizabeth Jennings Papers, Mss. 186, 282, 283, 284 (UD).

University of Texas, Harry Ransom Center, Robert Graves Miscellanea Collection, Mss. 2178 (UT).

Washington University at St. Louis, Department of Special Collections, Elizabeth Jennings Collection, MSS 061 (WU).

PRIVATELY HELD MATERIALS

Elizabeth Jennings, "Autobiography, 1986," Manuscript held by Roger Pringle. "For My Sister and Brother-in-Law." Held by Mark Albrow.

Health Records of Elizabeth Jennings: Oxfordshire Health NHS Trust. Clinical Notes 1978–2000 and Elizabeth Jennings Letters to Dr. Seymour Spencer, Consultant. Held by Mark Albrow.
Letters from Elizabeth Jennings to Anne Harvey. Held by Anne Harvey and given to the John Rylands Library.

MATERIAL GATHERED FROM THESE INFORMANTS THROUGH INTERVIEWS, EMAILS, OR TELEPHONE

I take full responsibility for this biography.

Mark Albrow
Alan Brownjohn
Duncan Campbell
Donald Hall
Christina Hardyment
Anne Harvey
Wendy Hill
Christopher M. Johnson
Grevel Lindop
Emma Mason

Robert Ombres
Gina Pollinger
James Price
Roger Pringle
Gillian Reynolds
Nicholas Scheetz
Michael Schmidt
Anthony Thwaite
Priscilla Tolkien

POETRY BY ELIZABETH JENNINGS ARRANGED CHRONOLOGICALLY

Elizabeth Jennings. Pamphlet Series, 1. Oxford: Oxford University Poetry Society, 1952.
Poems. With an introduction by Anne Ridler. Swinford: Fantasy Press, 1953.
A Way of Looking: Poems. London: André Deutsch, 1955.
A Sense of the World: Poems. London: André Deutsch, 1958.
Song for a Birth or a Death. London: André Deutsch, 1961.
Recoveries: Poems. London. André Deutsch, 1964.
The Mind Has Mountains. London: Macmillan, 1966.
The Secret Brother and Other Poems for Children. Illustrated by Meg Stevens. London: Macmillan/New York: St. Martin's Press, 1966.
Collected Poems, 1967. London: Macmillan, 1967.
The Animals' Arrival. London: Macmillan, 1969.
Lucidities: Poems. London: Macmillan, 1970.
Relationships. London: Macmillan, 1972.
Growing-Points: New Poems. Manchester: Carcanet, 1975.
Consequently I Rejoice. Manchester: Carcanet, 1977.
After the Ark. Oxford: Oxford University Press, 1978.
Selected Poems. Manchester: Carcanet, 1979.
Winter Wind. Newark, VT: The Janus Press, 1979.
A Dream of Spring. With illustrations by Anthony Rossiter. Stratford: Celandine Press, 1980.

Moments of Grace. Manchester: Carcanet, 1980.
Italian Light and Other Poems. With drawings by Gerald Woods. Eastbourne, Sussex: Snake River Press, 1981.
Celebrations and Elegies. Manchester: Carcanet, 1982.
Extending the Territory. Manchester: Carcanet, 1985.
In Shakespeare's Company: Poems. Shipston-on-Stour, Warwickshire: Celandine Press, 1985.
Collected Poems: 1953–85. Manchester: Carcanet, 1986.
An Oxford Cycle. Oxford: Thornton's, 1987.
Tributes. Manchester: Carcanet, 1989.
Times and Seasons. Manchester: Carcanet, 1992.
Familiar Spirits. Manchester: Carcanet, 1994.
In the Meantime. Manchester: Carcanet, 1996.
A Spell of Words: Selected Poems for Children. Introduction by Anne Harvey. London: Macmillan, 1997.
Praises. Manchester: Carcanet, 1998.
Timely Issues. Manchester: Carcanet, 2001.
New Collected Poems, edited by Michael Schmidt. Manchester: Carcanet, 2002.
The Collected Poems, edited by Emma Mason with a Preface and Afterword. Manchester: Carcanet, 2010.

PROSE, EDITIONS, AND INTRODUCTIONS BY ELIZABETH JENNINGS
ARRANGED CHRONOLOGICALLY

The Batsford Book of Children's Verse, edited by Elizabeth Jennings. London: B. T. Batsford, 1958.
Let's Have Some Poetry! London: Museum Press, 1960.
An Anthology of Modern Verse, 1940–1960. Edited and with an introduction by Elizabeth Jennings. London: Methuen & Co., 1961.
Every Changing Shape. London: Deutsch, 1961; Manchester: Carcanet, 1996.
Poetry To-day. London: Longmans, Green & Company, 1961.
The Sonnets of Michelangelo. Translated by Elizabeth Jennings with an introduction by Michael Ayrton. London: Folio Society, 1961.
Frost. Edinburgh: Oliver and Boyd, 1964.
Christianity and Poetry. London: Burns & Oates, 1965. Published in the U.S. as *Christian Poetry.* New York: Hawthorn Press, 1965.
The Story of My Heart, by John Jefferies. Introduced by Elizabeth Jennings. London: Macmillan, 1968.
A Choice of Christina Rossetti's Verse. Selected and with an introduction by Elizabeth Jennings. London: Faber, 1970.
Seven Men of Vision: An Appreciation. London: Visa Press, 1976.
Wuthering Heights and Selected Poems by Emily Brontë. Introduction by Elizabeth Jennings. London: Pan Books, 1979.
The Batsford Book of Religious Verse, edited by Elizabeth Jennings. London: B. T. Batsford, 1981.

In Praise of Our Lady, edited by Elizabeth Jennings, with a foreword by Cardinal Hume. London: B. T. Batsford, 1982.

A Poet's Choice, compiled by Elizabeth Jennings. Manchester: Carcanet, 1996.

Collected Poems of Ruth Pitter, with an introduction by Elizabeth Jennings. London: Enitharmon Press, 1996.

SELECT ANTHOLOGIES INCLUDING THE POETRY OF ELIZABETH JENNINGS

Adcock, Fleu, ed. *Twentieth Century Women's Poetry.* London: Faber & Faber, 1987.

Barker, Sebastian, with photographs by Christopher Barker. *Portraits of Poets.* Manchester: Carcanet, 1986.

Cosman, Carol, Joan Keefe, Kathleen Weaver, eds. *Penguin Book of Women Poets.* Harmondsworth: Penguin, 1978.

Davie, Donald, ed. *The New Oxford Book of Christian Verse.* Oxford: Oxford University Press, 1981.

Ferguson, Margaret, Mary Jo Salter, Jon Stallworthy, eds. *Norton Anthology of Poetry.* New York: W.W. Norton, 2005.

Harvey, Anne and Charles Causley, eds. *Poets in Hand: A Puffin Quintet.* Harmondsworth: Penguin, 1985.

Larkin, Philip, ed. *Oxford Book of Twentieth-Century English Verse.* Oxford: Oxford University Press, 1973.

Penguin Modern Poets: Lawrence Durrell, Elizabeth Jennings, R. S. Thomas. Harmondsworth, Middlesex: Penguin, 1962.

Pringle, Roger, ed. *A Garland for the Laureate: Poems Presented to Sir John Betjeman on His 75th Birthday.* Stratford-upon-Avon: Celandine Press, 1981.

Schmidt, Michael, ed. *An Introduction to Fifty Modern British Poets.* London: Heinemann, 1979.

Schmidt, Michael, ed. *Eleven British Poets.* London: Methuen, 1980.

Six Women Poets. Oxford: Merton College, 1952.

Stallworthy, Jon, ed. *Six Oxford Poets.* Oxford: Bodleian Library, 1977.

Stallworthy, Jon, ed. *Book of Love Poetry.* Oxford: Oxford University Press, 1986.

Wain, John, ed. *Anthology of Contemporary Poetry: Post-War to the Present.* London: Hutchinson, 1979.

SELECT ARTICLES, CHAPTERS, INTERVIEWS, AND REVIEWS BY ELIZABETH JENNINGS

"Author's Introduction to *Collected Poems, 1967.*" Reprinted in *Poetry Book Society: The First Twenty-five Years*, edited by Eric W. White, 40. London: Poetry Book Society, 1979.

"The Café Society of a B & B Poet," interview by E. Jane Dickson. *Daily Telegraph* (October 29, 1994): 16.

"Cloistered Reflections," review of *A Secular Journal*, by Thomas Merton. *The Times Literary Supplement* (May 22, 1959): 309.

"Dame Edith," The *Spectator* Archive (December 18, 1964): 9.

"A Difficult Balance." *London Magazine* 6, No. 11 (November 1959): 27–30.

"Elizabeth Jennings," interview by John Press. In *A Poet Speaks: Interviews with Contemporary Poets*, edited by Peter Orr. New York: Barnes & Noble, 1966: 91–6.

"Elizabeth Jennings." In *Authors Take Sides on the Falklands*, edited by Cecil Woolf and Jean Moorcroft Wilson, 114–15. London: C. Woolf Publishers, 1982.

"Elizabeth Jennings," interview by Jeni Couzyn. In *The Bloodaxe Book of Contemporary Women Poets: Eleven British Writers*, edited by Jeni Couzyn. Newcastle upon Tyne: Bloodaxe Books, 1985: 98–111.

"Elizabeth Jennings." In *Contemporary Authors Autobiography Series* 5, edited by Adele Sarkissian, 103–14. Detroit: Gale Research Co., 1987.

"Elizabeth Jennings," interview by Sue Lawley. *Desert Island Discs* (January 3, 1993), http://www.bbc.co.uk/programmes/p0093x99.

"Elizabeth Jennings," interview by Gerlinde Gramang, 93–101. In *Elizabeth Jennings: An Appraisal*. Lewiston, New York: Edwin Mellon Press, 1994.

"Elizabeth Jennings Writes…" *The Poetry Book Society Bulletin*, No. 29 (July 1961): no page.

"The Elusive Values: A Study of Contemporary Artistic Forms." *New Blackfriars* XLIV, No. 519 (1963): 373–8.

"Emily Dickinson and the Poetry of the Inner Life." *Review of English Literature* 3, No. 2 (April 1962): 78–87.

"Her Prize Money Is in the Bag," interview by Mark Davidson. *Daily Telegraph* (December 13, 1997): 7.

"Interview with Elizabeth Jennings," interview February 1982 by E. A. Sturzl. *Acumen* 1 (1985): 8–16.

"Introductions to *A Way of Looking* and *Song for a Birth or a Death*." In *Don't Ask Me What I Mean: Poets in Their Own Words*, edited by Clair Brown and Don Patterson, 132–5. London: Picador, 2003.

"A Life in the Day of Elizabeth Jennings," interview by Chris Oram. *Sunday Times* (July 27, 1980): 62.

"A Life in the Day of Elizabeth Jennings," interview by Rosalyn Chissick. *Sunday Times* (March 17, 1996): 53–4.

"Meeting-Points of Mysticism," review of *Ecstasy* by Marghanita Laski. *Time and Tide* (November 16, 1961): 1936.

"New Verse," review of *Choosing a Guest: New and Selected Poems* by Michael Schmidt. *The Spectator Archive* (January 26, 1985): 28.

"Not A-verse to Conviction," interview by Paul Goodman. *Catholic Herald* (March 1, 1991): 7.

Oxford Poetry VI, No. 3 (1992), interview by Sinéad Garrigan: 103–7. http//www.oxfordpoetry.co.uk/interviews.

"A Poet Argues that There Is No Such Thing as a 'Catholic Writer' Just a Plain and Simple Writer." *Catholic Herald* (August 18, 1967): 4.

"Poet At the Pictures," interview by Hermione Lakers. *Oxford Today* (Trinity issue, 1989): 34.

"Poetry and Mysticism: On Re-reading Bremond." *Dublin Review* 234 (1960): 84–91.

"Praying and Praising," review of *Religious Verse* edited by Helen Gardner. *The Tablet* (October 11, 1986): 16.

"Priest Poet," review of *Counterpoint* by R. S. Thomas. *The Tablet* (January 19, 1991): 17–18.

"Questionnaire on Rhyme." *Agenda* 28, No. 4 (1991): 24.

"The Restoration of Symbols: The Poetry of David Gascoyne." *Twentieth Century* 165 (June 1959): 567–77.

"Saved by Poetry." *The Tablet* (May 15, 1993): 13.

"The Secular Angels: A Study of Rilke." *New Blackfriars* 40, No. 476 (November 1959): 467–83.

"The State of Poetry—A Symposium." *Poetry Magazine*, Nos. 29–30 (Spring/Summer, 1972): 25–7.

"The State of Poetry." *Agenda* 27, No. 3 (1989): 40–1.

"Ten Years After: The Making of a Movement." *The Spectator* (October 1, 1964): 30.

"Three Score and Ten: Elizabeth Jennings," interview by Ian McMillan. *The Living Poet* Series 1, Episode 27 (May 1983). http//www.bbc.co.uk/programmes/b08oxzf4. Rebroadcast November 4, 2016. On air only through 2017.

"The Unity of Incarnation: A Study of Gerard Manley Hopkins." *Dublin Review* 234 (1960): 170–84.

"The Vision of Joy: A Study of Georges Bernanos." *New Blackfriars* 40, No. 472–3 (July 1959): 291–8.

"A Wanderer's Voice," review of *My Country: Collected Poems of Alistair Elliot*. *The Tablet* (May 26, 1990): 24.

"Water Music." Review of *The Kingfisher: Poems* by Amy Clampitt. *The Spectator* (August 3, 1984): 25.

"Wondering About the Individual Sheep: Susan de Muth in Bed with Elizabeth Jennings," interview by Susan de Muth. *The Independent* (October 21, 1994).

SELECT SECONDARY SOURCES ABOUT ELIZABETH JENNINGS

Abse, Dannie and Stephen Spender, eds. *New Poems: A PEN Anthology*. London: M. Joseph, 1956.

Adams, Anna. "Review of *Collected Poems*." *The Green Book* 2, No. 7, 1987.

Aeschliman, M. D. "Moments of Grace," review of *Collected Poems*. *Reflections* (Winter, 1990): 13.

Allen, Brigid. *Peter Levi: Oxford Romantic.* Oxford: Signal Books, 2014.

Amis, Kingsley. "Books Now for Christmas," review of *Collected Poems.* *The Spectator* (December 6, 1986): 34.

Amis, Kingsley. *Memoirs.* New York: Summit Books, 1991.

Arnold, Matthew. *The Study of Poetry.* http//www.poetryfoundation.org.

Bergonzi, Bernard. "Religious Poet," review of *Collected Poems 1953–85.* *The Tablet* (September 13, 1986): 13–14.

Bergonzi, Bernard. "Faith of a Poet," review of *Times and Seasons. The Tablet* (February 6, 1993): 14–15.

Bertram, Vicki, ed. *Kicking Daffodils: Twentieth Century Women Poets.* Edinburgh: Edinburgh University Press, 1997.

Bissett, William. "Elizabeth Jennings." In *The Dictionary of Literary Biography*, 27. *Poets of Great Britain and Ireland 1945–60*, edited by Vincent B. Sherry Jr. Detroit: Gale Research (1984): 163–70.

Blackburn, Thomas. *The Price of an Eye.* London: Longmans, 1961.

Boland, Eavan. *Object Lessons.* New York: W. W. Norton, 1995.

Bold, Alan. "Educating the Imagination," review of *Extending the Territory. The Scotsman* (August 24, 1985): 3.

Booth, Martin. *British Poetry 1964–84: Driving Through the Barricades.* London: Routledge & Kegan Paul, 1985.

Bradford, Richard. *The Odd Couple: The Curious Friendship between Kingsley Amis and Philip Larkin.* London: Robson Press, 2012.

Bradley, Jerry. *The Movement: British Poets of the 1950s.* New York: Macmillan, 1993.

Brooke-Rose, Christine. "A Poet Among the Mystics," review of *Every Changing Shape and Song for a Birth or a Death. The Times Literary Supplement* (October 6, 1961): 660.

Brownjohn, Alan. "Hymenoptera," review of *Growing-Points. New Statesman* (May 30, 1975): 732–3.

Brownjohn, Alan. "A Preference for Poetry: Oxford Undergraduate Writing in the Early 1950s." In *The Yearbook of English Studies*, 17. *British Poetry since 1945*. Special Number (1987), 62–74. London: Modern Humanities Research Association.

Buck, Claire. "Poetry and the Women's Movement in Postwar Britain." In *Contemporary British Poetry*, edited by James Acheson and Romano Huk, 81–111. New York: S.U.N.Y Press, 1996.

Buxton, Rachel. "Elizabeth Jennings, The Movement, and Rome." In *The Movement Reconsidered: Essays on Larkin, Amis, Gunn, Davie, and Their Contemporaries*, edited by Zachary Leader, 292–306. New York: Oxford University Press, 2009.

Byers, Margaret. "Cautious Vision: Recent British Poetry by Women." In *British Poetry since 1960: A Critical Survey*, edited by Michael Schmidt and Grevel Lindop, 74–84. Manchester: Carcanet, 1972.

Clayre, Alasdair. Review of *The Mind Has Mountains. Encounter* (November 1967): 76.

Coelsch-Foisner, Sabine. "Elizabeth Jennings: 'Against the Dark.'" In *English Language and Literature: Positions & Dispositions* 16, edited by J. Hogg, K. Hubmayer, and D. Steiner, 39–49. Salzburg: University of Salzburg Press, 1990.

Coelsch-Foisner, Sabine. "Denying Eros: Reading Women's Poetry of the Mid-twentieth Century." *Gramma: Journal of Theory and Criticism* 4 (1996): 55–76.

Coelsch-Foisner, Sabine. "The Mystic Voice in Elizabeth Jennings's Poetry." *Revolution in Poetic Consciousness: An Existential Reading of Mid-twentieth-century British Women's Poetry* 2, 578–610. Tübingen: Stauffenburg, 2002.

"Cool Comfort," review of *Collected Poems. The Times Literary Supplement* (September 21, 1967): 840.

Conquest, Robert. *New Lines.* London: Macmillan, 1956.

Crawford, Robert. "Locked and Barred," review of *New Collected Poems. London Review of Books* (July 24, 2003): 31–2.

Crewe, Candida. "Bag Lady of the Sonnets." *The Times* (November 23, 1991): 10–11.

D'Evelyn, Thomas. "Two Contemporary Poets. Graham and Jennings: Poles Apart in Form and Subject." *Christian Science Monitor* (August 12, 1987): 213.

Davis, Jane. "Praises." *The Reader,* 5 (Autumn/Winter, 1998): 41–4.

Dinnage, Rosemary. "Happy Cronehood!" review of *The Change* by Germaine Greer. *The Times Literary Supplement* (October 25, 1991): 6.

Dodsworth, Martin. "The Movement: Never and Always." Chapter V. in *The Oxford Handbook of Contemporary British and Irish Poetry*, edited by Peter Robinson. Oxford: Oxford University Press, 2013.

"The Dominican Friars—England & Scotland." http://godzdogz.op.org/godzdogz/fr-sebastian-bullough-o-p-1910-1967.

Dooley, Maura, ed. *Making for Planet Alice: New Women Poets.* Newcastle upon Tyne: Bloodaxe Books, 1997.

Dowson, Jane. "'There is a Sweetness in Willing Surrender': Self-loss and Renewal in the Poetry of Elizabeth Jennings, Kathleen Raine and Stevie Smith." In *Women's Writing, 1945–1960: After the Deluge*, edited by Jane Dowson, 217–32. New York: Palgrave, 2003.

Dowson, Jane. "Towards a New Confessionalism: Elizabeth Jennings and Sylvia Plath." In *A History of Twentieth Century British Women's Poetry*, edited by Jane Dowson and Alice Entwistle, 62–81. Cambridge: Cambridge University Press, 2005.

Dowson, Jane. "Poetry and Personality: The Private Papers and Public Image of Elizabeth Jennings." In *The Boundaries of the Literary Archive*, edited by Carrie Smith and Lisa Stead, 105–20. Burlington, VT: Ashgate, 2013.

Dowson, Jane. "What is the True Standing of Oxford Poet Elizabeth Jennings?" *Oxford Today* (October 23, 2016). http://www.oxfordtoday.ox.ac.uk/culture/events/what-true-standing-oxford-poet-elizabeth-jennings.

Dowson, Jane. The Elizabeth Jennings Project. http://elizabethjennings.dmu.ac.uk/home.html.

Dunn, Douglas, "Unremittingly Prolific Poet," review of *Celebrations and Elegies. Glasgow Herald* (May 5, 1982): 8.

Eagleton, Terry. "Adjusting the Art to the Self," review of *Lucidities. The Times Literary Supplement* (December 11, 1970): 1436.

Eagleton, Terry. "New Poetry: 'Growing-Points.'" *Stand* 17, No. 1 (1975): 79–80.

Eaves, Will. "Ceremonial Forms," review of *Times and Seasons. The Times Literary Supplement* (January 15, 1993): 23.

Enright, D. J., ed. *Poets of the 1950s.* Tokyo: Kenyusha Press, 1955.

Fenge, Gerry. "Journeys of the Self." *The English Review* (September 1, 2000): 26.

Fisher, Emma. "New Poetry," review of *Selected Poems* and *Moments of Grace. The Spectator Archive* (December 1, 1979): 29.

Forth, John. "Moving Houses," review of *Collected Poems. The London Magazine* (October 1986): 82–5.

Fraser, G. S. "Christianity and Poetry," review of *Christianity and Poetry. The Times Literary Supplement* (July 1, 1965): 559.

Fuller, R. C. "Sebastian Bullough O.P. 1910–1967." *Scripture: The Quarterly of the Catholic Biblical Association* XX, No. 49 (January 1968): 1–4.

Fuller, Roy. "In Search of an Audience," review of *New Poetry* edited by A. Alvarez. *The Times Literary Supplement* (April 20, 1962): 266.

Fuller, Roy. "Mysterious Clarities," review of *Growing-Points. The Times Literary Supplement* (July 4, 1975): 718.

Gardner, Timothy. "Learning the Lesson of Love: The Poetry of Elizabeth Jennings." *New Blackfriars* 83, No. 979 (September 2002): 401–7.

Gascoyne, David. "A Poet's Experience," review of *Extending the Territory. The Tablet* (September 14, 1985): 16.

Gilbert, Sandra. Review of *Collected Poems, 1953–1985. Poetry* CL, No. 2 (May 1987): 106–9.

Gramang, Gerlinde. *Elizabeth Jennings: An Appraisal of Her Life as a Poet, Her Approach to Her Work and a Section of the Major Themes of Her Poetry.* Lewiston, NY: Edwin Mellen Press, 1995.

Greer, Germaine. *The Change—Women, Aging and the Menopause.* New York: Knopf, 1992.

Hall, Donald and Robert Pack, eds. *New Poets of England and America.* New York: Meridian, 1957.

Hamilton, Ian. "The Making of the Movement." In *British Poetry since 1960: A Critical Survey,* edited by Michael Schmidt and Grevel Lindop, 70–3. Manchester: Carcanet Press, 1972.

Hamilton, Saskia, ed. *The Letters of Robert Lowell.* New York: Farrar, Straus & Giroux, 2005.

Haynes, Anthony. "Most Catholic Poet," review of *New Collected Poems. The Tablet* (April 13, 2002): 19–20.

Hays, Angelyn. "Elizabeth Jennings." In *British Writers* V, edited by George Stade and Sarah Hannah Goldstein, 205–21. New York: Charles Scribner's Sons, *c.* 1999.

Heaney, Seamus. "Words and Rhymes," review of *The Mind Has Mountains*. *The Times Literary Supplement* (July 14, 1966): 616.

Heath-Stubbs, John. "Poets and Poetry," review of *A Sense of the World*. *Encounter* (February 1959): 72–3.

Holroyd, Michael. *Works on Paper: The Craft of Biography and Autobiography*. Washington, D.C.: Counterpoint, 2002.

Hughes, Sian. "Except for Sudden Darks," review of *Timely Issues*. *The Times Literary Supplement* (November 23, 2001): 2.

Hunter, Jeffrey, ed. "Elizabeth Jennings," *Contemporary Literary Criticism* 131, 228–44. Detroit, MI: Gale Publishing, 2000.

JLeS. "Review of *Familiar Spirits*." *The Times Literary Supplement* (May 5, 1995): 29.

Jones, P. and M. Schmidt, eds. *British Poetry Since 1970*. Manchester: Carcanet, 1980.

Kaplan, Cora. *Sea Changes: Essays on Culture and Feminism*. London: Verso, 1986.

Kennedy, Madeline. "Childhood Brain Injury May be Tied to Anxiety and Depression Later in Life." *Washington Post* (June 20, 2017): E-8.

Kinsella, Thomas. "A Way of Looking." In *Prose Occasions, 1951–2006*, edited by Andrew Fitzsimons, 159–61. Manchester: Carcanet, 2009.

Larkin, Philip. "Reports on Experience." In *Further Requirements: Interviews, Broadcasts, Statements and Book Reviews, 1958–85*, edited by Anthony Thwaite, 178–80. Ann Arbor: University of Michigan Press, 2004.

Leader, Zachary, ed. *The Movement Reconsidered: Essays on Larkin, Amis, Gunn and Davie*. Oxford: Oxford University Press, 2009.

Levi, Peter. "The Sinews of Poetry," reviews of *Song for a Birth or a Death* and *Every Changing Shape*. *Time and Tide* (July 27, 1961): 1241.

Levi, Peter. "A Sense of Inward Fire," review of *Extending the Territory*. *The Spectator* (October 19, 1985): 33.

Levi, Peter. Review of *Collected Poems*. *PN Review* 53, No. 3 (1986): 89–90.

Levi, Peter. "Otherwise Engaged." *The Independent* (March 12, 1987): 12.

Levy, Edward. "The Poetry of Elizabeth Jennings," review of *Growing-Points*. *Poetry Nation* 5 (Spring, 1975): 62–74.

Lewis, Gwyneth. "Annunciations." *Poetry Review* 84, No. 4 (Winter, 1994): 60.

Lindop, Grevel. "Elizabeth Jennings," obituary. *The Guardian* (October 31, 2001). http//www.theguardian.com/news/2001/oct/31/guardianobituaries.books.

Lomas, Herbert. "Straight from the Heart," review of *Tributes*. *The Tablet* (March 25, 1989): 25.

Lucas, John. Review of *Extending the Territory*. *New Statesman* 110, No. 2851 (November 15, 1985): 28.

Lucie-Smith, Edward. *British Poetry Since 1945*. Middlesex: Penguin, 1970.

Luckins, Kirsten. "Differing Poetic Responses to the Big Questions." *The London Quarterly* 5 (February 14–May 15, 1995): 30.

Maclean, Alasdair. "Marble Fun," review of *Relationships*. *The Listener* 89, No. 2295 (March 22, 1973): 389–90.

Maio, Samuel. "The Revolt Against Free Verse." *The Formalist: A Journal of Metrical Poetry* 2, No. 1 (1991): 15–20.

Marghella, Maria Antonietta. "Bibliography." "Love, Knowledge, Art, Religion: An Analysis of Elizabeth Jennings' Poetry." Theses, Università di Roma "La Sapienza," 1988.

Matthias, John. "Pointless and Poignant," review of *Growing-Points*. *Poetry* (March, 1977): 347–50.

Maxwell, Glyn. "Faith in Form," review of *Tributes*. *The Times Literary Supplement* (May 5, 1989): 495.

May, Derwent J. "New Lines—or Sidelines?" review of *New Lines 2* by Robert Conquest. *The Times Literary Supplement* (September 6, 1963): 673.

McInerney, Stephen. "'Art with Its Largesse and Its Own Restraint': The Sacramental Poetics of Elizabeth Jennings and Les Murray." In *Between Human and Divine: The Catholic Vision in Contemporary Literature*, edited by Mary R. Reichardt, 207–25. Washington, D.C.: Catholic University of America Press, 2010.

Michaels, Amanda G. "The Mystic and the Poet: Identity Formation, Deformation, and Reformation in Elizabeth Jennings' 'Teresa of Avila,' and Kathleen Jamie's 'Julian of Norwich.'" *Christianity and Literature* 59, No. 4 (Summer, 2010): 665–81.

Mole, John. "Crepuscular and Plain," review of *Celebrations and Elegies*. *The Times Literary Supplement* (July 16, 1982): 770.

Montefiore, Jan. *Feminism and Poetry: Language, Experience, Identity in Women's Writing*. London: Pandora, 1987.

Moore, Chris. "Two Women, Two Voices." *The Tablet* (October 15, 1994): 21.

Moore, Chris. "A Clutch of Poems," review of *Praises*. *The Tablet* (March 20, 1999): 19.

Moran, Maureen. "The Heart's Censer: Liturgy, Poetry and the Catholic Devotional Revolution." In *Ecstasy and Understanding: Religious Awareness in English Poetry*, edited by Adrian Grafe, 40–1. New York: Continuum, 2008.

Morley, David. "Elizabeth Jennings." In *The Cambridge Guide to Women's Writing in English*, edited by Lorna Sage, 149. Cambridge: Cambridge University Press, 1999.

Morrison, Blake. *The Movement: English Poetry and Fiction of the 1950s*. Oxford: Oxford University Press, 1980.

Mott, Michael. "Recent Developments in British Poetry," review of *Animals' Arrival*. *Poetry* CXVIII, No. 2 (May, 1971): 110–11.

Murray, Les. "Letter—Selecting the Poet Laureate." *The Times Literary Supplement* (December 11, 1998): 17.

"Obituary of Elizabeth Jennings." *The Times*, London, October 31, 2001: 19.

"Obituary of Elizabeth Jennings." *The Tablet* (November 3, 2001), 31.

O'Neil, Michael. "Review of *Praises*." *The Times Literary Supplement* (December 25, 1998): 28–9.

Oxley, William. "Review of *Collected Poems*." *Acumen* (April 5, 1987): 81–3.

Padel, Ruth. "The Sunday Poem." *The Independent* (October 17, 1999): 13.

Padel, Ruth. "Fortunes of War, Love and Peace," review of *New and Collected Poems*. *Financial Times* (April 20, 2002): 4.

Perkins, David. *A History of Modern Poetry: Modernism and After*. Cambridge, MA: Harvard University Press, 1987.

Pitter, Ruth. *The Letters of Ruth Pitter*, compiled by Don W. King. Newark, DE: University of Delaware Press, 2014.

"A Poet Honoured." *The Tablet* (March 21, 1987): 9.

"Poet Whose Verse Drew on Her Christian Faith but Offered Experience Rather than Sermons," obituary of Elizabeth Jennings. *Daily Telegraph* (October 30, 2001): 25.

"Poet's Toy Passion Will Help Children." *Oxford Mail* (May 27, 2002). http://www.oxfordmail.co.uk/news/6593609.

Porter, Peter. "Cassettes of Atrocity," review of *Extending the Territory*. *The Observer* (September 1, 1985): 19.

Powell, Neil. "Degrees of Seriousness," review of *Consequently I Rejoice*. *PN Review* 6, Vol. 5, No 2. (January–March 1979).

Powell, Neil. "Elizabeth Joan Jennings." In *The Dictionary of National Biography*. Oxford: Oxford University Press. 2005. https://doi.org/10.1093/ref:odnb/76379.

Press, John. *Rule and Energy: Trends in British Poetry Since the Second World War*. London: Oxford University Press, 1963.

Rae, Simon. "Overwhelming Questions," review of *Extending the Territory*. *The Times Literary Supplement* (May 30, 1986): 586.

Redgrove, Peter. "Representative Poets," review of David Stacton's *An Unfamiliar Country* and Elizabeth Jennings' *Poems*. *The Times Literary Supplement* (December 4, 1953): 778.

Reeves, James. "Poet's Corner," review of *Let's Have Some Poetry*. *The Times Literary Supplement* (November 25, 1960): 768.

Reid, Louis Arnaud. "Review of *Every Changing Shape*." *British Journal of Aesthetics* 2, No. 3, (1962): 287–9.

Regan, Stephen. "Larkin and the Movement." In *The Cambridge History of English Poetry,* edited by Michael O'Neill, 879–96. Cambridge: Cambridge University Press, 2010.

Richardson, Graeme. "Shining Years Ago," review of *The Collected Poems*. *The Times Literary Supplement* (October 12, 2012): 22–3.

Ross, Alan. "In the Shadows," review of *A Sense of the World*. *The Times Literary Supplement* (October 31, 1958): 628.

Sail, Lawrence. "Recapturing Hope," review of *Collected Poems*. *Poetry Review* (December 1986): 42–3.

Sail, Laurence. *Review of Tributes. Stand Magazine* 31, No. 4 (Autumn, 1990): 48–50.

Schmidt, Michael. "Elizabeth Jennings." In *An Introduction to Fifty Modern British Poets.* London: Pan Books, 1979.

Schmidt, Michael. *Lives of the Poets.* New York: Knopf, 1999.

Schmidt, Michael. "Obituary: Elizabeth Jennings." *The Independent* (October 31, 2001): 6.

Schmidt, Michael. "Elizabeth Jennings." *Woman's Hour.* B.B.C. Radio 4 (November 3, 2001).

Schmidt, Michael. "Editorial." *PN Review* 143, Vol. 28, No. 3 (January–February 2002).

Schmidt, Michael. "Preface." In Elizabeth Jennings, *New Collected Poems.* Manchester: Carcanet, 2002: xix–xiv.

Schmidt, Michael and Grevel Lindop, eds. *British Poetry since 1960.* Oxford: Carcanet Press, 1972.

Scupham, Peter. "Sacred Encounters," review of *Consequently I Rejoice. The Times Literary Supplement* (December 30, 1977): 1530.

Scupham, Peter. "Circumambient Weathers," review of *Collected Poems. Poetry Review* 102, No. 2 (Summer, 2012).

Sheppard, Robert. "Review of *Collected Poems.*" *New Statesman* (August 21, 1987): 22.

Short, Edward. "A Faithful Poet: From the Darkness of Her Existence, Elizabeth Jennings Comes to Light." *The Weekly Standard* 18, No. 22 (February 18, 2013). http://www.weeklystandard.com/a-faithful-poet/article/700492.

Simms, Gemma. "Secret Poets Revealed." *Oxford Mail* (June 18, 1998): 14.

Sisson, C. H. "Divine Rhyme," review of *The Batsford Book of Religious Verse. The Spectator* (June 26, 1981): 23.

Sisson, C. H. "How Spirit Speaks to Spirit," review of *Tributes. The Spectator* (September 2, 1989): 30.

Sloan, Barry. "Poetry and Faith: The Example of Elizabeth Jennings." *Christianity and Literature* 55, No. 3 (Spring, 2006): 393–414.

Smith, David. *St. Anne's College, Oxford: A Brief History.* http//www.st-annes. ox.ac.uk.

"The State of Poetry." Survey sponsored by *New Poetry Magazine*, compiled by Norman Hidden. London: Workshop Press, 1978.

Stevens, Wallace. Aphorisms from Adagia. http://giveitaname-giveitaname. blogspot.com/2009/04/from-adagia-wallace-stevens.html.

Stevenson, Anne. "A Need for Reverence," review of *Growing-Points. The Listener* 94, No. 2430 (October 30, 1975): 51–73.

Stevenson, Anne. "Snaffling and Curbing," review of *Consequently I Rejoice. The Listener* 98 No. 2530 (October 13, 1977): 486–7.

Stevenson, Anne. "A Rage for Order," review of *Collected Poems. Sunday Times* (September 14, 1986), 55.

Sturzl, E. A. "'Here Is a Humility at One with Craft': The Thematic Content of the Poetry of Elizabeth Jennings." In *On Poets and Poetry*: Fifth Series, edited by James Hogg, 63–96. Salzburg: Institut für Anglislik und Amerikanistik, 1983.

Symons, Julian. "Clean and Clear," review of *Collected Poems*. *New Statesman* (October 13, 1967): 476.

Symons, Julian. "A Distilled Despair," review of *Moments of Grace* and *Selected Poems*. *The Times Literary Supplement* (February 1, 1980): 112.

Teller, Joseph R. "'The Misrule of our Dust': Psychoanalysis, Sacrament, and the Subject in Elizabeth Jennings's Poetry of Incarnation." *Christianity and Literature* 57, No. 4 (2006): 531–57.

Thwaite, Anthony. "Forms of Assurance," review of *A Sense of the World*. *The Spectator* (September 4, 1958): 24.

Thwaite, Anthony. *Contemporary English Poetry: An Introduction*. London: Heinemann, 1964.

Thwaite, Anthony. "How to Confess," review of *Recoveries*. *The Times Literary Supplement* (June 11, 1964): 512.

Thwaite, Anthony. "Elizabeth Jennings." In *Contemporary Poets*, 2nd ed. Ed. James Vinson, 776–8. London: St. James Press, 1975.

Thwaite, Anthony. *Twentieth-Century English Poetry: An Introduction*. London: Heinemann, 1978.

Thwaite, Anthony. *Poetry Today: A Critical Guide to British Poetry, 1960–1984*. London: Longman, 1985.

Thwaite, Anthony. "'Angel' into 'Bag-lady.'" *Sunday Telegraph* (April 21, 2002). http://www.telegraph.co.uk/culture/4727712/Angel-into-bag-lady.html.

Tolkien, Priscilla. "Beginnings and Endings." *PN Review* 31, No. 1 (September–October 2004): 9–10.

Wain, John. "Green Fingers: For Elizabeth Jennings in Oxford." *Critical Quarterly* 9, No. 3 (1967): 197–9.

Wakefield, Gordon S. "God and Some English Poets: Elizabeth Jennings." *Expository Times* 109, No. 1 (1997): 10–14.

Walczuk, Anna. "Among the Admirers of G. K. Chesterton: Elizabeth Jennings and the Poet's Metaphysical Intuition." *The Chesterton Review* XXXXI, Nos. 1 and 2 (Spring/Summer, 2015): 179–95.

Walczuk, Anna. "The Poetic Magnificat of Elizabeth Jennings with a Polish Priest Poet in the Background." Conference paper delivered at The Power of the Word International Conference, Rome, June 2015.

Walczuk, Anna. "Elizabeth Jennings and the Mysticism of Words." In *Poetic Revelations: Word Made Flesh Made Word*, edited by Mark Burrows, Jean Ward, and Malgorzata Gregorzewska, 69–85. London: Routledge, 2017.

Walczuk, Anna, *Elizabeth Jennings and the Sacramental Nature of Poetry*. NY: Columbia University Press / Jagiellonian University Press, 2018.

Ward, Jean. "Elizabeth Jennings: An Exile in Her Own Country?" *Literature and Theology* No. 21, 2 (June 2007): 198–213.

Ward, Jean. *Christian Poetry in the Post-Christian Day: Geoffrey Hill, R. S. Thomas, Elizabeth Jennings.* New York: Peter Lang, c.2009.

Wedgwood, C. V. "Poet of Changing Moods," review of *Growing-Points. Daily Telegraph* (April 17, 1975): 13.

Wedgwood, C. V. "Tuscan Idylls," review of *Celebrations and Elegies. Daily Telegraph* (June 3, 1982): 14.

West, Paul. "Tutors: My Many Mentors at Oxford, from Lincoln College to All Souls, Linger Like Spirits in the Mind." *The American Scholar* 83, No. 1 (Winter, 2014).

Wheeler, Michael. "Elizabeth Jennings and Gerard Manley Hopkins." In *Hopkins among the Poets: Studies in Modern Responses to Gerard Manley Hopkins*, edited by Richard Giles, 104–6. Hamilton, ON: International Hopkins Association, Series No. 3, 1985.

White, John P. "At Some Imagined Limit," review of *Consequently I Rejoice. The Tablet* (May 27, 1978): 10.

White, John P. "Fragments of Insight," review of *Moments of Grace* and *Selected Poems. The Tablet* (March 8, 1980): 15.

Wilmer, Clive. "Poetry and Prayer," review of *In the Meantime* and *Every Changing Shape. Times Literary Supplement* (July 25, 1997): 25.

Woolf, Virginia. *A Writer's Diary.* New York: Harcourt, Brace, 1954, 84–5.

Index

awards and prizes (*cont.*)
   W. H. Smith Award xix, 152,
      154, 157
"(The) Awkward One" 121
Ayrton, Michael 67

B 76, 78, 80
Baker, Kenneth 154
Balcon, Jill 74, 89
Barker, Sebastian 150
*(The) Batsford Book of Children's
   Verse* 62
*(The) Batsford Book of Religious
   Verse* 94, 115, 135, 139
Baycock, Jack (imaginary brother)
   5, 92
B. B. C. 38, 88, 148, 163, 164, 171
Beat poetry 47
Beauvoir, Simone de 96
Beckett, Wendy 27
Bednarowska, Dorothy 28, 29
Beer, Patricia 137
Belloc, Hilaire 94
Bernanos, George 69
Bernard, Oliver 119
"Beseeching" 129
Betjeman, John 41, 124, 138
Birch Court 169, 175, 176, 181
Bishop, Elizabeth 96, 137, 150–1
"Bitter Fruit" 146
Blackfriars 61, 78, 112, 170
Blake, Father Simon 75
*(The) Bloodaxe Book of Contemporary
   Women Poets* 151, 152
Blunden, Edmund 100
Bodley Head 114
Boland, Eavan xvii
"(A) Book of Spells" 154
Boston, Lincolnshire 1, 3, 6, 7, 158
"Bread" 173
Bremond, Henri 69
*(A) Brief Study of Eliot and His
   Life* 97, 104–5
Bristol 5
Brontë, Emily 95, 106, 151
Brooke-Rose, Christine 69–70

Brownjohn, Alan 37, 120, 154
Bryson, John Norman 31
Bullough, Father Sebastian 61–73,
      75, 77, 78, 98
Bury Knowle library 62
Butler, Dom Cuthbert 68
Butterfield, John and Isabel 75, 79,
      82, 85, 109, 110
Byers, Margaret 111

Caetani, Princess Marguerite 54
"(The) Call of the Sea" 19
Calvert, Tim 179
Camus, Albert 79
Caravaggio, Michelangelo Merisi
      da 92, 158
Carcanet magazine 107
Carcanet Press 107, 114, 117, 119, 125,
      154, 163, 171, 227
Catherine of Siena 71
Catholic Herald 163
Catholicism *see* Roman Catholicism
Causley, Charles 150, 157
CBE, awarded 1992 xiii, 160–2
Cecil, Lord David 28
Celandine Press 150
Celebrations and Elegies 135,
      137, 140
Cézanne, Paul 128
Chagall, Marc 92
Chapman, Dom John 68
Chardin, Jean-Baptiste-Siméon 158
chastity xvi, 92, 112, 218, 226–7
Chatto & Windus 73, 74, 75, 78, 104
Cheltenham Literary Festival 41
Chesterton, G. K. 18–19, 94
Chettle, Peter 33
childhood xvii–xviii
   Boston 2–6
   early poems 10, 20, 23–4
   Oxford 9–19
children's poetry 62, 89, 91, 130, 150,
      154, 171
"(The) Child's Story" 149
Cholmondeley Award 169
Christianity and Poetry 89, 93–4